THE SUCCESSFUL EQUIPMENT LEASE BROKER

THE SUCCESSFUL EQUIPMENT LEASE BROKER

The Leasing Expert, Inc.

ISBN 978-0-9742691-0-8

PREFACE

This book is intended for those with no former education in the equipment leasing business and for people already in the equipment leasing business interested in ways to improve their profitability.

For equipment leasing beginners, this book is an easy way to learn, step-by-step, how to start and build your own equipment lease brokerage using capital from funding sources to finance leases and generate profits. By applying the methods described in this book, you will be taking advantage of a rare short cut to the top. This is the only book available on the market that describes in detail how to begin and profit from an equipment lease brokerage.

For the equipment leasing professional, this book can help you boost your business to a higher level, maximizing your efficiency while minimizing your expenses and growing pains.

With the proper tools and education, anyone can build a very lucrative equipment leasing business. This manual teaches you how to make over $100,000 yearly in today's equipment leasing marketplace. It was written for entrepreneurs by an entrepreneur in the leasing business. The Successful Equipment Lease Broker book is packed with real world advice. It includes three complete paper trails of actual lease transactions from start to finish, and it is packed full of sample documents and worksheets to help your new or existing business hit the ground running.

Work this business hard for six months, then begin to enjoy the rest of your career working minimal hours per week while generating a positive income in a business that is fun, dynamic and lucrative!

*The author of this book is not responsible for any accounting or legal advice given herein. We advise you to consult your own attorney or accountant with any specific questions you may have regarding laws and/or accounting regulations as laws differ from state to state.

Acknowledgements

The Successful Equipment Lease Broker

Written & Published By:

The Leasing Expert, Inc.

Table of Contents

- Receive and Process Documentation
- Funding the Lease
- Getting Paid

- Broker Commission Fee
- Lease Payments
- Converting Rate Factor to Interest Rate

- (See Table of Contents for details)

- Collection Assistance
- Commission Refund
- Fraudulent Transactions

- Vendors
- Funding Sources
- Past Lessees
- Other Leasing Companies
- Lease Organizations

- Register Your Business
- Telephones & Fax Lines
- Opening a Bank Account
- Stationary
- Setting Up Funding Sources
- Customize Processing Documentation for Use

- A Quick & Easy Transaction
- A Lease that Required Tax Returns and a Little Extra Work
- A Tough lease That Required Determination

- Documentation Examples

Index of Exhibits

SECTION 1

EQUIPMENT LEASING 101

In This Section:

- Key Leasing Terms
- History of Leasing
- An Overview of the Leasing Industry
- The Current & Future Market Climate
- Key Factors to Your Success

Equipment Leasing 101

Key Leasing Terms

Before you begin, there are a handful of key terms that you must read and understand:

Equipment

Tools, machines, or other things that you need for a particular job or activity. Tangible property used to carry out the operations of a business.

Equipment Lease Broker

An equipment lease broker is an intermediary between the lessee (buyer of equipment) and lessor (funding source). The broker arranges a leasing transaction. A funding source pays the broker for its services.

Funding Source

A funding source is sort of like a bank. It exists to fund leases. Funding sources use equipment lease brokers to get their business. Funding sources pay the broker a commission for their services.

Lease

A lease is a binding contract between the owner (lessor) and the user (lessee) that conveys the right to use equipment for a specified period of time. Some specific leases are classified as a "true lease" that meets all IRS requirements and allows the lessee a dollar-for-dollar tax write-off of the monthly payments. A "master lease" is a flexible lease that will allow the lessee to acquire additional future equipment under the same basic terms and conditions without negotiating a new contract. The lease end purchase options vary from a fair market value estimated at ten percent of the equipment's original cost to a fixed one dollar buyout. The choice is up to the lessee on how they want to structure the lease purchase option.

Lease Application

The lease application is the application that a prospective lessee completes in order to obtain financing on a desired piece of equipment.

Lessee

A lessee is the user of the equipment that is the subject of the lease agreement. The lessee is the person or business responsible for the lease payments.

Lessor

The lessor is the owner of the equipment that is the subject of the lease agreement. This is typically the financial institution that lends the money to the lessee.

Term

The term usually defines how long the lease has been written for and details the residual at the end of a lease. The term states whether a lease is two years long or five years long.

Vendor

The vendor is the seller of the property; commonly, the manufacturer or distributor of equipment.

The History of Equipment Leasing

Though often mistaken for a new field due to its rapid growth in the past fifty years, equipment leasing actually has a recorded history dating back to 2011 BC. Equipment leasing transactions have been documented amongst farmers and priests who administered governmental rental programs of agricultural tools. Other lease transactions from antiquity occurred in Rome, Babylon, Egypt and Greece.

The first recorded equipment leases in the United States appeared in the 1700's for horses, buggies and wagons in the livery stable industry. Contemporary leasing began to take shape in the 1870's with the financing of barges, railroad cars, and locomotives. The railroads in particular gave rise to the first true leases, including conditional sale contracts and contracts in which the railroad car manufacturers, as the lessors, retained ownership of the cars at the end of the lease.

The 1900's brought economic stimulus that further broadened the leasing industry. Various equipment manufacturers in the 1920's adopted leasing to boost equipment sales as they still do today. World War II also encouraged manufacturers to acquire capital in ways that didn't involve heavy investment in war machinery production equipment, as it would have no use in peacetime. The war also produced formalized operating leases for equipment, such as a truck, leased with an operator included.

The first non-manufacturing company formed to conduct general leasing business was the U.S. Leasing Corporation in 1954. A number of companies followed including Boothe Leasing Corp. (now part of Greyhound Corp.), Chandler Leasing (now owned by Pepsi-Cola), General Electric Credit Corp., and Commercial Credit Corp.

Since then, the percentage of capital acquired via leasing has continued to grow, representing $169.9 billion of the $566.2 billion of U.S. capital acquisition in 1996. The development of the computer industry spurred leasing into the realm of computer and office equipment, with IBM and Xerox leading the way with leasing programs. In 1970, the amendment of the Bank Holding Company Act expanded bank activities, enabling them to form holding companies and conduct business in leasing. This development brought leasing to many other industries, popularizing leasing as a financially attractive way to acquire equipment. The process of financing is much simpler and faster than standard financing methods.

An Overview of the Leasing Industry

Who are the Leasing Companies?

There are over 2,500 companies that provide leases to American business. They are industrial finance companies, banks, and independent companies, both large and small. Many of these companies specialize in certain equipment or industries. As mentioned above, they offer a wide range of services including the provision, maintenance, operation, managing, and re-marketing of equipment.

Why Do Companies Lease Equipment?

About 32 percent of all new business investment equipment is financed through leases in the United States (this number has hardly varied in ten years), with 80 percent of U.S. companies leasing all or some of their equipment.

A recent study examining why companies lease showed the following percentages: 36 percent chose cash flow reasons, 18 percent chose dollar value, 14 percent chose ease and convenience, 12 percent chose maintenance options, 10 percent chose tax benefits and 8 percent chose latest technology and transferring the cost of upgrading to the lessor.

* Cash flow and financial reasons. Leasing enables rental payments to be closely matched to the income produced by the leased equipment. Leasing also allows a company to use its debt lines for working capital instead of capital expenditures.

* Efficiency and convenience. Businesses have come to recognize the value of equipment in its use, not its ownership. They make money by using equipment -- ownership being incidental depending on business factors. Additionally, leasing companies offer many services (like acquisition, disposition, maintenance, and upgrading) related to equipment that permit a company to keep its focus on its central business activities, not on dealing with its equipment. Leasing is also especially efficient for certain industries as it protects against technological obsolescence.

* Stimulating investment and serving growth. Federal and state tax laws give incentives to companies to invest in new equipment, but often companies could not take advantage of these incentives if burdened by the expense of new purchases. With leasing, however, depreciation or credit incentives can be used by a leasing company who then passes them on to the lessee in the form of low rental payments.

The Current & Future Market Climate

The U.S. economy is currently in a downturn, and the demand for equipment and leasing services has slowed a bit. However, there are always industries that weather downturns well, like food processing, waste management, and non-luxury clothing manufacturing. And there are still profitable opportunities and growth in industries dealing with computer networking, software, websites, internet providers, franchise lease financing, etc. Economic expansions and contractions form a continuum, and the savvy equipment lease broker adjusts his business to the economy, creating opportunities in the changing environment.

Due to the economic downturn, a lot of funding sources are tightening up their credit window. This means they are taking less risk on deals they used to consider for approval. Many lease professionals have the experience that there is less funding available for risky and tough deals. I have found, however, that there is almost always a home for a lease if you are willing to work on it for a long time, make a lot of phone calls, and send a lot of faxes. Again, your success is largely the product of your own determination and attitude, especially in a challenged economy.

In the future, increasing technological innovations will constantly create demand for equipment leasing as an economical means of acquisition. The internet especially is changing the industry. It is streamlining communication between customers and vendors, reducing costs, and allowing deals to be processed and funded more quickly.

To conclude, those leasing professionals who stay committed and resourceful during economic downturns will profit even more during economic expansions thanks to their firmly established leasing industry relationships in hardy and future-oriented industries

Key Factors to Your Success

In today's leasing climate, you should focus on a niche or portion of market share. Decide what your company's main focus is going to be: Competitive Advantage, Specialized Industries. Unfortunately for leasing professionals still working the business on a daily basis, there have been some serious changes that must be understood. "In the '70s, the industry was capable of providing the 'value-add' of transferring tax benefits, and, in the '80s and '90s, through securitization, the industry provided the "value-add" of an additional low cost capital source. Today, the tax benefits have been reduced through changes in the tax codes and customer profits and are less integral to customer decision-making."

Leasing will continue to have a significant role in financing equipment acquisitions. Growth opportunities will remain evident throughout the decades. As mentioned above, realizing this growth potential will require strong management skills, niche marketing and focus.

SECTION 2

UNDERSTANDING LEASES AND THEIR BENEFITS

In This Section:

- Variable Elements of Leases
- The Benefits of Leasing
- The Tax Benefits of Leasing

Variable Elements of a Lease

Leases vary in many ways. One way a lease can vary is by the way it terminates or ends. This is known as the "end of lease" option. Leases also vary by the way the payments are structured and by the interest rate.

"End of Lease" Options

Below is a description of the different "end of lease" options and why a lessee would choose one option over the other. The "end of lease" option would be the residual of the lease. How the lease terminates, and how the lessee becomes the owner of the leased equipment at the end of the lease, is defined as the "end of lease" option.

There are three common "end of lease" options to choose from:

$1.00 BUY OUT

The first "end of lease" option is known as a $1.00 buy out, or a capital lease. It may also be called a finance lease. This type of a lease is the closest lease to straight bank financing. The lessee makes his/her payments for the agreed term of the lease, and then becomes the owner of the equipment after completing the payments and paying $1.00.

With a capital lease, the equipment must be shown as an asset and depreciated. Some lessees choose to write the payment off as a rental expense, however, it is not recommended that they do so. The lessee has the option to purchase the equipment for $1.00 with no further obligations. The rental payments are somewhat higher than an operating lease, but the equipment will belong to the lessee at the end of the lease for only a $1.00.

Many lessees will choose this option because of how simple it is. I personally do not like this option as much as the following options, because it does take full advantage of the benefits of leasing (see Exhibit 1 for Benefits of Leasing).

FAIR MARKET VALUE

The second "end of lease" option is known as the fair market value lease or an operating lease.

An operating lease may be tax deductible under IRS guidelines where as the payments are written off as a cost of doing business. The equipment can be purchased at lease end for its then fair market value, which is typically estimated at ten percent (10 percent or greater), or the equipment can be returned back to the lessor with no further obligations.

10% PUT or Purchase Option

The third "end of lease" option is the 10% PUT or Purchase Option (can be 10 percent, 15 percent, 20 percent, etc) which is a combination of the capital lease and operating lease. The lessee leaves a predetermined percent of the original equipment cost owing at the end (typically 10 percent of the original lease amount) of the lease. The lessee has the option to keep the equipment and pay the amount of the option (10 percent of the original cost) or walk away.

It would be silly to pay the entire lease and all its interest to walk away at the end. Most lessees' pay the option at the end and buy the equipment from the lessor.

A 10% PUT is the most common type of lease. It is common because, by leaving a residual at the end of the lease, the lessee lowers his/her monthly payments and can take advantage of the tax benefits of leasing.

An example of a 10% PUT is when a lessee guarantees at the beginning of a lease to pay 10 percent of the original equipment cost at the end of the lease and keep the equipment. The larger the residual buyout is at the end of the lease, the lower the lease payments will be. 10 percent residuals are the most common, however, funding sources sometimes offer 20 percent and 30 percent residuals as well (usually at special request).

Payment Structures

Funding sources offer many different types of programs for you to utilize as marketing tools for your equipment lease brokerage. The more programs you offer as a leasing company, the better. It is rare that this will happen, but sometimes a lessee will require a flexible payment plan. Common flexible payment plans that funding sources will offer are as follows: 90 days deferred, 7 × $100.00, 6 × $99.00, Annual Payments, Step Payments, etc. Descriptions of these payment plans are as follows:

90 Days Deferred

The 90 Day Deferral Plan is extremely helpful for those customers acquiring equipment that will not generate income during the first ninety days. With this program, the lender may require minimal contact payments of $25.00 for each of the first 3 months followed by the normal term at a predetermined rate factor.

7 X $100.00

The 7 × $100.00 program is a great selling tool for vendor promotions (if your funding source offers such a program). The lessee pays a $100.00 security deposit and has their first six "contact" payments at a fixed $100.00. The remaining 30, 42 or 54 payments are at the determined rate factor. The lessee can generate money with the equipment for seven months while only paying $100.00 per month.

6 X $99.00 Program

Another exceptional tool to market to your customers is the 6 × $99.00 Program. With this program, the customer pays two security deposits totaling $198.00. Their first six payments are $99.00 followed by 30, 42 or 54 payments at the determined rate factor.

Step Program

The Step Program is a payment plan in where the payments begin low, and gradually rise during the term of the lease as the customer generates income from the leased equipment.

Annual, Semi-Annual & Quarterly Payment Plans

For those customers who request annual, semi-annual or quarterly payments, most funding sources will handle those needs. This would require that the lessee pay one (one, two or four) large sum(s) every year. It is rare that a lessee requests this, but good to know about. This is typical in the farming industry due to the seasonality of its revenues.

Interest Rates

Interest rates will fluctuate from lease to lease depending upon a number of factors including: personal credit of borrower, dollar amount of equipment, equipment being leased, the type of business applying for the lease and the time that the borrower has been in business.

Personal Credit of Borrower

Everyone with a social security number begins establishing credit from the first time they use a credit card or sign a cell phone contract. One's entire credit profile is easily accessible by creditors. If a borrower has a poor credit history, i.e. late payments, collection accounts, unpaid parking tickets, judgments, tax liens, bankruptcy, etc., they will be approved with limitations, higher rates or not approved at all.

Dollar Amount of Lease

Generally as the dollar amount increases, rates drop. Each funding source has their own rate chart based on the rate of return or yield they wish to receive for lending the money. These charts display dollar amounts at which rates decrease. Typically the rates will drop at $15k, then again at $40k, and then again at $75k. This will vary from funding source to source.

The Equipment Being Leased

Funding sources have restrictions on certain equipment types; depending upon resale value of equipment, its life, etc. For example, forklifts and heavy machinery will last for ten years or more, while other equipment such as computers are only valuable for 36 months before they are obsolete. Equipment that is over seven years old may have a higher interest rate than newer equipment.

Type of Business Applying for the Lease

Funding sources also restrict certain types of business due to the nature of the industry. For example, funding sources rarely finance health clubs and restaurants due to the high turnover and low success rate in the business. Therefore, these businesses and others that are similar pay higher rates and have a much tougher time getting approved for financing/leasing. Desirable and undesirable industries change on a yearly basis as the economy and markets change in the United States. Restricted equipment will have higher rates (see Exhibit 3).

Time in Business

This is a huge factor in leasing. Most businesses must be in business at least two years to qualify for standard leasing interest rates. With businesses under two years in age, few funding sources will approve them. The funding sources that will approve them charge a higher rate to offset the risk involved in funding a brand new venture. These rates will commonly start at 16-18 percent.

The Benefits of Leasing

The benefits of leasing are vast. Provided is an exhibit (Exhibit 1), which compares leasing and bank financing. Reading and understanding this exhibit will help your lease salesmanship for years to come.

Exhibit 1

Leasing Versus Bank Borrowing

Leasing	Bank Borrowing
1. Sales tax payable over term of lease	1. Sales tax due up-front
2. Conserves valuable working capital	2. Short term money is not used for long term purpose
3. Conserves Cash – 100% Financing	3. Requires large down payment (Usually 20% - 30%)
4. Fixed rate for life of lease	4. Floating interest rate
5. Keeps credit lines open	5. Uses credit lines that could be utilized for operations.
6. Transfers risk of equipment obsolescence to lender	6. 100% obsolescence risk
7. Leasing can save you money	7. May be more expensive than leasing
8. Eliminates risk of alternative minimum tax	8. Potential liability to alternative minimum tax.
9. Recorded off the company's balance sheet	9. Booked on balance sheet
10. Payments can be structured to creatively fit the borrower's needs	10. Inflexible Payments
11. Provides a quick and simple financing solution that can close in days	11. Normally requires more time and paperwork to execute
12. Saves Bank credit lines for growing the business	12. Uses bank lines for depreciable assets
13. Term of lease can be longer (60-72 months)	13. Term of loan is restricted (12-36 months)
14. Asset can be upgraded easier	14. Asset harder to dispose of
15. Payments may be 100% tax deductible	
16. Finance soft costs: freight, warranties, installation, training, etc.	
17. Reduces taxable income as lease is paid for with before-tax monies.	

The Tax Benefits of Leasing

Tax Benefits of Leasing vs. Paying Cash or Bank Loan

The following three paragraphs illustrate the tax benefits of leasing by explaining the different taxable situations your client will be involved in depending upon whether he/she paid cash, utilized a bank loan or leased equipment:

Paying Cash

The first method of obtaining equipment is to pay cash. This method is very expensive because it uses after-tax dollars. In other words, if lessee is in a 34 percent tax bracket, the lessee must earn $15,152 to be left with $10,000 for buying new equipment. The lessee must then depreciate his/her investment over its useful life. Therefore, the economic cost is $15,152 plus the loss of interest that could have been earned if the money remained in the bank.

Bank Loan

The second method is bank borrowing. The lessee is allowed to deduct the interest as an operating expense, and the only way he/she can recoup their investment is through long-term depreciation. The lessee must depreciate the equipment over its useful life. This means the lessee will still be taking depreciation on the equipment years after the bank note is paid off.

Leasing

The third method is leasing. [1]Each lease payment comes from pre-tax money and each payment is fully deductible as a direct operating expense (FMV or 10% Option). The lessee is not depreciating their equipment over its useful life. Instead, the lessee is writing off the entire cost of the equipment during the term of his/her lease agreement, normally three to five years. Therefore, the lessee has sheltered considerably more income during the term of the lease agreement, than they would have through bank borrowing or outright purchase. Since the lessee has sheltered more income, the lessee has earned more money. Once the lease is over, the lessee transfers the asset to his/her balance sheet. Depreciation can be deducted off of the remaining value of the equipment.

When Is Leasing Tax Deductible?

IRS Classification

It is important to understand the different types of leases before giving advice to a customer on the tax advantages of leasing. For IRS purposes, equipment leases generally fall into two categories, each with a different type of purchase option:

- Non Tax-Oriented Leases: Legal ownership resides with the lessor, however because the lessor is not considered to be at risk at the end of the lease because the lessee has a nominal purchase option at the end of the lease, the lessee receives the tax benefits of ownership. (Lease is intended as security.)

---

1 A lease can typically be written off as a rental expense if there is no intention to purchase. That is, the equipment is simply being rented. Your lessee or client is urged to consult an Accountant. Do not offer advice unless you are trained in the field, as you could be held liable.

- <u>Tax-Oriented True Leases</u>: Lessor maintains ownership, fair market value purchase option for lessee at the end of the lease.

Accounting Classification

For a lessee's book purposes, equipment leases also fall into two separate categories.

- <u>Operating Lease</u>: The equipment acquisition is treated as a rental. Lease obligations are kept "off-balance sheet." (True Lease)

- <u>Capital Lease</u>: The equipment acquisition is treated as a purchase and the asset is included on the balance sheet and depreciated.

Classification is determined independently at the inception of the lease by both the lessor and lessee. Generally, the lessee is attempting to achieve operating lease treatment because they wish to keep the obligation off their balance sheet and to charge the lease payments to expense accounts as they become payable.

True Tax Lease vs. Non-Tax Lease

When leases are structured as true leases, the lessee may claim the entire lease payment as a tax deduction. The equipment write-off is tied to the lease term, which can be shorter than IRS depreciation schedules, resulting in larger tax deductions each year. The deduction is also the same every year, which simplifies budgeting.

- The true lease offers all of the primary benefits commonly attributed to leasing. It is a tax-oriented lease in which the lessor claims the tax benefits of ownership through depreciation deductions, but passes through to the lessee those benefits in the form of reduced rentals (Rentals are lower because a percentage of the original equipment cost has been deferred to the end of the lease). The lessor owns the leased equipment for the life of the contract.

- The non-tax lease passes the tax benefits of ownership to the lessee. While the lessor is legally the owner, the lessee may claim the depreciation and interest deductions. At the end of the lease term, the IRS expects that the lessee will choose to exercise their purchase option.

A True Tax Lease Must Meet All of the Following Criteria?

- At the start of the lease, the fair market value of the leased property projected for the end of the lease term equals or exceeds 20 percent of the original cost of the leased property (excluding front-end fees, inflation and any cost to the lessor for removal).

- At the start of the lease, the leased property is projected to retain a useful life at the end of the initial term that both exceeds 20 percent of the original estimated useful life of the equipment and is at least one year in duration.

- The lessee must not have a right to purchase or re-lease the leased property at a price which is less than its then fair market value.

- The lessor cannot obligate the lessee to purchase the leased property at a fixed price.

- At all times during the lease term the lessor must have a minimum unconditional "at risk" investment equal to at least 20 percent of the cost of the leased property.

- The lessor must show that the transaction was entered into for profit, apart from tax benefits resulting from the transaction.

- The lessee must not furnish any part of the purchase price of the leased property, nor have loaned or guaranteed any indebtedness created in connection with the acquisition of the leased property by the lessor.

Internal Revenue Code Section 179

This Code allows a sole proprietor, partnership or corporation to fully expense tangible property in the year it is purchased. Property eligible for the Section 179 deduction are as follows: machinery and equipment, furniture and fixtures, most storage facilities, single-purpose agricultural or horticultural structures, etc. Many leasing representatives mention Section 179 in their sales pitch to help motivate a customer to buy equipment using leasing.

The Section 179 deduction isn't automatic. Lessees/taxpayers who want to take the deduction must choose to do so.

Maximum Section 179 deduction increased

As you can see from the numbers below, the Small Business Job Protection Act increases the maximum annual Section 179 deduction on a yearly basis. The following table shows how the amount that can be deducted has increased almost $1,000.00 yearly:

- 1999: $19,000
- 2000: $20,000
- 2001: $24,000
- 2002: $24,000
- 2003: $25,000
- 2004 – 2010 The numbers have increased dramatically

Conclusion: Advantages of Section 179 deduction

You do not need to know too much about this, because you will not be giving tax advice, however, it is good too know a little bit about the subject in case a lessee brings it up, or you choose to use it as a selling point.

SECTION 3

THREE TYPES OF EQUIPMENT LEASING PROFESSIONALS

In This Section:

- The Equipment Lease Broker
- The Lease Discounter
- Financing Your Own Leases

Three Types of Equipment Leasing Professionals

In the equipment leasing business, as well as other types of business, i.e. real estate, mortgage lending, etc, there are a variety of approaches to making money. Some are riskier than others. Some require more hours, more stress, start-up capital, commission only, income vs. salary, etc.

In the equipment leasing business, there are three common career paths from which to choose. The easiest and quickest path is becoming an equipment lease broker. Another, somewhat more risky way to make money in leasing is to become an equipment lease discounter. The riskiest and potentially most lucrative path is to fund leases using your own money.

This section will describe the three different equipment leasing professionals, with emphasis on the equipment lease broker. I believe that this is the best way to enter into the business. Once you have become an equipment lease broker, the other two paths become easy options for growing and expanding your operation into a lucrative empire.

The Equipment Lease Broker

The equipment lease broker's role is to match an equipment buyer with a funding source (lender) to finance the acquisition of desired business equipment. The lease broker builds in a fee (commission) for successfully matching the funding source with the equipment buyer (lessee). This fee is known as a broker fee.

Brokering leases is the easiest way to get started in the leasing business and close to risk free (see section 8). Once you begin working the business and receiving commission checks, you will be amazed at how superb this business is. You use one company's money to finance another company and earn a commission for doing so (some commissions will be very large and you do not need to be a rocket scientist to put a deal together).

The risk to the equipment lease broker is minimal. If you do the best you can to screen you customers (as seen in the following sections) then you should not have a problem. Each funding source has their own set of rules that determine your risk. Typically, if a lease that you arrange goes bad within six to eight months, you may have to pay back your commission. If the funding source finds that you had reason to believe the lease was a fraudulent one, you will be responsible for the entire dollar amount.

The equipment lease broker business is not a get rich quick scheme. Anyone who applies the methods set forth in this manual can definitely make money within the first couple months of making their first call

How Does an Equipment Lease Broker Fund Its Leases?

What is a Funding Source?

A funding source is a party who provides financing for a lease transaction. The term is most commonly used by equipment lease brokers in referring to lessors, but it can also be used by lessors in referring to those parties who provide lessors with the funds lessors use to purchase equipment.

The first thing you will do when you complete this manual is start gathering funding sources. In order to get set-up with a funding source, you will be required to complete a Broker Application. The Broker Application (provided by funding sources) will request your company name and address, as well as personal information on yourself. Expect funding sources to check your personal credit and bank references. [2]<u>Be aware that some funding sources will not take new brokers</u>, while others just want to see that your credit is in good standing.

Where Do You Find Funding Sources?

Funding sources can be found on the internet and in leasing periodicals. The Monitor Daily is the greatest source for funding sources and other information. Their website is free and you can search their entire database for funding sources at www.Monitordaily.com. Another site that has some funding source information on it is www.ELAonline.com. ELA online may charge you a membership fee to search their funding source database (a lot of the same ones that are free at the Monitor Daily).

Funding Source Programs & Services

Funding sources offer a lot of different programs. The best ones will offer programs that no other sources offer. These programs give you a competitive advantage when lessees or vendors require specialized financing.

Some "Common Programs" you must make sure you have:

- Application Only to $75,000.00
- Prefunding
- Corporation Only Programs
- New & Used Equipment

Some "Special Programs" you should try to get:

- Start-up Businesses or Businesses under two years
- Seasonal Payment Plans
- 90 Day Deferral
- Step-Up Program
- 7 × $100 Program
- 6 × $99 Program
- Annual Payments
- Leasing for Restricted Industries
- Franchises
- Title Vehicles (New & Used)
- Tough Credit Programs

---

2 If a funding source does not allow you to work with them because of your new status, ask them if they can recommend an equipment lease broker for you to work through until you establish yourself. They will usually refer you to a "super broker." A super broker is an equipment lease broker who allows other lease brokers to send them business and in turns offers rates almost as good as the funding sources.

The Lease Discounter

Lease discounting is when you use your own money to fund the lease with plans to later sell the lease to a specified funding source, bank or insurance company. You are the lessor and loan underwriter (you approve or decline the deals). The documentation you use is all up to you. However, if you plan to discount your leases to a particular funding source or bank, the agreements you use better coincide with what that entity will accept as a legal binding contract.

Discounting leases may be more profitable than brokering leases, but it's a lot riskier and more difficult.

When you sell the lease to the bank, you can either hold title to the equipment on lease and its purchase option (residual) or release the title and residual to the party buying the lease from you. Holding the title to the equipment may be more profitable for you in the long run. On the other hand, holding the title of the equipment puts you at more risk for the entire term of the lease. You are responsible for the lease as it matures if you continue to hold title to the equipment.

The other option is to sell the lease and your rights to the equipment entirely. In this situation, you release yourself from any liability to the said lease, while also sacrificing a larger return and some nice tax breaks.

As you can see, a lease discounter has much greater risk than an equipment lease broker. While an equipment lease broker may only be on the line for the lease commission a few months after the lease commences, the lease discounter is on the line for the entire dollar amount until it is off his/her books.

If you are interested in discounting leases, learn as much as you can about it first. Talk to professionals, banks, funding sources, competitors, etc. Simply brokering equipment leases will be a good start in your education process.

Financing Your Own Leases

Financing your own leases requires you, the lessor, to accept applications yourself, analyze the credit data of your applicant and decide whether you will invest in the applicant. Then you must decide on a yield that you desire to receive relative to the risk that you are taking to lend the customer the money on the equipment. Then you must fund the lease yourself and wait out the entire term of the lease to get your money back and your desired return (assuming that your customer makes all of the payments).

In financing your own leases, you are responsible for drawing up a lease agreement between yourself and the lessee (see documentation examples J-1 through J14, and Lease Scenarios 1-3). You must also pay the vendor for the equipment and bill the customer for however long the lease term is (thus servicing the loan).

Sample lease agreements are provided that may be usable in your state; however, it is important that you have the lease agreements proofed by an attorney in the state that you wish to lease in before using them. Laws are subject to change from state to state.

At this advanced stage of leasing, you may have already been brokering leases; perhaps you have discounted them too. It is not a good idea to finance leases on your own without complete knowledge of the leasing business and lease accounting and its legalities. Because laws differ so much between states, you will need to be aware of collection issues, the proper documentation, lessee rights, liability insurance on the equipment that you lease, titling equipment, etc. Since this book is not centered on financing your own lease portfolio, I recommend that you take a look at some of the suggested readings provided for more information on this type of leasing.

SECTION 4

A BRIEF SUMMARY OF THE LEASE PROCESS AS AN EQUIPMENT LEASE BROKER

In This Section:

- The Leasing Process: Application through Funding

The Leasing Process: Application through Funding

A Summary of the Equipment Lease Broker's Role

Step 1:   **Marketing for Lease Applications**

A lease begins with a completed lease application, which may be faxed, mailed or taken via telephone. You receive the completed application from an individual who desires to procure equipment.

As described in the next section, there are various ways to market for lease applications. Depending upon how you choose to market for lease applications, you will get them from two main sources: The vendor &/or the lessee (end-user).

Upon receipt of a lease application from an equipment vendor, it is important to call the vendor (equipment salesman) and notify him/her that you received a lease application for the specified equipment.

If the lease application came to you from the vendor, then get the vendor's permission to contact the customer to go over any missing or unclear information on the application.

Lease applications are often illegible and incomplete. You may need to call the customer to clarify the social security numbers, phone numbers, bank account numbers, etc.

Step 2:   **Process the Application**

Pull a credit report on the customer to determine if the lease application is workable. Once a credit report is analyzed and you decide to move forward, you will get the bank and trade references and prepare the application to be submitted to a funding source of your choice.

Step 3:   **Prepare the Application for Submittal**

Once you have obtained and reviewed the bank reference and trade references you should be able to determine on your own if the deal is approvable and with which funding source.

Decide which funding source to send the lease for approval consideration

Type the application and fax with references to the desired funding source

Step 4:   **Funding Source Response**

Funding sources respond within 24-48 hours on a typical application only transaction with an approval, decline or pending. Pending means that you will have to request extra information and documentation from the customer and get it to the funding source to be re-considered for approval.

Step 5:   **Sell the Terms**

If approved, you will need to contact the customer and sell the terms offered by the funding source. Contact the vendor and let him/her know that the customer is approved right way.

Step 6:   **Prepare & Send Lease Documentation**

Lease documentation should be overnighted to the customer (lessee) in accordance with the terms, vendor sales invoice and your documentation request worksheet. Either you or your funding source will prepare and send out lease documents.

Step 7:   **Receive & Review Completed Lease Documents**

Make sure the lessee has completed the documents accurately and that they submitted a check for the deposit on the lease.

Step 8:   **Process Documentation**

Go through and make sure that all the signatures are where they should be. Contact vendor and let him/her know that documents have been received and are being processed.

* It is important that you get an original invoice from the vendor before the funding source will issue you your commission. The invoice must designate the lender as the "Bill To" and lessee as "Ship To."

Step 9:   **Overnight Documentation to Funding Source**

Step 10:   **Funding Source Funding Update**

Funding sources typically respond within 24 hours with a funding report to tell you whether the deal funded or if any further action or information is required to fund.

Step 11:   **Verbal & Funding**

Upon receiving verbal verification of the equipment delivery and acceptance, the funding source overnights a check to the vendor for the equipment cost, and one to you for the commission that you built into the deal.

Step 12:   **You Receive Your Commission Check & Get Another Deal!**

SECTION 5

THE LEASE PROCESS IN DEPTH

In This Section:

- Marketing
- Getting the Application
- Processing the Application
- Submitting the Application
- Funding Source Response
- Selling the Terms
- Documentation
- Receiving & Processing Documentation
- Funding the Lease
- Getting Paid

Marketing

Who are You Marketing to?

Vendors or Lessees?

Emphasis of your marketing efforts should be placed on vendors, because vendors provide repeat business. However, in recent years, leasing companies have been experimenting with emphasis on lessee marketing because vendors are getting inundated with marketing calls from leasing companies.

This section will show you ways to market to vendors and lessees. I suggest doing both. I have gotten customers both ways. Lessees are good for one deal here and there, but vendors are for life (unless you upset them).

Choose an Industry

When you choose an industry to market to, you must consider the following factors: Are the dollar amounts of the equipment in this industry between $5,000 and $75,000+, and will funding sources like the equipment?

You can figure out the dollar amounts of the equipment in a couple of phone calls or with some quick research online. You may not want to pursue cash registers or televisions sets or other small items. You should instead consider heavy equipment like coin-operated laundry equipment, forklifts or printing presses, etc. which will allow you to earn more money.

When it comes to the types of equipment funding sources will consider, each source has their own list of approved equipment that they will consider and restricted equipment, which they will not consider (unless you pre-arrange a special "vendor program" with the funding source). A "vendor program" is a program designed especially for your company by a funding source which gives you a competitive advantage over other leasing companies. In some cases you must obtain a written commitment from a vendor to give you first-right-of-refusal on all of his/her deals in order for a lender to give you a vendor program. He in turn gets a higher approval ratio and better interest rates from your funding source. You sit in the middle processing the deals and collecting the cash.

Below are examples of both commonly approved and restricted equipment:

Approved Equipment (See Exhibit 2)

Exhibit 2

APPROVED EQUIPMENT BY MOST FUNDING SOURCES

Addressing Machines
Automotive Repair Equipment
Automotive Electric Equipment
Bakery Equipment
Baling Equipment
Beauty Salon Equipment
Bending Machinery
Blueprint Equipment
Bookbinding Equipment
Bowling Lane Equipment
Brake Service Equipment
Bulldozers
Cash Registers
Check Protection Equipment
Collating Equipment
Compacting Equipment
Computer Equipment
Computer Furniture
Concrete Braking Equipment
Contractors Equipment
Conveying Equipment
Copying Machines
Counting Machines
Cranes
Dairy Equipment
Data Processing
Degreasing Equipment
Dental Equipment
Die Cutting Equipment
Dredging Machinery
Drying Equipment
Dry Cleaning Equipment
Duplicating Equipment
Electrical Discharge Machinery
Embroidery Equipment
Excavating Equipment
Facsimile Equipment
Fitness & Health Club Equipment
Folding Machinery
Food Processing Equipment
Forklifts (New & Used)
Garbage Collecting Equipment
Golf Course Equipment
Hoists
Hospital Equipment
Hotel Equipment
Ice Making Equipment
Industrial Equipment
Irrigation Equipment
Knitting Machines
Labeling Equipment
Laboratory Equipment

Lamination Equipment
Laundry Equipment
Lettering machines
Lighting Systems
Lithographers Equipment
Loading Dock Equipment
Machine Shop Equipment
Machine tools
Marine Equipment
Materials Handing Equipment
Metal Fabrication Equipment
Metal Forming Equipment
Office Furniture & Equipment
Packaging Equipment
Paving Equipment
Perforating Equipment
Photographic Equipment
Physicians Equipment
Plastic Molding Equipment
Plating Equipment
Printing Equipment
Refrigeration Equipment
Restaurant Equipment
Roof-Top Heating & Cooling Systems
Sandblasting Equipment
Screen Printing Equipment
Service Station Equipment
Sheet Metal Equipment
Sign Making Equipment
Store Fixtures
Telephone Equipment
Textile Equipment
Tire Equipment
Typesetting Equipment
Video Equipment
Wheel Alignment Equipment
Wood Working Equipment
Word Processing
X-Ray Equipment

Restricted Equipment (See Exhibit 3)

Often you will find a funding source that will do tough equipment/industries like underground fuel tanks, fitness equipment, surveillance equipment, etc. You should take advantage of those rare situations and work closely with that funding source to corner those markets. Market share in a rare industry will give you a competitive edge over other leasing companies (the ability to finance equipment other leasing companies cannot). This is an example of a niche.

Exhibit 3

RESTRICTED EQUIPMENT BY MOST FUNDING SOURCES

Air Conditioners/Heating Systems
Aircraft
All Roof-Top Equipment
Amusement Equipment
Antennas
Archery Simulators
Artwork
ATM's
Bingo Equipment
Boats
Bowling Equipment
Bullet Proof Booths for Convenience Stores
Car Carousels
Cellular Phones
Charter Buses
Concrete Ramps
Credit Card Terminals
Emergency/Ambulance Response Systems
Emissions Equipment/Smog Machines
Energy Management Controls
Fencing
Fire or Gas Alarm Systems
Fire Detectors
Fitness Equipment
Fluorescent Lights
Games (jukeboxes, pool tables)
Golf Simulators
Hair Removal Systems
Ice Machines
Invasive Medical Equipment
Lead Testers
Leasehold Improvements
Mobile Kiosks
Mobile Homes/RV's
Oil Field Equipment
Pagers
Pay Phones
Pet Displays
Playground Equipment
Predictive Dialers
Radio Towers
Satellites/ Satellite Dishes
School Buses
Shelving Customized
Small Hand Tools
Solar Energy Equipment
Sport Utility Vehicles

Tanning Beds
Theatrical Equipment/Stage Lighting
Toxic Waste Equipment/Containers
Underground Fuel Tanks
Used Audio, Visual, Survaillance Equipment
Used Computers
Used Irrigation Equipment
Vending Machines
Water Coolers
Websites

Marketing for Leases

Summary of the Different Marketing Methods

Mailers

Flyers and postcards are a common item to send out to potential vendors and lessees. It is very common now, and unfortunately, not very effective. If you choose to use this method, you can save money by creating a card stock flyer that utilizes four parts of a normal sheet of paper (post cards). The printing expense will be four times more cost effective and the postage rates will decrease to postcard rates rather than letter. You can also take advantage of the bulk rates that the U.S. Postal Service offers. Bulk mailing requirements tend to be too tedious, so I have found small local mailing service companies to be more advantageous. These companies will save you money from the normal postal rate and do all of the stamping and mailing for you. You just hand them a stack of flyers or postcards, and they do the rest. Your time is better spent on the phone, not licking envelopes.

If you send a flyer, fold it in three and address one of the sides. Do not waste money on envelopes for a procedure that may not show much return.

Create a Professional Website

It is very inexpensive to build a website today. Prices have come down, and web-building programs have gotten easier to use. In addition, you can purchase high-end website templates online for around $100.00 per site. You purchase the website template design that you think most represents what you want to do and then fill in the blanks with your business info. Whether you desire to develop a major web store for potential clients to read information and complete lease applications or just build a simple one page website (information page that has contact information), it is always a good idea to expose your business in as many places as possible.

On-line applications make it easy for your customers to apply for leases. (Results are, however, debatable).

Internet marketing has grown rapidly in the last decade. It would highly recommend taking advantage of the technology and creating a high-end website. The better your website is, the more reason for someone to stay on the page and eventually contact you. A great website will give you a competitive edge in the leasing industry. If you do some research online at other leasing companies, you will find that most leasing websites are terrible and look like they were created and designed by children. I was blown away at how unprofessional leasing websites looked when I last checked. Websites are extremely important today. Do not make the mistake that most other leasing companies are making and allow your website to appear unprofessional and boring.

Once you have a website online, you need to know how to make it work for you. There are several ways to do this:

SEO Rankings:

Invest some money into a company that can help boost your SEO rankings. SEO is the well known abbreviation for Search Engine Optimization. When someone types equipment+leasing+forklift into the Google search engine, websites with the best SEO rankings will pop up first. It is even easier and less expensive if you focus your SEO work on an industry or city (equipment+leasing+seattle). Since most people seek out services online, you would be wise to invest in a good website and SEO service.

Online Networking and Link Building:

Another way that people are building their businesses today is by networking with other companies and people online. Try linking your website to other sites and directories. Create a Facebook page for your company and link to as many other people as you can. Create a blog page on your website and be sure to add information to it weekly. This will boost your SEO rankings dramatically so that your website pops up more frequently when people seek out leasing companies.

Broadcast Faxing

Fax numbers are available from mailing list companies that you can purchase in bulk by industry, state, company size, etc. Faxing alone will not make your phone ring off the hook. In fact, you may get more calls from people telling you to remove their fax number from your list, than you do for business. However, if you can put together a nice simple flyer on your computer combined with a faxing program (I prefer Winfax) you can contact over four hundred people a day. You will eventually get some business, and the money earned will outweigh your phone bill. I recommend faxing to equipment vendors and potential lessees on a regular basis, but do not rely on this type of marketing alone. *Check the laws in your state before doing this. Unsolicited emails could get you in trouble or fined.

Broadcast Emailing

Email marketing is becoming more popular as more and more people get involved in the super information highway. The effectiveness is too new to rate. The good part is: it is free to send email. The bad thing is: there is no piece of paper to put in a file. Once someone realizes they are getting marketing literature, they just delete the email (with a click it is gone) or it goes to their junk file. If you fax them or mail them a piece of information, they may file it for the future when they need your service. I am not sold on emailing as a source of business, but it is definitely worth a try to see what results you can get. Companies exist that both sell email lists and actually send the emails. There is a variety of software available that will allow you to send multiple emails from your computer if you want to do it on your own.

    You may also try searching industries on the web. Look at different websites and email the salespeople listed. Ask them if they are happy with their leasing source. Inform them of your niche. You may get a better response from this emailing option versus the shotgun approach just mentioned.

Trade Shows & Conventions

In almost any equipment industry there are trade shows a couple of time per year in different regions of the United States. There are three ways to utilize a trade show for marketing:

    First, you can have a booth for your company. A booth is nice, but expensive. You have to pay for the booth space ($2,000 to $20,000 depending on the show). You have to have a nice, professional looking booth made for your company ($10,000 or more). Though pricey, the advantage to a trade show booth is that you have a lot of customers walking by your booth for 2-3 days straight, walking away with a polished impression of what you have to offer. It is good to be prepared with a lot of business cards, applications and brochures on your programs and services.

    The second option is to go to attend trade shows as a guest with a pocket full of business cards and talk to as many people as you can meet. Talk to people looking at equipment, buying coffee, eating lunch, etc.

    I have also offered to sit in my vendors' booths and talk to the potential equipment customers about leasing. This method is great; you have a shoe in with people and don't have to pay to be there. You do not have to walk up to anyone and make conversation, they come to you.

In conclusion, trade shows can be a great way to market. It can be costly or inexpensive; your results will vary with the amount that you are willing to spend. A trade show is also a great way to meet vendors that you have been doing business with over the phone. Be sure to make appointments to meet these people when you go.

Paid Advertising

Some advisable places to purchase advertising are:

- Industry Journals

- Industry Magazines

- Bi Monthly's

Ads in Industry magazines or Journals are a great example of effective paid print advertising, because of their precise targeting. Let's say, for example, that you are marketing in the fitness equipment industry. There are only five industry magazines that market equipment to owners of health clubs. If you placed an ad in one of these magazines, you are almost sure to get response. A large ad can be costly, so choose wisely and hire a graphic designer to make your ad look superb.

You may also experiment with cable television, radio, or the yellow pages if you feel that your target market is truly reachable via these media. I do not otherwise recommend them.

Business Cards

Print professional business cards and hand them out to everyone. Let everyone know that you provide financing for equipment. People love to do business with people they know rather than strangers. A referral creates immediate business, whereas business developed through phone solicitation requires more time. This brings us to the next technique: Referrals.

Referrals

Some of your best, most reliable vendors will come from referrals. A perfect scenario is as follows:

A vendor sends you a deal. You get the customer approved and discover that the customer is buying one piece of equipment through your vendor, but then needs another piece from another vendor you've never met before. GREAT! A new vendor! If you can do a smooth deal with this new vendor, he/she may do business with you again and again because they are familiar with you.

Great referral tip!

Ask your customers for three referrals. In return, you waive their processing fee on their documents. There is typically a $75.00 funding source charge for documents. Offer to waive that fee if the customer gives you three names and phone numbers of friends of his that may need leasing. When you call these people, you can use your customer's name as a referral and it creates immediate trust and credibility.

Telephone Solicitation to Develop Equipment Vendor Relationships

I don't know anyone who likes to telemarket, however, in this business, telemarketing is the most effective way to build your business if done properly. This section illustrates how to develop a daily flow of lease applications through telemarketing. It describes how you will develop relationships with equipment vendors nationwide, creating a consistent flow of lease applications using the "3-Call Prospecting Cycle."

This marketing method will be the main engine for promoting your business. If this method is followed correctly, you can potentially earn in excess of $100,000 yearly. Some equipment lease brokers will use this method to get their business off the ground during their first year in business. When done properly, these people never have to do this again. In some cases, others find that due to changes in vendor relationships (i.e. vendors going out of business or discontinuing lines) they end up telemarketing again to build a database of new relationships.

What is Your Intention with the 3-Call Prospecting Cycle?

There are essentially two groups to market leasing to: End-users (lessees) and vendors. Vendors have proven to be the most profitable. Vendors provide repeat business monthly/yearly whereas end-users will typically lease once every 3-5 years. Hence, you must develop a vendor base to take advantage of continuous repeat business.

Almost all vendors offer some sort of financing to their clients. 70-80 percent of equipment vendors use outside sources like you, the equipment lease broker. When a vendor's customer inquires about how to finance their equipment, the vendor refers to a file of leasing companies he/she has on hand. These are typically equipment leasing companies that have solicited his/her business. Your goal is to first, get into that file of lease companies. And second, be the first company chosen by the vendor every time the vendor's customers request leasing. The 3-Call Prospecting Cycle shows you how to develop this type of a profitable relationship with a vendor.

No matter what you learn from the 3-Call Prospecting Cycle, the vendor is going to have to like you, trust you and enjoy working with you. If your personalities clash, he/she may not be worth your time pursuing.

I recommend that you use a contact manager/database program with your computer in conjunction with telemarketing. My favorite database program is ACT. Many people use Outlook or Excel. Both are simple and work well with Winfax and other common programs making it easy to get the job done without a fuss. A database program will assist you in organizing the relationships that you are building and helps you organize follow-up calls to maintain these relationships. Database programs also work in conjunction with faxing and emailing programs so you can stay in contact with your database of clients easily on a regular basis through periodic or frequent marketing faxes (monthly, quarterly, etc.).

Structural and organizational skills are a key element to your success. A database program, such as a current version of ACT, Outlook or Excel, will greatly assist you in organizing your contact.

Telemarketing lists are available through different mailing list firms, online and at libraries. For example, one mailing list firm that you can use to get started with is InfoUSA. They have a product called, "Power Business" which costs today approximately $300.00, and includes a Cd-Rom, with 2,000 downloadable contacts for your own for marketing purposes. These lists include business phone numbers, fax numbers, key contacts, etc. You can tailor your own prospecting lists from these disks to meet your individual needs. You can choose the industry, city, state, etc. If you do some research you will find a few different "leads" companies around. You can have specific lists sent to you, or a Cd-Rom to customize your own.

3-Call Telephone Prospect Cycle for Vendors

FIRST CALL: Vendor Qualification

This is the initial prospect call to obtain information to qualify your prospective vendor to determine whether they meet your defined market niche. You will utilize the "Lead Qualification Sheet: Vendor" (Example Y in this book).

When calling your prospects, ask for the individual listed as "Main Contact" on your call sheets, or you could ask for the "Sales Manager." Once you have this key person on the phone, find out if the equipment type, average transaction, and number of potential leases per month qualify this vendor as someone you want to do business with. Typically, the right answers would be: heavy leasible equipment, $5k - $75k average transaction size, one plus lease transactions per month, etc. You also need to find out which of your funding source's services are the most valuable to this prospect (these valuable services are called the "Hot Buttons"). Find out how you benefit them by increasing their sales and providing excellent equipment leasing support. You must concentrate on developing a full understanding of the operation of their business and product and on marketing so you become a valuable leasing partner. If they are not a qualified vendor or you cannot develop a mutually beneficial partnership, do not pursue this prospect further.

The two most destructive habits are chasing prospects who are not qualified but who love to set-up and talk lease programs, and spending time pursuing qualified prospects that you cannot locate a mutual benefit.

> Don't get excited about a vendor that only leases twice a year, or does 20 leases a month at $1,800 each. Those are not good prospects. You will accelerate the growth in your vendor network by making more prospect calls with the extra time saved avoiding these vendors.

> Many times, a vendor will be highly qualified (beneficial to you), but because they are already working with a list a good leasing companies, may not find your service beneficial. Do not spin your wheels on these vendors unless you can identify a special leasing program that they can use.

In conclusion, if you reach a qualified prospect, who has an interest in your services, send a presentation package and fax immediately following the telephone conversation. Include a hand-written note on your fax cover sheet referencing the "Hot Buttons" which you have identified in the conversation.

Presentation Folder & Fax:

Gather your paperwork from all of your funding sources and make a combined list of all the services they offer you and your customers. You will end up with a summary of "programs & services" to market and fax to your vendors (as you add and lose funding sources, this list will change). Send this list along with a business card and a friendly note to your prospective vendor. As mentioned in the paragraph above, you should also fax a note and the list of "programs & services" immediately following your phone conversation in case the vendor has a deal for you prior to receiving your package.

SECOND CALL: Vendor Follow-up & Close

You should make this call about one and a half weeks following the time your package was sent to the vendor to make sure they received their materials and to ask them to submit a lease application to you.

It is time to emphasize the "Hot Buttons" discussed in your initial conversation, and to obtain a verbal commitment that they will use you for their next leasing transaction. Do everything possible to keep them from saying no.

Example:"Mr. Vendor, we have established in our last conversation that we indeed have the programs to best meet your customers' needs. Not only can we offer your customers' zero payments for ninety days, but we can also pre-fund all of your lease transactions before you ship the equipment to the customer! Will you send us your next lease application?"

If you hang up the telephone before obtaining the commitment for the next lease, your valuable time, prior telephone call and information sent was likely wasted. You need to go back into your summary of "Programs and Services" and relocate new "Hot Buttons" not accurately found in your initial call before terminating the telephone call. You must obtain the verbal commitment for the next lease or put together a re-defined lease program and then follow-up again for the vendor commitment.

THIRD CALL: Thank You or Vendor Accountability

This is an essential call you must make to thank your new vendor for the application(s) sent, or to find out the reason you have not received a lease application. A thank you call is always appreciated. It can smooth out any obstacles during the lease process, and most of all, it is always memorable when the next lease comes across the vendor's desk. This third call should be made within thirty to forty five days of the second call.

On the other hand, if you have not received an application you can [3]confront the vendor on the issue in this third call. You know the amount of leasing your prospect does from your first call and you have obtained a commitment for the next lease in your second call. It is never improper to confront someone on a promise not fulfilled after you spent your valuable time and energy setting up a lease program to meet the vendor's specific needs. You have shown your potential vendor much respect, and you should accept nothing less in return. You will gain your highest credibility from people when you have expectations for commitments you receive. This way of doing business shows great pride, commitment, care, and responsibility on your part. You may discover that their lease volume or potential originally stated in your first call was not correct. You then need to go back to step one, re-qualify your vendor, and get a new realistic commitment.

You should set yourself a goal to fax or mail out five to ten presentation folders a day to qualified vendors. Keep this up until you reach over two hundred vendors in your database. You can then maintain your database by faxing newsletters and promotions to your vendors every couple of months to remind them of your existence. You can also set reminders for yourself to follow-up on certain vendors every couple of months.

The Lead Qualification Worksheet (Example Y)

The Lead Qualification Worksheet has been created to aid you in your vendor prospecting phase. The worksheet addresses all of the important vendor qualification questions in reference to "The 3-Call Prospecting Cycle."

In accordance with the worksheet, a qualified vendor is one that:

- **Currently offers leasing**. If you have to educate them, they probably have never been asked, care about it, nor want to understand it. There are plenty of vendors out there who already offer leasing, understand it and are looking for a good leasing company.

- **Sells equipment that your funding source will like.** Virtually all equipment can be leased. Check your funding source's list of approved & restricted equipment before choosing industries.

- **Dollar Range:** $5,000 to $1 million
  Typically $10k to $75k is the best.

- **At least one (1) lease per month. Preferably 2-6.**

- **They have something negative to say about their current leasing source**. All vendors have something negative to say about the leasing company they currently use. Capitalize on that.

---

3 Since you are trying to establish a relationship with this vendor, you do not want to confront them with a negative tone your first time. Give the vendor the benefit of the doubt; ask why they have not submitted a lease first. Behave in a service-full manner. Then if they continue to make false promises, you can lay down the law and/or move on.

Getting the Application

A completed lease application (example A) is a direct result of your marketing efforts, and the number of applications you receive will depend upon the quality of your marketing efforts.

Lease Applications Are Taken in Three Ways

Facsimile

Faxing is the most common vehicle for receiving lease applications. In most cases, the vendor will provide their customer (the lessee) a lease application to complete and forward to you. The customer will either complete the application and fax it from the vendor's office or head to his/her office to complete and fax it to you at a later date.

Mail

In some cases, although very rare, an applicant may wish to mail you his/her lease application. This is common in certain industries where the customers don't have offices like trucking and agriculture. You will have to mail the customer an application. Provide a return envelope with the application to assist them in returning it to you (you need their signature). In the meantime, I would recommend getting all of the information that you can over the phone and beginning what credit work you can until you get the signature to pull credit and bank references.

Phone

Approximately 15 percent of the time someone will give you the information over the phone so that you can begin working on the application. The only problem with this method is that you cannot pull an individual's credit report without a signature allowing you to do so. You will need the application with the signature before you can obtain crucial data used in the decision-making process.

Proofing the Application

(Refer to the Lease Application Example A while reading this section).
There are a few key elements of the application that must be completed before funding sources will review it. It is your responsibility as an equipment lease broker to make sure you have all of the information that is required by your funding source completed on the application. For some reason, applicants almost always leave certain portions of the application blank or the applicant's handwriting may be poor. Here are the important elements of an application that must be completed before moving to the next step (Processing the Application):

Vendor Information

The vendor information shows who the vendor is, including address, phone and contact person. This is important, because on all transactions, the funding source will want to do some background research on the strength of the vendor. It is important for the funding source to make sure they are sending money to a legitimate business.

Lessee Information

Make sure that the applicant includes the name of his/her company, address, contact, phone, type of business and [4]years in business. It is imperative that you have the exact name of the business and

---

4 If the lessee's company is 10 years old, but the current owner bough the business from the former owner 1 year ago, then the "years in business" is only 1 year. A different business owner means a different business. No 2 owners are the same, so

correct spellings. The exact name of the business is important because the funding source is going to research the company in Dun & Bradstreet using the exact company name.

Personal Information of Lessee

This section must include names of officers and owners of the business applying for a lease including addresses and most importantly, social security numbers. If there are more than two owners, try to find out what percentage of the business each officer owns.

Bank Information

This is an extremely important part of the application which displays the applicant's business bank, account number, branch phone number, and contact person. Try your best to get a phone number and contact. The applicants do not always fill this part out completely. The information obtained from a business bank account can tell you and your funding source a lot about an application as discussed in the following section of this chapter.

Trade References

While not always needed, it is a good idea to make sure that you have 2–3 trade references on the application before you begin working on it. A trade reference is a referral from a business which has extended credit to the applicant. For example, a lumber company allows a construction company to pick up lumber throughout the month by simply signing a purchase order. The lumber company bills the construction company on a monthly basis. The lessee (a construction company in this example) establishes a credit history with the lumber company which can be referred upon by anyone with the construction company's authorization.

Signature

It is imperative that there be a signature at the bottom of the lease application. Without a signature, you are not allowed, by law, to do any credit work on the applicant. The signature gives you permission to pull a credit bureau, call the bank, and obtain trade references. Don't be afraid to fax the application back to the customer for a signature, or use the "credit authorization sheet" (Example E) to obtain a signature by fax.

Equipment Description

Provide a complete and accurate breakdown of the equipment and its cost somewhere on the application. Part of the funding sources decision to approve your customer for financing is based on the strength of the equipment. If there is a lot of equipment, you can forward the vendor's quotation along with the application to the funding source.

Re-Brokered Transactions

If your funding source will allow re-brokered transactions (where another equipment lease broker sends you deals) then you must put the name and address of the original broker somewhere visible on the lease application or fax cover.

---

a funding source will consider this business 1 year old. There are some exclusions to this if the current owner managed the company for a long time, etc.

Processing the Application

Once you have received all of the required information on the lease application, it is time to collect as much positive credit data as you can and prepare the application for submittal to the 5proper funding source.

Processing the application entails a combination of pulling a credit bureau on the owners of the company together with obtaining bank, trade, and loan references.

Credit Bureaus

It is preferable to pull credit bureaus prior to obtaining bank, trade, and loan references. If the personal credit bureaus are really bad, then you can stop right there and save yourself the time and energy on phone calls and faxes that could be focused towards working on a potentially profitable deal with someone else.

In order to pull credit bureaus, you must sign up with a local credit reporting agency that allows you to pull your own credit bureaus. You will have to have your leasing company in place with a business license to do this. Currently there are three places that you can call to pull bureaus directly from your computer: Equifax, Transunion and Experian. These credit reporting agencies are the three most commonly used for their data on individuals with any sort of credit history in the United States. They can be found in the white pages under the business section. If you call any one of them, they will be able to instruct you further on how to set your company up to pull credit bureaus. It is very easy.

A credit bureau shows if a person pays their bills on time, how much available credit they have, etc. Negative results include late payments, high revolving debt, tax liens, civil judgments, bankruptcies, foreclosures, repossessions, etc. If a person pays their bills on time, has not over extended him or herself, is a homeowner, etc., they are considered to have good credit. A credit bureau will also show you and your funding source how many inquiries your applicant has had recently. Every time someone pulls a persons credit bureau, it is called an inquiry. For example, if a man gets a car loan at a dealership and the dealership tries five different banks before the man is approved, then the man will have five different inquiries on his credit report listing each of the banks that the dealership attempted to get approval at. The same goes with funding sources. If your customer has a bunch of inquiries from other funding sources, chances are, there is something wrong and he/she is not getting approved, or your customer is getting approved but is trying to get a lot of leases at once. Either way, a lot of inquiries do not look good to your funding source. The funding source may actually decline your customer unless you get explanations of all of the recent inquiries (within 3–6 months). If the funding source thinks the deal is worth pursuing, they will request the explanations.

The credit bureau is a great starting point to building a file on your lease applicant. Credit will be pulled on all owners of a company as long as they own over 20 percent of it (this varies from funding source to funding source). If there are three partners, three credit bureaus will be pulled. However, sometimes, in a corporation, if two people own 40 percent and one person owns 20 percent, it may not be that important to pull credit on the 20 percent owner (check with your funding source). If the credit bureaus are clean and positive, then there is a high probability that the applicant(s) will run their business well and pay their bills on time.

The three different credit-reporting agencies (Transunion, Equifax and Experian) each report a little differently. The credit reporting agencies, as well as your funding sources will gladly assist you in reading and understanding the data on the reports.

---

[5] It will be up to you to decide which of your funding sources will be the best match for the lease application based on your credit findings (applicant's time in business, credit, bank reference, trade reference, etc.).

Bank References

The bank reference is the second most important element of the application, because it tells you several key things. The bank reference will tell you how long the applicant has been in business and how well they manage their account. For example, you are looking to see if the applicant's average balance in their business bank account is high enough to be approved by your funding source and whether they had any Non-Sufficient Funds (NSF) or Overdrafts (OD) in the last year. It is common to have several bank accounts on a lease application. The more bank accounts provided the better. If a bank balance is low or contains NSF's or OD's, try to get other bank accounts from the applicant.

Example B is what a bank reference request sheet looks like. To get the reference, you simply call the phone number for the bank that the applicant provided on the application and ask for the contact person. If your applicant does not have a contact person, simply ask for someone that can give a reference on a bank account. Typically what a representative of the bank will give you a fax number and a person's name (or department) to send the reference request to. Once you have received this information, complete the top of the bank reference request form with the bank on the top left and the applicant information on the top right including the account number (if you use the reference form provided with this manual). Fax the form to the appropriate person or department at the bank and you should receive it back within 24 to 48 hours. You may be requested to send the lease application (containing the customer's signature) with the bank reference form so that the bank knows that they are allowed to release information to you. I like to call after 24 hours and follow up on the reference if I have not received it. Sometimes it gets lost at the bank, or the person who was supposed to do the reference is out sick. If you are friendly with the bank staff, you should be able to get someone else at the bank to do the reference for you. It is important to process a lease application quickly because the customer and vendor are depending on your to close the deal fast in most cases.

In some situations, the credit people at the bank will give you the information over the phone. This is nice because you get it immediately. Other times, they will request it by mail and refuse to give the reference any other way. In this situation, call the lease applicant and request his/her last three months bank statements. Most funding sources will allow you to sub the bank reference with bank statements if the reference is hard to get.

Things to examine when you get the bank reference back: date opened, average balance, NSF/OD activity (non-sufficient funds/overdrafts) and name exactly as it appears on account.

Date Opened

This is very important. For the best rates, a company must be in business for at least 2 years. Hopefully this date will be over two years old. If it is not, and they claim to be an older company, then ask them if they have another bank account to give you, or ask if they switched accounts within the last two years. If they switched accounts sometime in the last two years, try to get a copy of an older statement dating back two years or more with the company name on it.

Non-Sufficient Fund (NSF) / Over Draft (OD) Activity

It is extremely hard to approve a company for a lease when they bounce checks and overdraft their account. These numbers will fluctuate from zero to eighty or more. When these numbers exceed five, it becomes very difficult to approve the deal unless there is a legitimate excuse. If there is an excuse, then have the customer put the reason in writing and fax it to you. If they cannot fax, do the best you can to write a brief summary of why the NSF or OD activity took place (it better be good).

Name Exactly As It Appears On Account

This tells you if the account is personal or business AND verifies the business name. Always make sure you get this information. Whatever the bank tells you the name of the business is on the account must be the same name on the customer's business check that you receive when you process the lease documents. Later in this Section, you will see why this is important.

Do not ever cross out, correct, or change information on a bank reference form once completed by a bank representative. All bank reference information will be verified by your funding source, and if they find out that you changed any information on the reference, they will prohibit you from doing business with them. What would you change? Well you might consider increasing the dollar amount in their account, or deleting the NSF's or OD's with white out. Don't do it; they will find out and your relationship with the funding source will be destroyed.

Trade References

Trade references are not usually required on approval requests under $25k, however all funding sources are different, so you should review the required credit criteria for each of your funding sources. I always try to get 3 references (as requested on the lease application).

An example trade reference sheet has been provided for you (Example C). You may use the generic one, or create your own.

Basically, a trade reference shows you if the applicant pays his creditors in a timely fashion. As you can see on the trade reference request form, it asks for date opened, high credit, current balance, terms and payment history. These factors combined help you and your funding source determine whether you have a viable applicant or not.

Date Opened

Just like the bank reference request, date opened shows an amount of time that an applicant has been in business. Again, it is preferred that a company is in business for over two years, however, there are programs for applicants under 2 years in business.

High Credit

The high credit is the highest amount of credit that the reference allowed the applicant. For example, if a manufacturer orders boxes for his product from a cardboard box company, his orders may fluctuate monthly. He may need $2,200 in boxes on month and $3,200 the next. In that two month period, $3,200 was the high credit. Hopefully, when you get your reference, you will get the highest credit over the entire relationship between your applicant and the trade reference.

Current Balance

This is where the trade reference states if the applicant is carrying a balance. Hopefully it is lower than the high credit. If not, there is a problem. Your applicant is not paying and interest is accruing.

Terms & Pay History

This is the part on the reference request sheet where the trade reference gets to tell all. They state whether the applicant pays within 30 days, or is a bit slow.

Comparable Credit)

This is the last of the references that may be helpful in approving your customer. A loan reference includes any business loans or leases. I provided a generic form that you may use (Example D). I don't ask for these unless there is a problem getting an approval, or the funding source requests it.

Loan references are great to have when submitting an application to your funding source. It shows your funding source that other funding sources and banks believe in your customer and if your customer pays those loans well, then they will probably pay another loan well. Loan and lease references are great; if you can get them, be sure to do so.

For all of the above, it is important that all of the information on the application relates to a business. Funding sources are uninterested in personal bank accounts (unless there is a lot of money in them, as a second reference), credit cards accounts, personal loans, phone bills, etc. Make sure that everything on the lease application pertains to the business applying for the lease, not the business owner's personal accounts or credit card loans.

Submitting the Application

Once you have completed processing the application, it is time to submit the application for approval through the appropriate funding source.

By this point you should have the original application from the applicant, the credit bureau, the bank reference, up to three trade references, and any other pertinent data to accompany the deal (i.e. explanations of questionable items, proof of liens paid, judgment settlements, bank statements, etc.).

You must choose the best possible funding source to submit your deal to. Each funding source, when you set your leasing company up with them, will give you a list of credit criteria or parameters upon which they base their approval decisions upon. It is very simple. You just need to look at all of the information that you have obtained and pre-evaluate which source will most likely consider your lease transaction and approve it? Does the bank reference date back far enough for Funding Source A? Or should I send it to Funding Source C, because they will approve newer companies? Is the credit strong enough for Funding Source B? Will Funding Source A consider the equipment being leased?

Upon choosing the proper funding source to send your deal, it is ready for submittal and you must package your deal to them in the following order:

1. **Cover page / Fax Transmittal Sheet to Funding Source**

   You should have a standard fax cover letter (Example U.) that you always use for your company that includes your company name, address, phone, fax, logo, etc. Address it to your contact at the funding source and include a brief summary of the transaction at the bottom of the facsimile sheet. Include strengths & weaknesses. Do not hide anything from a funding source. They will confirm all of the data.

2. **Typed Lease Application and Handwritten Original**

   I suggest that you always type up a fresh lease application onto a blank lease application for your funding source. It looks so much more professional than sending the original handwritten application. Send the original along anyhow so that your funding source has the signature in case they need to re-verify your credit work.

3. **Credit Bureau(s)**

4. **Bank Reference(s)**

   Make sure they are legible, whether you handwrote them, or they were faxed to you.

5. **Trade References**

   Again, make sure they are legible.

6. **Any additional documentation strengthening the deal.**

Now it is time to submit the transaction by fax to your chosen funding source and await an answer. This typically takes 24-48 hours, sometimes sooner, sometimes later, depending upon the funding source.

Funding Source Response

You will receive one of three answers: Declined, Pending or Approved.

Declined

No one wants to receive this answer and you want to try not to. If you can avoid it, try not to send a deal to a bank that will likely decline the deal. The idea of the processing or pre-evaluation is to try to figure out exactly which bank will approve the deal, giving the customer the best possible payment. Unfortunately, there will be times where your research (the typical processing expected of a broker covered in the previous section) does not completely uncover all the details about a client. Funding sources do research on their own using a company called Dun & Bradstreet to pull a report on the business itself. This usually uncovers things that you never knew existed about the customer if you don't pull this report yourself. For example, Dun & Bradstreet may have in their files that your customer pays all loans and creditors over thirty to sixty days late. Or there may be information that the customer is holding back, like number of years in business, a pending tax lien or a secret partner with terrible personal credit. Sometimes you can address a funding source's concerns and actually turn the deal into an approval, especially if the funding source sees potential in the deal and faxes you a Pending notice, rather than a flat out decline.

You may end up submitting a deal over 3-4 times before finding a funding source that will finance your customer. If you believe in the deal, your determination will get it done somewhere. There is certainly no shortage of funding sources looking for deals all over the country.

Pending

When a bank faxes you a pending notice, they basically do not like the deal as it is, or have questions about your findings or the strength of it. They will express how the deal could be more desirable to them. They do this by having you answer a couple of questions about the customer and commonly ask for additional documentation to clarify questions they have on the deal.

Here are some common additional documentation requests you will come across:

- Full Financial Package (two years tax returns, personal financial statement.)

- Business License (Need proof that applicant's business exists or has existed over two years)

- Directory Assistance (Can't find phone number in directory assistance.)

- Article of Incorporation (Need to know breakdown of ownership.

- Equipment Description (unclear as to what equipment is: Get vendor invoice or brochures.)

- Vendor Profile (Uncomfortable with vendor, need more info (Example F).)

- Additional Application from partner not mentioned

- Need Clarification on NSF/OD Activity.

- Need Clarification on business structure.

- Need Clarification on what type of business the applicant is in.

- Need Clarification on old bankruptcy (why did they file?)

- Proof of Release of Tax Lien, Judgment or lawsuit.

- Etc.

If you are eager to get the deal approved, then with just a little work, you usually can. The funding source will not make a deal pending if they do not believe in some way that it has merit. They are expressing interest in the transaction and are asking you to go one step further to help them feel more comfortable with putting their money into it. The other option is to try sending the deal to an alternative funding source.

Otherwise, if you send a deal to your funding source that meets all of their criteria, then there is a great chance that you will have an approval sitting on your fax.

Approved

Congratulations. You are almost done with the transaction. All you need to do now is follow up with the vendor to notify him/her that the customer is approved and notify the customer that he/she is approved.

When notifying the customer that they are approved, you should be prepared to quote some payments for different terms and end of lease options. I like to calculate a thirty month payment and a sixty month payment before I call so that I am prepared for them to ask what the payment is. Be sure to calculate the complete payment with tax to avoid misleading the client with a payment lower than actual.

Respond to the Vendor

It is important at this point to call the vendor and notify him/her as well as the customer that they are approved.

Next you sell the terms.

Selling the Terms

Selling the terms of the lease can be the most challenging part, aside from getting the application in the first place. The deal is approved and now for the first time, the customer is going to find out exactly what his payment is going to be over different terms and using different "end-of-lease" options. Typically, you can charge up to 15 percent commission (fifteen points) per deal with the funding sources. However, more specialized funding sources may only allow 5 percent to 10 percent commission to keep their exposure (risk) down. To figure out payments and build in your commission see Section 6.

How Much Commission Do You Charge?

How much commission you charge is entirely up to you. Typically, if the customer is easy to approve, has great credit and strong business history, you will not be able to charge more than 4 percent to 7 percent. If the deal just barely approved and you put a lot of work into it, then you might decide to charge 10 percent to 15 percent commission.

Quoting Your Customer

When I quote a customer, I usually start with the lowest possible payment, which is based on 60 months with a 10% PUT (typically the longest term available). Your customers will usually go for that to enjoy lower payments. Some want to be done with their lease earlier, so you can quote them 24 or 36 months. Find out what the customer wants.

Utilize The Benefits To Sell Tough Customers

The biggest factor that comes to play is rate. What is the rate? This is a question you do not want to encounter; yet you almost always have to. You can refer to Section 7 for some help answering this and other questions. I found that if you give lessees a ball-park figure they are happy with that. Interest rates in the equipment leasing business have always been higher than regular bank loans. The reason is; equipment leasing monies are easier to get, which puts funding sources at a higher risk. Funding sources do not require a lot from a customer to approve them. Also, the collateral for a lease is a depreciating asset that is being used daily by a company that may or may not stay afloat. There are many good reasons why equipment lease rates are a little higher than bank loans, as you will learn through time. Once you learn them and understand them, it will be easier for you to sell your lease payments to your customers. The only inexpensive lease rates you will encounter are manufacturer's specials like John Deere, CAT, etc. These companies will offer super low finance rates to good customers on new equipment. You cannot compete with that, so don't try to go head-to-head with manufacturers' lease incentive programs at 5 percent.

Once you have sold the payment and the terms to your customer, you will need to prepare documentation and overnight it to your customer to sign and send back.

Documentation

Generic Versus Funding Source Generated Documents

There are two ways to prepare the documentation on your lease. Depending upon the relationship that you have with your funding source, you will either have the funding source prepare documents, or do them yourself. Preparing documents yourself, using your company name and logo, means you are using "*generic documents.*"

Your documentation duties will vary depending upon which documentation procedure you choose.

Funding Source-Generated Documents:

Complete a Documentation Request Worksheet (Example I.)

Fax the documentation worksheet to the funding source that approved the transaction along with:

- Completed Lease Application

- Vendor Invoice

- Copy of Approval

- Vendor Profile (if Pre-funding is required)

The funding source sends documentation out to the customer and waits for the return of the completed documents. Your job is to follow-up with the lessee and make sure they sign and send documents back properly. You will have to familiarize yourself with the funding source's documents in order to answer questions from the customer about them.

Generating Generic Documents: You Do the Documentation Yourself

1. Complete a Documentation Worksheet for yourself.

2. Complete the generic documents provided for you by your funding source. Each funding source has their own generic lease documents that you can fill in with your company name and logo. A lot of funding sources have a documentation program that they will send you on disk, or that you can utilize via their website. They are very easy to use. You type in the pertinent data regarding the particular lease (payments, purchase options, lessee name, etc.)

and then you can print the documents right out of your computer. Even better, some banks allow you to email or fax documents.

3. Ship the documents to the customer or the vendor via an overnight courier. Speed is important. Your vendor will be eager to sell his equipment. And you will be eager to earn your commission and close this deal. The same goes for the return. Enclose a return overnight envelope with the documents that you send out so that the lessee can overnight the completed documents back to you at no cost to them. It would be in your best interest to set up an account with an overnight courier like Federal Express, Airborne or UPS.

Here are some things to consider when making your decision on whether to utilize funding source-generated documents, or to do them yourself using generic documents provided by the funding source:

Control

If you prefer total control over your lease transactions, it is best to do documents yourself. You can track them, hold yourself responsible for errors, control the flow of money, etc. I like to be in control of the documentation process myself.

Timing

When you do your own documents, you can control the speed at which they are produced and sent out. However, when you rely on a funding source to do the documentation and overnight it to the customer for you, this may not always be the case. Often a funding source may take a day, two, or even more to prepare documentation and send it out. This is a long time in the leasing business.

Convenience

One good thing that I will take advantage of every once in a while is having the funding source complete the documents for me when I am busy with a lot of leases or when I am traveling. Sometimes it is nice to have those things handled for you.

Professionalism

Having your company name on the documents that you send out is great. Lessees can provide repeat business. It is a good idea to have your name in front of them at all times. Until they make their payments, they will think that you are the funding source.

Strength of Your Leasing Entity

Most funding sources will not allow you to do your own documents if your company is new. Larger funding sources may want your leasing brokerage to be at least two years old.

Receive and Process Documentation

Tips on Getting Documents Back

After you send your lease documents via overnight to your lessee, it is good business to follow up on them to verify that the customer has received them and to answer any questions they may have. Of course, you can always track the documents if you sent them overnight, but this gives you an excuse to call and see how quickly the customer intends to complete and send the docs back. Here are some ways to encourage the lessee to send his/her documents back right way (create urgency):

Equipment Delivery

The lessee is excited about the equipment; remind him/her that the equipment will not be delivered until the documents have been sent back and processed. Also, equipment that has to be manufactured or customized will not be ordered by the salesman until documents are back to lender.

Rate Change

In rare cases, rates will change while the documents are out with the customer. If a funding source raises rates, they will usually allow you a certain amount of time to get the documents back prior to increasing the rate on your particular deal. A hint of about rates increasing will definitely encourage your lessee to send documents back in a timely manner.

Approval is going to Expire

This is a very common way to create urgency when needed. Most approvals last for ninety days, while others may last for thirty or sixty days. I have had a lot of lessees wait until the last minute to send docs back. The expiring approval gives you a good reason to call the lessee and urge him/her to send the documents back for his/her benefit. Mention that you will have to start the process all over again in order to re-approve the lease.

Reminder Calls

Follow up with the customer every two or three days; especially if they seem excited to do the lease. Some business people need reminders when they are really busy. If you tastefully pester them, you will get the documents back. This method is common because a lot of people are afraid to sign long-term contracts. You will discover that several reminder calls are necessary to get the documents back on almost all of your deals.

May Lose Equipment to Another Customer

Sometimes lessees hold the documents so long, they lose the equipment that they originally wanted. This is especially the case with used machinery. Because the price is so good on quality used machinery, the equipment is in high demand. The vendor cannot wait for a lessee who is reluctant to send documents back when the vendor has cash customers calling every day for the same piece of equipment. Eventually, the vendor is going to sell it and tell you and your customer to have a nice day. Don't let this happen. Stay on top of your customer to prevent this from happening.

Overall, it is imperative that you go over the payments and terms with the customer before you send documentation out. Make sure they are excited about moving forward with the lease. Always quote the customer before sending documents and let them know when they are coming. Also, let them know that you are inserting an overnight envelope with the documents so that they can send them back immediately for processing.

Processing Generic Documents

Once documents have been received, it is now your job to thoroughly check that the customer has done everything correctly. The following is a short list of some common completed documentation requirements:

1. Lessee Advance Check
2. Photocopy of Driver's Licenses of all required personal guarantors.
3. Federal Tax ID#
4. All correctly signed documentation: Lease Agreement

Insurance Request
Purchase Option Letter
Personal Guarantee(s)

Here are some things that can go wrong when receiving signed documentation, and how to correct them:

1. Advance check is for the wrong amount
   Have the lessee overnight another check for the difference (you pay for overnight).

2. Advance check was written from the wrong account
   Have the lessee overnight a check from the proper account, or get a bank rating on the account they wrote the check from and approve it with the funding source.

3. Lease agreement or complimenting documentation is missing signatures.
   Send or fax it to the customer for signatures, then have them overnight back to you.

4. There is white out on the documentation, or a correction.
   Send or fax new documents to the lessee to redo and overnight back to you.

5. No drivers license.
   Lessee can make a good photocopy and fax it to you.

6. Missing Documents
   Send or fax new documents and have them complete and overnight them back to you.

Once all of the documents are in order, you must overnight them to the funding source along with the following documents:

1. Broker Fee Invoice   (Example S)
2. Assignment of Lease   (Example J-11)
3. Insurance Binder   (See Scenarios)
4. Original Vendor Invoice   (See Scenarios)

The more documents that you process, the better you will understand each funding source's requirements. Until then, expect to do a little bit extra work after you send the documents to the funding source. If you miss any of the mistakes above, the funding source will let you know that they need to be corrected prior to funding. They usually notify you with a fax.

Before a deal will fund, the funding source will be waiting on:

1. Original Vendor Invoice   (Example R & Scenarios)
2. Insurance Binder   (Example K & Scenarios)
3. Verbal Delivery & Acceptance

Funding the Lease

Original Vendor Invoice(s)

It is your responsibility to get the vendor to make and send you an original invoice for the lease at hand. Ask your funding source how they want the invoice made out. Typically, it will include the "Bill To: (the lessor)," a "Ship To: (the lessee)," the "Equipment Description" and "Total with Tax." If you do generic documents with your company name, then you are the lessor (Bill To &/or Ship To).

The Insurance Binder

You have to show the funding source a copy of the insurance binder before they will fund the lease and pay you your commission. The insurance binder shows the funding source that the lessee has liability insurance on the subject equipment for lease. This liability insurance protects the leasing company's investment/equipment if anything were to happen to it (fire, theft, injuries, etc.). There is an insurance request (example K) that you or the funding source sends to the lessee with the documentation. This request, when completed, has the lessee's liability insurance provider on it with phone numbers. All you have to do when you get that is fax it to the insurance carrier along with the vendor invoice, and they will fax you back an insurance binder within a day or so. This may sound difficult, but it is very easy and becomes second nature after awhile. If the funding source does your documents, then they may handle this procedure for you.

Site Inspection

On rare occasions, a lease will be approved by a funding source requiring that a site inspection be done prior to funding the lease. This means that once the lessee receives equipment, they must notify you so that you can notify your funding source to do the inspection. Your funding source will call a local site inspector who usually inspects the equipment within 24-48 hours. A report is faxed to your funding source stating whether the equipment has arrived and the condition it is in. If there is going to be a site inspection, it will be stated on the approval, and the customer has to pay for it (typically $150 to $250). The only bad thing about a site inspection is that it delays the speed in which you and your vendor get paid by the funding source after the vendor has delivered.

Verbal Delivery & Acceptance

If the equipment has been delivered and your funding source has all of the pertinent documents in hand, they will call the customer and verify equipment delivery. In this phone call, they will also inquire whether the customer is satisfied with the equipment and go over terms one last time.

Once the above three items have been handled, you and the vendor(s) get paid. The funding source will pay you the commission owed per your broker free invoice.

Getting Paid

By this point, the documentation is all clear for funding. The following has to happen for you to get paid:
1. All documentation including your assignment of lease is accurately completed and sent to the funding source.

2. Insurance binder has been faxed to the funding source.

3. Original invoice has been sent to the funding source (sometimes a fax is okay).

4. Your broker invoice has been faxed or mailed in with the documents instructing how much the funding source owes you and how to send you the money.

5. Verbal acceptance of equipment has taken place.

All funding sources overnight the vendor check and your commission check if you request it. They will either use your overnight account number to do it, or overnight and pay for it themselves. Each funding source handles overnight charges differently. It not, you can have them take $10 or $20 off of your commission to cover their costs. I have never had a problem with this.

If you made any agreements with referral sources or vendors to pay them a fee for the deal that closed, now would be the appropriate time to take care of them for their services.

Conclusion

The lease process in depth can appear very difficult, however, it is not. Once you go through the process a couple of times, you will find it to be very easy. This does not mean that you will not get discouraged or aggravated dealing with certain aspects of the process. The most challenging part is the documentation. You have to be extremely accurate when creating the documents. Make sure you do everything correctly before sending them to the lessee. When I first begin doing documentation for a funding source, I usually go over the documents with a documentation specialist at the funding source over the phone to be sure everything is correct before sending them out to the customer. Sometimes a caring specialist will have you fax or email your documents to them for review before you send them out to the customer. This can save you a headache later on, especially when you are doing a new funding source's documents for the first time.

When documents come back, there are many things that can be wrong. Be patient and work through them. It seems like funding sources always find something wrong at the last minute. Or they decide they need something in addition to the documents that they did not request ahead of time. All funding sources vary this way. Some funding sources are very easy to work with, while others can be difficult.

Overall, the process is easy and fun. Personally, I am addicted to the leasing business. I find myself working at night and on the weekends sometimes. I love closing deals. The best part is watching a Federal Express truck park in front of your office to deliver a large commission check to you!

SECTION 6

IMPORTANT LEASE CALCULATIONS

In This Section:

- Calculating Broker Commission Fee

- Calculating Lease Payments

- Converting Rate Factor to an Interest Rate

Important Lease Calculations

There are only a few calculations that you will need to know that are not typical calculator functions. You will want to purchase a financial calculator or one that is a little more advanced that your standard calculator[6].

Calculation One: Broker Commission Fee

Commission must be figured out before one calculates the lessee's lease payment, because the lease payment is dependent upon your commission. For example, the customer's payment will be higher if you charge 10 percent commission rather than if you charge 5 percent commission. The amount you decide to charge is up to you. Typically, your funding source will allow you to charge up to 15 percent (fifteen points) per lease transaction. The rate of commission allowed will vary among funding sources and dollar size of the transaction (as mentioned earlier). The funding source will clearly state what they will allow you to earn.

Funding sources will provide you with rate factor sheets (see Example V). On rate factor sheets are decimal numbers called factors. Factors are numbers provided to you by funding sources, which already have a built in yield to the funding source. It is then your responsibility to add 1-15 percent commission to the factor. This is easy. The factor you base your payments on depends upon the terms that your client requests. If your client wants $20,000 at 60 months ($1.00 Buy Out) then you find the appropriate factor on the funding sources factor chart. It is standard that factor charts are provided to you by your funding source.

For this example, let's say the funding source rate factor is .02251 (using rate factor sheet from example V). To add your commission you simply multiply the factor by 1.X (X is your desired commission percentage in decimal format).

Two Examples:	You want 8%	Multiply .02251 × 1.08 = .02431
	You want 10%	Multiply .02251 × 1.10 = .02476

Calculation Two: Lease Payments

Once you have built in a commission to the factor, it is easy to calculate the customer's payment. Simply multiply your new factor (w/commission included) times the total dollar amount of the lease.

Two Examples:	If you chose 8%	Multiply .02431 × $20,000 = $486.20
	If you chose 10%	Multiply .02476 × $20,000 = $495.20

Calculation Three: Converting Rate Factor to Interest Rate

This formula produces a high interest rate it doesn't necessarily mean that it is a bad lease: Rate Factor x 2400

This "lease calculator" takes no account of the following:

- The size of loan.
- Your company's circumstances.
- A start-up company may need to have additional security to secure lease finance.
- Other potential costs that an asset lender may charge.

---

[6] A calculator that allows you to insert numbers to the right of the decimal point is required. The first thing that you will need to do is read the directions to your new calculator and figure out how to insert 5 zeros to the right of the decimal point instead of the standard two. This is the only function that requires a better than average calculator.

Examples are documentation or "change of title" fees, which do vary but are generally minimal. Other factors that may affect the rentals include:

- The residual value of any asset to be leased
- Quarterly, Half Yearly or Annual Rentals.
- The amount of deposit you may wish to put down.

The equipment leasing process is faster, simpler, and often less costly than other financing alternatives.

SECTION 7

ANSWERS TO COMMONLY ASKED QUESTIONS

In This Section:

- Answers to Commonly Asked Questions

Answers to Commonly Asked Questions

The following several pages touch on some of the most commonly asked questions about equipment leasing. These are questions that you, your lessee and your vendor may need clarification on. Make sure that you read through all of the following questions and answers to better prepare yourself for any questions that may arise. Refer to this section for your first couple months of business until you are comfortable with the answers.

Question: **What is the interest rate on a lease?**

Answer: One of the main differences between a lease and a bank loan is that with a lease the entire payment can be tax deductible. (Your customer should consult an accountant regarding deductions. Do not attempt to give tax advice). That is why leasing companies do not quote interest rates. The leasing company owns the equipment during the term of the lease. There is a way to show the customer how much the cost would be per year, over and above the equipment cost.

Let's say the equipment was $7,500.00 and the monthly lease payment for 60 months is $193.50 (factor = .0258).

$$\$193.50 \times 60 \qquad = \qquad 11,610$$

$$-7,500 \text{ equipment cost}$$

$$\$ \quad 4,100$$

$$\$4,100 / 5 \qquad\qquad = \$ \qquad 820 / \text{year}$$

$$\frac{\$ \ 820}{7,500} \qquad = 11\% \text{ per year is the lease cost}$$

If the customer exercises the 10% purchase option at the end of the lease, this is also divided by 5 and gives 2 percent per year more, so the 11 percent becomes 13 percent.

Question: **Can a lessee pay the lease off early?**

Answer: Although funding sources allow early payoffs, caution the customer that an early payoff might be expensive.

When the lessee signs the lease agreement, he/she is committing to pay a certain amount of payments (12, 24, 36, 48 or 60 payments). This is the difference between a loan and a lease. With a loan, the borrower can pay off the principle balance at any time with no interest. With a lease, the lessee is required to pay all payments (all principle and interest) as agreed through the term of the lease. If a lessee decides he/she must pay the lease off early, they must contact the funding source for the remaining balance on the lease. There is no penalty for early pay off, however the customer is exercising their purchase option in addition to paying off the net lease balance. If this occurs early on in the lease agreement, the payoff could be higher than the original equipment cost.

To get a payoff amount, the lessee must calculate the sum of the remaining payments on the lease. On some occasions, the funding source will offer a small discount off the sum of the remaining payments due on the lease. This is more common once half of the lease has been paid off and dependent upon a good pay history.

If it is important to the client to pay off early, you should recommend a shorter term (12 or 24 months).

Question: **What do you lease?**

Answer: The sum of all the equipment that your funding sources will finance (per their credit guidelines). Examples of leasible equipment are: Fitness & health equipment, medical & dental equipment, dry cleaning & laundry, computers, telecommunications, surveillance, construction, office furniture, packaging equipment, forklifts, heavy machinery, and more.

Question: **Why would a lessee choose a 10% purchase option versus a $1.00 buy out at the end of the lease?**

Answer: The IRS guidelines on leasing call for a purchase option of 10 percent or greater in order to be considered a true lease. With anything less than 10 percent the IRS considers the transaction a conditional sale contract, and you could lose the tax write-off if audited.

Sometimes a lessee will choose the $1.00 buy out at the end of the lease because they do not want to pay a large sum at the end (10 percent or greater). In some cases lessees will deduct the payments as a rental expense even though the lease is considered a conditional sale contract and they are at risk of getting in trouble with the IRS.

Question: **Who provides service on the equipment?**

Answer: All warrantees and vendor guarantees are passed along to the lessee. Beyond the warranty time frame, the customer would contact the dealer or manufacturer. A funding source simply buys the equipment for the lessee, but does not take liability of the equipment.

Question: **Can a lessee return the equipment to the leasing company during the lease if they do not like it?**

Answer: No, an equipment lease is a contract for a specified number of payments. The only way to terminate the agreement prematurely is to payoff the lease.

Question: **Is the payment on the lease the only monthly cost?**

Answer: The lessee's payments may include use tax. Use tax is calculated by multiplying the payments times the lessee's local tax rate. Sometimes tax is included in their payment. Other times it is billed separately on their monthly bill.

Questions: **Is a lease assumable?**

Answer: Sometimes, it depends on the funding source. The funding source reserves the right to approve the new lessee from a credit standpoint. Once the new lessee is approved, the funding source will provide an assumption form for all parties to sign.

Question: **Can a lessee add equipment to the lease?**

Answer: Sometimes (depending again upon the funding source), the lessee can add equipment at a later date by signing a separate lease agreement or amendment for the additional items. The customer will still receive only one bill each month, and it can be arranged where all leases terminate at the same time. However, if twelve months or more pass, it is best to write a new lease all together. This varies from funding source to funding source.

Question: **Can a lessee upgrade the equipment during the lease term?**

Answer: This varies from funding source to source. The lease would have to be paid off, and then rewritten. The amount that it would cost to pay off the lease and write another one depends on whether the lessee is going to do another lease and upgrade, or pay it off and walk away. This can be an expensive route.

In some cases, if the lessee wants to amend the lease within thirty days of the start, it can be done at a minimal cost.

Question: **Can a lessee lease equipment from multiple vendors?**

Answer: Yes, almost all funding sources will allow a lessee to purchase from multiple vendors on one lease. For example, a lessee acquiring an oven, refrigeration unit, and point of sale computer system for their restaurant may need to buy each of those items at different places (vendors). In this situation, the oven and refrigeration unit will come from one vendor, while the point of sale computer will come from another.

For an equipment lease broker, your job becomes a little more difficult doing a multiple vendor transaction. You will be required to coordinate the invoices from the different equipment vendors prior to doing documentation. Here are some things you should be aware of as an equipment lease broker transacting a multiple vendor deal:

Last minute changes

One vendor can cause problems sometimes. Imagine negotiating for three vendors with numbers constantly changing, etc. For the broker, the less vendors, the better. However, you must always try to do what ever the lessee needs to get deals done for yourself and your vendor (to continue the relationship).

Why not write three leases if your customer has 3 vendors? If you wrote three different leases, your customer would have 3 different lease bills coming each month for three to five years. It is always best to try to get all the vendors on to one lease. Plus, the interest rates drop as the dollar amount rises. One lease at $60,000 will have a lower interest rate for your customer versus 3 leases at $20,000 each.

Invoices

Prior to funding you will need to get all of the original invoices in order. This will mean calling different vendors and coordinating with all of them how to correctly complete their invoices.

Delivery Times

All vendors have different delivery dates. The worst thing that can happen is to have three vendors on a lease. One delivers early, another won't deliver for six weeks because of a special order. This could be bad because your funding source may not pay the vendors until all vendors have delivered. This means that the vendor who pays first has to wait the longest for their money. Sometimes, funding sources will pay vendors as they deliver. Funding sources will not be so lenient on transactions under $20,000.

Funding Requirements

All vendors have there own funding requirements. Some want their money upfront, others require 50 percent upfront and the best do not require it until the equipment is delivered.

Do not be discouraged by the warnings of he multiple vendor deals. They are done all of the time, but just take a little bit more paperwork. The little extra work that is required is not worth passing on a lease deal. These are very common.

Question: **What is prefunding?**

Answer: Prefunding is a requirement for a lot of vendors. This is when a vendor requires that they get paid a certain percentage of the invoice amount prior to shipping, delivering or manufacturing the equipment for the lessee. Some vendors require 25-50 percent while others require 100 percent. Not all funding sources will allow prefunding. The funding sources that do allow it will require that a vendor complete a vendor profile (Example F) and get approved for prefunding.

Question: **Can a lessee cancel a lease?**

Answer: 99 percent of the time, a lease in non-cancelable unless negotiated prior to documentation with a specialized funding source. The lessee is required to make all the payments as agreed per the lease agreement.

Question: **What types of equipment can be leased and from whom?**

Answer: A lessee can lease virtually any business or professional equipment. Equipment is ordered from any reputable vendor specified by the lessee. Equipment leasing is available for all types of equipment from major manufacturing equipment to smaller equipment, such as computers. Equipment leasing financing is available from banks, finance companies and from equipment manufacturers or retailers.

Question: **Who is leasing good for?**

Answer: Companies that have to make major investments in equipment that don't want to tie up large sums of money, companies that need to change their equipment frequently, and companies with good cash flow that can easily afford the monthly payments but don't have the money to lay out for the purchase of equipment.

Question: **How are lease payments determined?**

Answer: The monthly payment is based on the risk factors associated with the industry, time in business, cost of equipment, and the terms requested by the lessee. The initial terms of a lease are normally twelve to sixty months and will also impact the payment terms. Leasing rates can be determined by factors such as:

- The cost of the leased asset.
- The lease term.
- The lease rental structure.
- The credit strength of the lessee including their history of other term debt.
- The financial strength of the lessee including term debt requirements and available cash flow.

Question: **Is a down payment required?**

Answer: A security deposit, normally equal to one or two months lease payment, is generally needed. This differs from a down payment since the amount is generally much less. It is a true deposit, which can be applied to the purchase price of the equipment at lease-end, or returned if there are no other payments due.

Question: **What happens at the end of the lease?**

Answer: What happens at the end of an equipment lease is up to the lessee. The lessee decides at the beginning of the lease which type of lease they want or, more likely, they'll want to choose a lease that allows them the flexibility of waiting until the end of the lease to decide. Generally it will be one of these choices:

- Return the equipment at the end of the lease with no further obligation. Assuming the equipment is in normal working condition; any security deposits paid will be refunded back to the customer.

- The lessee may re-lease the equipment. Many leases offer annual or monthly renewals at renegotiated lease payments. Because the leasing company has already gotten a good deal of their investment back, the lessee can generally look for drastically reduced lease payments.

- The lessee may trade in or upgrade the equipment for a lease on newer equipment. The lessee may effectively get the value of a trade-in on equipment they didn't even own.

- The lessee may purchase the leased equipment. In the case of the so-called "$1.00 Buyout" lease, they will take ownership for $1.00.

SECTION 8

YOUR RISK AS AN EQUIPMENT LEASE BROKER

In This Section:

- Commission Refund
- Collection Issues
- Fraud Transactions
- Conclusion

Your Risk as an Equipment Lease Broker

While you may not actually be personally guaranteeing the leases that you are transacting, you do have some liability to the funding sources that fund your deals and pay you a commission. It is rare that a lease that your funding source approves will go bad, unless you intentionally fund a deal that you knew was fraudulent. Illustrated below are three risks that you need to be aware of as an equipment lease broker from least serious to the most critical: collection assistance, commission refund and fraudulent transactions.

RISK LEVEL 1: Collection Assistance

Sometimes, your lessee may, at sometime during the duration of his/her lease term, have difficulty making payments on the lease for one reason or another. In this situation, you are not necessarily responsible (typically after six months you have no financial liability); however, the funding source may call you for assistance on getting the lessee to send in some payments. This entails a simple phone call to the lessee. You will often find that a lessee will take your call, but not the funding source collection department's call, because you are less threatening. This will enable you to find out why the customer/lessee is not making their payments. Hopefully, you can urge the customer to continue making payments and give a positive report (Estimated Time of Payment) to your funding source. Sometimes, the reason is simple and 90 percent of the time, the customer continues making payments again. I have seen this happen before due to communication errors, slow months, missed billing invoices, etc.

RISK LEVEL 2: Commission Refund

A commission refund is as bad as it sounds. It is a very discouraging moment having to give the funding source back your commission, especially if you split the money with another party (vendor, referral source, sales representative, or other equipment lease broker). All funding sources have their own policies on this. Basically, according to most funding source agreements, if you earn and get paid a commission on a lease that goes bad within six months, you may have to pay 100 percent of your commission back to the funding source. "Goes bad" would mean that a customer went bankrupt immediately after funding of the lease, or they just decided they weren't going to make anymore payments due to equipment dislikes, a dispute with the vendor or a negative change in business activity.

RISK LEVEL 3: Fraudulent Transactions

This would be considered breach of warranty or representation. A breach of warranty or representation would mean that you represented the deal to the funding source in a way that was untrue in order to get an approval. If the misrepresentation was in the lessee's favor and the deal goes bad, you will be responsible for the entire lease amount. As your relationship develops and grows with your funding sources, they begin to stand by your word more and more. The entire lease amount ("Repurchase Price" as funding sources like to refer to it) includes the unpaid balance of the lease, including accrued charges, plus all amounts subsequently added to the lessee's obligations under the lease (including your commission), plus the funding source's expenses in enforcing the lease or in repossession the equipment (including repossession, recovery and storage fees, court costs, and attorney's fees) less any applicable refund of earned finance charges. As you can see, this is a horrible situation for you. This can only happen due to your own fraudulent behavior, for very rare instances where a vendor and lessee conspire and use you as a puppet to transact a fraudulent deal. Be Careful. Though rare, it does happen. It never happened to me, however, friends of mine in the business have had to pay back deals that were fraudulent and they did not even know.

In conclusion, you hope that you can rely on the funding sources to do good background checks on all of the deals that you send them, so you do not have to encounter a fraudulent transaction payback. Most importantly, do not ever lie to your funding source about a lease applicant.

SECTION 9

RELATIONSHIPS

In This Section:

- Vendors
- Funding Sources
- Past Lessees
- Other Leasing Companies
- Lease Organizations

Relationships

In the equipment leasing business, all you have is your relationships. The more relationships you can maintain, the better. Relationships with vendors, funding sources, past lessees, other leasing companies, and equipment leasing organizations are all key to your success as an equipment lease broker.

Vendors

Vendors, as you learned in section 5, are the most crucial relationships for your survival in the leasing business. These are the people that regularly put food in your mouth. A good vendor will give you lease applications monthly. Take them to lunch, remember their birthdays, or send them something on the holidays. If you can establish a great relationship with a vendor you should never have to worry about that vendor using another leasing company. However, if you take them for granted, do not expect them to stick around. Make the vendor your friend.

Three Keys to Vendor Relationships:

- Constant Communication

- Vendor Bonuses

  A vendor bonus is a monetary bonus given to an equipment vendor from the commission you earned as a result of a referral that ended in a new lease. It can be a constant 2 to 5 percent per lease transaction, or it can vary depending on your agreement with the vendor. Some vendors will never ask for money. Some vendors will tell you that they are getting a certain amount, say 3 percent, on every deal they do with your competitor. If a good vendor tells you this (you can verify that they refer a few leases per month), offer them 4 percent. If you can charge 10 percent commission per lease transaction and walk away with 6 percent on a few leases a month, then you are doing great. Be careful guaranteeing a percentage though. Not all deals will warrant a 10 percent commission. Sometimes you may only be able to charge 5 percent commission because of the strength of the lessee. Your vendor will have to understand that if you only earn 5 percent, you cannot give him or her 4 percent.

- Friendship Building

Funding Sources

Your relationships with funding sources are almost as important as your relationships with vendors. You can make even more money by also being friendly with the funding source's staff. If the folks evaluating the credit worthiness of your transaction like you, the funding source may be more likely to approve a lease transaction that would otherwise be declined. It is true, a funding source will sometimes stretch their credit guidelines if you develop a good relationship with their staff. If you are difficult, they may tighten their credit window, or discontinue your broker relationship.

Things will not always go your way with your funding source. You need to watch your temper and be aware of how you are representing yourself. Always submit clear and legible lease application packages. Don't ever lie to them. If they ask for additional information, don't give them half of what they requested. A good funding source with a lot of flexibility will define your company. Do everything you can to keep them.

You should also know that if you repeatedly submit deals to a funding source that are outside their credit window, they will eventually cut you off for wasting their time. Some funding sources are stricter on this than others. Each source will give you warning and educate you on the type of applications they are looking for to help improve your approval ratios with them before terminating your relationship with them.

Three Keys to Funding Source Relationships:

- Cooperate with Requests and Collections
- Maintain High Approval Ratios (higher number of approved and funded transactions versus declined applications)
- Represent Applicants Honestly and Accurately

Past Lessees

Keep a consistent record of your past lessees in a computer database or filing cabinet. Leasing companies do not use this source enough. You know that these people utilize leasing to acquire equipment, so keep in touch with them once or twice each year so you can get that next lease. These people make good referrals also.

Three Keys to Past Lessee Relationships:

- Follow-Up with Old Customers at Least Once a Year
- Be Their Friend
- Be Honest

Other Leasing Companies

Believe it or not, your competitors can be lucrative for you as well. There are three reasons why you want to have good relationships with your local competitors:

1. You can share funding-source information
2. They can be a great source of lease applications (re-brokered transactions)
3. Maintaining their friendship can ensure they will not try to steal business from you.

When you are trying to find a local funding source to handle a special deal, it is nice to be able to call your friend at XYZ Leasing, and ask if he/she has any sources to recommend you.

Re-brokered transactions are rarely allowed with most funding sources. When you find a good funding source that other leasing companies don't know about, you will find it easy to be given deals from other equipment lease brokers who hope to profit from your relationship with these special funding sources. If this happens, show your appreciation and give them some deals too, or pay them 50 percent of your commission on the re-brokered deal.

I have found that the more people you know in the leasing business, the less you lose deals to other leasing companies. Often a lessee you are working with will decide at the last minute to check out rates with another leasing company. If the lessee happens to speak to a friend of yours, your chance of losing that deal is slim. Also, a friendly competitor will rarely try to take one of your vendors if they know the vendor is working with you.

Lease Organizations

Lease organizations provide Websites full of information (funding sources, news, industry statistics, event calendars, and more). Some of them have monthly and bi-monthly newsletters which can be educational. Everyone knows each other in the leasing business and news gets around fast, especially within lease organizations. These organizations hold events each year where you can meet people, ask questions, go to sales seminars, and improve your business connections. You may want to consider joining one of these organizations. The most popular one is the United Association of Equipment Leasing (see section 14).

Be good to as many people as you can. The more people like you, the more profitable your business can be.

SECTION 10

SETTING UP YOUR BUSINESS

In This Section:

- Register Your Business
- Telephone & Fax Lines
- Opening a Bank Account
- Stationary
- Set Up Funding Sources
- Customize "Processing Documentation" for Your Use

Register Your Business

You will need to register a trade name for you company. Come up with a few names that you like and search the secretary of state to be sure the name that you want is available in your state. You will also need to decide on and choose the business structure for your new company: sole proprietorship, partnership, LLC, corporation, etc. The process of registering and setting up a new business entity varies from state to state. The type of business structure you choose is solely dependent on you, your lifestyle, how big your want to grow your leasing company, whether you have partners, how you choose to handle taxation and accounting, etc. Consult an accountant or attorney to discuss the different types of business structures to help decipher which is best for you. There may be tax advantages to starting out as a corporation or LLC. You might prefer the limited liability of a corporation, or the simple accounting methods of a sole proprietorship.

Telephones & Fax Lines

You must have a dedicated line for leasing and another for your fax machine. If you want to save money, use your personal phone lines for business until you are ready to pay more for the same thing. A phone company will charge almost double if you tell them it is a business line. Not only will you get charged more, but your business phone number gets sold over and over again to telemarketers. You will get tons of unsolicited calls that waste your valuable time. The downside to not using a dedicated business phone line upfront is that your company name will not be listed in the white pages or yellow pages. In my experience, however, the only calls you will get out of the yellow pages are people wasting your time. The most important phone calls you are going to get will be a result of your marketing efforts, not someone picking a random leasing company out of a huge list in the yellow pages.

Opening a Bank Account

Once you have received your business registration and trade name registration in the mail, you can open a bank account under the name of your business. All commission checks will be paid to your business name, not your own. Also, once you begin generating your own leasing documents, the lessee's deposit will be sent to you as well. Your business bank account is crucial. Try to find a business account that does not charge you a monthly fee. For every large bank trying to charge you a monthly fee for your business checking account, there are other banks trying to earn your business that charge nothing.

Stationary

Envelopes, business cards and letterhead; these are the only things most people will ever see of your company. You will not need a storefront, an office with a lobby, etc. This business is done over the phone and fax. Sometimes, in rare occasions, you will actually meet a lessee or vendor in person to go over documents. Make the local coffee shop your conference room. Nobody will ever know that you are running your business out of the spare bedroom in your house or on top of the dining room table.

Make sure your envelopes, business cards and letterhead look professional and cohesive. Have a logo made if you can afford it and use it everywhere. While some companies charge thousands for logos, there are many start-up graphic designers that will be happy to create a logo and branding for less than $500.00.

Setting Up Funding Sources

Refer to Section 5, "The Lease Process In Depth." It is important to begin filling out applications for funding sources right away.

I recommend that you get the following five types of funding sources:

2 sources with good rates and App Only programs up to $75k   (strict credit guidelines)

2 sources that consider start-up lease applicants   (Not as Strict, higher rates)

1 local source that you can send tough local deals to

You can build from here. After a year you will have found new sources, dropped some sources and strengthened relationships with one or two of your initial sources. Things always change. Funding sources will come and go out of business. Funding sources will also change their appetite for deals. Your favorite funding source one month may tighten up their credit window and become your least favorite source the next month. Try that same source again in a couple of months; it may become your best source again when they loosen up the credit window a bit. This happens all of the time. This is why you need five sources to bounce around from one to the other.

Customize Processing Documentation for Use

In the last half of this book, I have given you all the forms that you will need to process applications. All you need to do is put your logo and phone numbers on the forms. Make them your own. They have proven to work well for me with all of my funding sources.

You should begin customizing the following forms:

Lease Application	Example A.
Bank Reference Sheet	Example B.
Trade Reference Sheet	Example C.
Comparable Loan Reference Sheet	Example D.
Credit Authorization	Example E.
Vendor Profile	Example F.
Documentation Request Sheet	Example I.
Fax Cover Letter	Example U.

NOTE:

Visit our website www.Theleasingexpert.com to purchase our Cd-Rom which includes a special section for those of you who use Microsoft Word Version 9.0 or greater. You can open all documents in their original format and use them right away without much editing. Otherwise, there is another folder with the same documents in text format that will take some editing before they will be usable.

SECTION 11

THREE EXAMPLE LEASE SCENARIOS

In This Section:

- Scenario 1: A Quick & Easy Lease Transaction
- Scenario 2: A Lease that Required Tax Returns & a Little Work
- Scenario 3: A Tough Lease that Required Determination

Three Example Lease Scenarios

I have put together three real lease scenarios for you to review. These were real transactions that I transacted in the past. The real names, addresses and phone numbers are replaced with fictitious ones in order to protect the privacy of the involved parties. At the end of each scenario description are sample documents for you to review.

The three example lease scenarios represent three of the many different ways a lease can go down. Lease transactions will sometimes be very easy and other times, very difficult and time consuming. Some lease transactions will require a lot of paperwork, while others will only require a little paperwork. Some lease transactions will close over a duration of seven business days, while others take three months. If a transaction takes three months, it is usually because the equipment had to be manufactured or shipped overseas before being delivered and funded.

Scenario 1: A Quick & Easy Transaction

Scenario 1 examines a quick and easy lease transaction. A quick and easy transaction is one where you do the least amount of work for your money. This happens when your applicant's credit and banks check out well and the customer goes along with everything comfortably.

The fictitious companies for Scenario 1 are as follows:

Lease Broker:	Lucrative Leasing (Hereafter referred to as LL)
Lessee:	Company A 1234 Main Street Seattle, WA 98100 Contact: Joe Smith, President
Vendor:	PacificForklift Sales 5000 Broadway Avenue Seattle, WA 98110 Contact: Jimbo, Sales
Funding Source:	Funding Source
Insurance Company:	All Good Insurance

Facts of Lease Scenario 1:

Equipment:	GEHL 8,000 lb Forklift
Dollar Amount:	$43,500.00 (plus tax)
Terms:	60 Months
Residual:	10% PUT

To start, LL received an application from one of their vendors, Pacific Forklift Sales. Joe Smith, President of company A, went to Pacific Forklift Sales in search of a large forklift to handle his toughest jobs. He did not have $43,500 sitting in the bank, so he asked Jimbo, the salesperson at Pacific Forklift, if he had any recommendations. Jimbo mentioned "Lucrative Leasing." Jimbo refers all of his leases to LL. Joe said he was interested and completed a lease application that Jimbo provided him, and faxed it to LL that same day.

LL then completed all missing information over the phone with Joe and retyped the application for processing (see Scenario 1, Lease Application).

The next step was to pull a credit report (see Scenario 1, Credit Report). The application that LL received had a signature on it, so LL went ahead and pulled the credit report (attached). The report scored well. According to the report, this applicant can handle a lot of debt and pays all of his bills in a timely manner.

With the credit report being so good, LL can move onto bank and trade references (see Scenario 1, Bank A, TRADE A, B & C). The lessee input one bank reference and three trade references on the application, so LL went ahead and got the references. The bank reference was great. The account was opened over two years ago and the average balance was "Low 6 Figures," which means that Company A has an average balance between $100,000 and $350,000 in the bank over the last six months. Once this reference was obtained, LL knew this would be an easy deal if they could sell the lease payments to Company A. LL also obtained all three trade references, which were stellar.

The typed application, credit report, bank reference, and trade references were then typed and faxed to LL's best funding source for consideration. As you can see, the funding source approved the deal (copy of actual approval, see Scenario 1, Lease Approval).

Once LL received the approval, they calculated some payment term options with 6.5 percent commission built in. They quoted the customer several different terms. The customer ended up choosing sixty months with a 10% PUT (guaranteed buyout at the end of the lease). LL created a documentation request worksheet. Usually a documentation worksheet is not needed if you create the documents yourself, however, creating one can make things easy and by organizing all of the important data for the lease onto one page (see Scenario 1, Documentation Request).

LL used generic documents provided by the funding source that approved the lease to prepare documents. LL has been approved with this funding source to do documentation in their name, and then assign the lease to the funding source once all documentation is in.

The documentation was created and sent by an overnight courier. The documentation cover letter (see Scenario 1, Documentation Cover Letter) that LL always uses with their documents went out with the documentation. As you can see, it covers some important reminders for the customer to follow: copy photo ID, who to make the check to and for what amount, Federal Tax ID #, etc.

The lease documents (see Scenario 1, Lease Agreement & Page 2) illustrate the criteria of the lease: monthly term, payment amount, addresses, etc. The lessee has to sign all of the lease documents and send them back with a check. The guaranteed 10% buyout (see Scenario 1, Guaranteed 10% Buyout) is a document for the lessee of the equipment that shows he will only owe 10 percent of the original booked value (the original total dollar amount that the lease was based on) at the end of the lease term if he wishes to obtain the rights to the equipment. The equipment schedule "A" (see Scenario 1, Equipment Schedule "A") is a list of the equipment on the lease. In this example, there is only one piece of equipment. In some cases, the Equipment Schedule "A" will be many pages long.

The insurance request (see Scenario 1, Insurance Request) must be signed at the bottom by the lessee, so that when the lease broker (LL) receives documents, they can obtain an insurance binder to give to the funding source, showing that the equipment under lease is protected by the lessee's insurance carrier. By signing the bottom of this form, the lessee is authorizing his/her insurance company to follow your instructions for insuring the leased equipment.

When LL received the documentation, the first thing they did was check to make sure there were no errors, missing signatures, etc. Was the check made out for the correct amount? Did the customer whiteout or scratch anything out? Everything checked out, and LL completed the assignment letter (see Scenario 1, Assignment Letter) provided by the funding source. This letter assigns the entire lease to the funding source making the funding source the lessor, and not LL.

Prior to sending the documentation to the funding source, LL had to include their broker fee invoice (see Scenario 1, Broker Fee Invoice) outlining the terms of the lease and invoicing the funding source for their commission (once the deal funds). As you can see, the funding source charges a $77.50 processing fee. LL charged $150.00 so that they will get $72.50 to cover some of their postage and processing costs. This amount gets figured into the total commission, as per the broker fee invoice.

LL sent the signed documentation to the funding source with a photocopy of the lessee's check that they deposited the day they received documentation. At the same time the documentation was being shipped, the insurance binder came across the fax (see Scenario 1, Insurance Binder). This binder, from All Good Insurance, displays all of the pertinent liability information required by the funding source to proceed.

LL then received the original vendor invoice (see Scenario 1, Vendor Invoice) in the mail that afternoon. LL then faxed the vendor invoice and insurance binder to the funding source so they would have all the information they needed.

In order to fund, the funding source needed the original vendor invoice in their hands, so LL had to overnight that after faxing a copy, in order to fund the deal right away. The insurance binder can just be faxed.

The funding source received all of LL's documentation and proofed it to make sure everything was in order. In this example, everything was perfect, from the documentation to the insurance and invoice. In order to fund the lease (pay the vendor and LL their commission), the funding source had to call the lessee and obtain a verbal "delivery & acceptance" to make sure Joe Smith had his forklift and to go over the terms with him once more.

Everything checked out with the verbal the following day and checks were overnighted to the vendor and LL. LL only received a check for $567.22, because they had already received $2,573.12 from the lessee with the documentation (per the Broker Fee Invoice). LL earned a total of $3,140.34 on this transaction that took about six to seven days to transact from start to finish. Not a bad week. This deal probably took a total of five hours of actual work from beginning to end.

Scenario 1

Completed Lease Application

LUCRATIVE LEASING

Lease Application

VENDOR INFORMATION

Vendor Name	Equipment Cost $43,500.00
PACIFIC FORKLIFT SALES	Initial Term 48 Months
Vendor Address 5000 Broadway Avenue, Seattle, WA 98110	Equipment Description
Contact Person Jimbo	Telephone number (800) XXX-XXXX

	(1) GEHL 883 Forklift

LESSEE COMPANY INFORMATION

Company Name COMPANY A	
Company Address 1234 Main Street, Seattle, County WA, State 98100 Zip	Special Requirements
Signor Joe Smith, President Title	Telephone number 800, XXX-XXXX
Nature of Business Roofs	Type of business __ Non-Profit __ Proprietorship __ Partnership X Corporation	No. of Years in Business 7 Years

PERSONAL INFORMATION ON OFFICERS, PARTNERS, OR GUARANTORS

Name Joe Smith	Title President	Social Security Number XXX-XX XXXX		Driver's License Number
Home Address N/A	City	State	Zip	How Long? Home Phone Number
Previous Address	City	State	Zip	Own / Rent Present Home?
Name	Title	Social Security Number		Driver's License Number
Home Address	City	State	Zip	How Long? Home Phone Number
Previous Address	City	State	Zip	Own / Rent Present Home?

COMPANY BANK REFERENCES - TWO YEAR HISTORY

Name of Bank/Branch Bank A	How Long?	Chkg. Acct. # Loan Acct. # XXXXX-XXX	Telephone No. (800) XXX-XXXX	Contact Officer Charlie
Name of Bank/Branch	How Long?	Chkg. Acct. # Loan Acct. #	Telephone No. ( )	Contact Officer
Name of Bank/Branch	How Long?	Chkg. Acct. # Loan Acct. #	Telephone No. ( )	Contact Officer

TRADE REFERENCES - TWO YEAR HISTORY

Name of Supplier TRADE A	City/State Seattle, WA	Telephone No. (800) XXX-XXXX	Contact Person Credit
Name of Supplier TRADE B	City/State Bellevue, WA	Telephone No. (800) XXX-XXXX	Contact Person Charlene
Name of Supplier TRADE C	City/State Spokane, WA	Telephone No. 800, XXX-XXXX	Contact Person Credit

I/we hereby authorize you to whom this application is made, or your agents, to investigate my/our credit worthiness and will provide financial statements, tax returns, etc., as you deem necessary. I/we agree that the security deposit is not refundable unless the application is rejected by Lessor. By the execution of the lease agreement, I/we warrant that the information submitted herein is true and correct and hereby authorized references contained herein to release any necessary information. Further, I/we warrant it is understood that Lessor reserves the right to reverse any credit decision if the information contained herein is found to be incorrect, and I/we will indemnify Lessor for any and all costs incurred with this application for credit including any cost incurred in the placement or reservation of the intended leased equipment based on the information contained herein.

Signature X	Date:

Scenario 1

Credit Report Page 1

```
User ID :  ▮▮▮▮▮▮                          Date : 06/03/2002

Report Name : Bureau Data (Record ID # ▮▮▮▮       Page : 0001
-----------------------------------------------------------------
▮▮▮▮▮▮▮   Department : ▮▮▮
Record Number : ▮▮▮▮▮
Report Type : Credit ▮▮▮▮▮▮▮▮▮▮
Tracking:
S .........,.....HC
▮▮▮▮▮▮▮▮▮▮▮▮▮▮
▮▮▮▮▮▮▮▮▮▮▮▮▮▮▮
▮▮▮▮▮▮▮▮▮▮▮▮▮▮▮▮

                           ▮▮▮▮▮▮CREDIT REPORT

<FOR>          <SUB NAME>      <MKT SUB> <INFILE>  <DATE>    <TIME>
▮▮▮▮▮▮▮▮▮▮▮▮▮▮▮             10 WA    2/82    06/03/02   18:03CT

<SUBJECT>                                <SSN>         <BIRTH DATE>
▮▮▮▮▮▮▮▮▮                        ▮▮▮▮▮▮      12/56
                                                      <TELEPHONE>
                                                      ▮▮▮▮▮▮

<CURRENT ADDRESS>                                     <DATE RPTD>
▮▮▮▮▮▮▮▮▮▮▮▮▮▮▮                                11/98
<FORMER ADDRESS>
▮▮▮▮▮▮▮▮▮▮▮▮▮▮▮                                 3/98
-----------------------------------------------------------------
S P E C I A L   M E S S A G E S
****HAWK-ALERT:INPUT SSN ISSUED: 1971 - 1972; STATE: AK
          :FILE SSN ISSUED: 1971 - 1972; STATE: AK; (EST. AGE OBTAINED:
          14 TO 16)***
-----------------------------------------------------------------
M O D E L   P R O F I L E
***EMPIRICA 95 SCORE +683  : 010, 013, 008, 002 ***
-----------------------------------------------------------------
C R E D I T   S U M M A R Y    * * *   T O T A L   F I L E   H I S T O R Y
PR=0  COL=0  NEG=0  HSTNEG=2-2  TRD=27 RVL=16 INST=9 MTG=1  OPN=1  INQ=8
            HIGH CRED  CRED LIM  BALANCE  PAST DUE  MNTHLY PAY AVAILABLE
REVOLVING:  $468K      $510K     $261K    $0        $2359      49%
INSTALLMENT: $272K     $         $203K    $0        $1758
OPEN:       $5953      $         $0       $0                   100%
TOTALS:     $766K      $510K     $464K    $0        $4117
-----------------------------------------------------------------
T R A D E S
SUBNAME        SUBCODE    OPENED  HIGHCRED TERMS    MAXDELQ  PAYPAT  1-12 MOP
ACCOUNT#                  VERFIED CREDLIM  PASTDUE  AMT-MOP  PAYPAT 13-24
ECOA COLLATRL/LOANTYPE CLSD/PD BALANCE  REMARKS           MO 30/60/90
▮▮▮▮▮▮▮▮▮▮▮▮        10/96   $10.0K   MIN92           111111111111 C01
                          5/02A   $10.0K   $0              1X1111111111
C    LINE OF CREDIT        $9212                         48   0/ 0/ 0
```

Scenario 1

Credit Report Page 2

```
████████████████         5/98    $16.5K   MIN244           111111111111 R01
                         5/02A   $15.0K   $0               111111111111
     C   CREDIT CARD             $12.2K                         48   1/ 0/ 0

████████████████         7/98    $20.4K   MIN231           111111111111 R01
                         5/02A   $25.0K   $0               XXXXXXXX1111
     I   CREDIT CARD             $20.3K                         47   0/ 0/ 0

████████████████         6/98    $10.0K                    XXX1          C01
                         5/02A   $10.0K   $0
     C   LINE OF CREDIT  6/00C   $0       ACCT CLSD BY CONSUMER  4  0/ 0/ 0

████████████████         5/98    $49.9K   MIN118           111111111111 C01
                         4/02A   $50.0K   $0               111111111111
     C   UNSECURED               $11.4K                         48   0/ 0/ 0

████████████████         6/98    $241K    MIN1674          111111111111 C01
                         4/02A   $250K    $0               111111111111
     C   █████████               $208K                         47   0/ 0/ 0

████████████████         11/98   $222K    240M1758         11111X11X1X1 I01
                         4/02A            $0               1X11111X11X1
     C   RECREATIONAL MERC       $203K                         42   0/ 0/ 0

████████████████         1/99    $5953                     111           O01
                         4/02A            $0
     A   CREDIT CARD     1/02F   $0                              3   0/ 0/ 0

████████████████         8/96    $1.3M    37M                            I01
                         9/00A            $0
     C   AUTOMOBILE      9/99C   $0       CLOSED               11   0/ 0/ 0

████████████████         5/95                              XX1211111111 R01
                         7/00A   $7200    $0               111111111111
     I   CREDIT CARD     3/99C   $0       ACCT CLSD BY CONSUMER 43  1/ 0/ 0

████████████████         2/97    $4000                     111111111111 R01
                         3/00A   $4800    $0               11111111
     C   COMBINED CREDIT P 4/97F $0                             20   0/ 0/ 0

████████████████         2/87    $15.0K                    111111111111 R01
                         8/99A   $15.0K   $0               111111111111
     C   CREDIT CARD     6/98C   $0       ACCT CLSD BY CONSUMER 34  0/ 0/ 0

████████████████         2/96    $39.9K   180M381          X11111111111 I01
                         11/98A           $0               1X1111111111
     C   RECREATIONAL MERC 11/98C $0      CLOSED               34   0/ 0/ 0

████████████████         8/94    $0       MTN50            111111111111 I01
```

Scenario 1

Credit Report Page 3

User ID : [redacted]   Date : 06/03/2002

Report Name : Bureau Data (Record ID #[redacted]   Page : 0003

		6/98A	$150K	$0		
C	JR MTG 1 4 80 LTV	6/98C	$0	CLOSED	12	0/ 0/ 0
[redacted]		8/95			111111111111	R01
		9/97A	$1400	$0	1111	
I	CHARGE ACCOUNT	12/96C	$0	CLOSED	16	0/ 0/ 0
[redacted]		7/94	$138K		111111111111	C01
		8/97A	$150K	$0	111111111111	
C	CREDIT LINE SECUR				24	0/ 0/ 0
[redacted]		4/96	$2635		111	R01
		7/96A	$3800			
I	CHARGE ACCOUNT		$0		3	0/ 0/ 0
[redacted]		8/95	$1147		1	R01
		4/96A	$1400			
I		11/95P	$0		3	0/ 0/ 0
[redacted]		2/94	$44			R01
		4/95A	$500	$0		
I	CHARGE ACCOUNT	1/95P	$0			
[redacted]		10/87	$53.8K	360M643		M01
		2/94A		$0		
P	FHA LOAN	2/94P	$0			
[redacted]		3/92	$49.7K	180M		I01
		1/94A		$0		
C						
[redacted]		2/87	$3919			R01
		12/92A		$0		
C						
[redacted]		1/99	$600K	1M		IUR
		9/00A		$0		
C	AUTOMOBILE	3/99C	$0	ACCT CLSD BY CONSUMER	1	0/ 0/ 0
[redacted]		8/95	$1400			RUR
		10/99A	$1400	$0		
I	CREDIT CARD	12/96C	$0	CLOSED	1	0/ 0/ 0
[redacted]		5/96	$636K	3M		IUR
		4/99A		$0		
C	AUTOMOBILE	8/96C	$0	CLOSED	1	0/ 0/ 0
[redacted]		2/94	$90.0K	180M831	111111111111	IUR
		12/96A		$0	1111	

Scenario 1

Credit Report Page 4

```
User ID :████████                          Date : 06/03/2002

Report Name : Bureau Data (Record ID #█████)          Page : 0004
-------------------------------------------------------------------------
C                     12/96C   $0      CLOSED            16   0/ 0/ 0

    ████████████████6/91   $16.2K   49M418                    IUR
                     2/94A            $0
C      91CHEV ███████/94C   $0      CLOSED

- - - - - - - - - - - - - - - - - - - - - - - - - - - - - - - - - - - - -
I N Q U I R I E S
DATE      SUBCODE        SUBNAME       TYPE    AMOUNT
 6/03/02  ████████████████████████
 4/24/02  ████████████████████████
 3/28/02  ████████████████████████
 1/15/02  ████████████████████████
 1/15/02  ████████████████████████
 7/24/01  ████████████████████████
 7/17/01  ████████████████████
 9/20/00  ████████████████

- - - - - - - - - - - - - - - - - - - - - - - - - - - - - - - - - - - - -
E N D  O F  C R E D I T  R E P O R T  -  S E R V I C E D  B Y :  ███████
████████████████████████████████████████

            END OF ████████ REPORT
```

Scenario 1

Bank A

BANK RATING REQUEST

TO: _Bank A_   RE: _COMPANY A_

   FAX # (800) XXX–XXXX   _____

ATTN: _Charlie_   _____

                                            ACCOUNT #: _XXXXX–XXX_

CREDIT MANAGER,

THE ABOVE NAMED PARTY HAS APPLIED FOR CREDIT IN CONNECTION WITH AN EQUIPMENT LEASE/PURCHASE. WE WOULD APPRECIATE RECEIVING THE FOLLOWING INFORMATION AS A CREDIT REFERENCE ON THEIR ACCOUNT. ANY INFORMATION PROVIDED WILL BE HELD IN THE STRICTEST CONFIDENCE.

DATE OPENED: _12/00_   AVERAGE BALANCE: _Low 6 Figures_

OF NSF'S: _0_   # OF OD'S: _0_   IF CLOSED, WHEN? _NA_
            (within last 6 months)   (within last 6 months)

RATING AND/OR COMMENTS: _____

NAME EXACTLY AS IT APPEARS ON THE ACCOUNT: _____

            COMPANY A

ARE THERE ANY LOANS/NOTES/LINES OF CREDIT?   (YES)   NO
IF YES, PLEASE DETAIL BELOW:

TYPE	OPEN DATE	HIGH CREDIT	BALANCE	(UN) SECURED?	RATING
Line of Credit	10/2000	Low 7 Figures	High 6	Secure	As Agreed

INFORMATION SUPPLIED BY: _Charlie_
                  TITLE: _Vice President_

AS A COURTESY TO OUR MUTUAL CUSTOMER, PLEASE REPLY BY FAX OR PHONE WITHIN FOUR HOURS FROM THE TIME YOU RECEIVE THIS REQUEST.
PLEASE FAX TO: (YOUR FAX #)   OR   CALL (YOUR PHONE #)

THANK YOU!

_____   _____   _____
CREDIT MANAGER   **DATE**   **TIME**

Scenario 1

Trade A

TRADE REFERENCE REQUEST

TO: TRADE A   RE: _____ COMPANY A _____

   FAX # (800) XXX-XXXX _____   _____

ATTN: Credit _____   _____

                                     ACCOUNT #: _____

CREDIT MANAGER,

THE ABOVE NAMED PARTY HAS APPLIED FOR CREDIT IN CONNECTION WITH AN EQUIPMENT
LEASE/PURCHASE. WE WOULD APPRECIATE RECEIVING THE FOLLOWING INFORMATION AS A CREDIT
REFERENCE ON THEIR ACCOUNT. ANY INFORMATION PROVIDED WILL BE HELD IN THE STRICTEST
CONFIDENCE.

DATE OPENED: May 1995 _____   HIGH CREDIT: $15,210 _____

BALANCE? $428.00 _____   CURRENT? (YES) NO   TERMS: N30 _____

PAYMENT HISTORY: (PROMPT) SLOW   If slow, how many days on average: _____

GOODS / SERVICES YOU SUPPLY TO THEM: _____ Lumber _____

COMMENTS:

_____

_____

_____

INFORMATION SUPPLIED BY: _____ Carol _____
                  TITLE: _____ Credit Manager _____

AS A COURTESY TO OUR MUTUAL CUSTOMER, PLEASE REPLY BY FAX OR PHONE WITHIN
FOUR HOURS FROM THE TIME YOU RECEIVE THIS REQUEST.

PLEASE FAX TO: (YOUR FAX NUMBER)   OR   CALL (YOUR PHONE NUMBER)

THANK YOU!

_____   _____   _____
CREDIT MANAGER   **DATE**   **TIME**

Scenario 1

Trade B

TRADE REFERENCE REQUEST

TO: _____ TRADE B _____   RE: _____ COMPANY A _____

_____ FAX # (800) XXX-XXXX _____   _____

ATTN: _____ Charlene _____   _____

ACCOUNT #: _____

CREDIT MANAGER,

THE ABOVE NAMED PARTY HAS APPLIED FOR CREDIT IN CONNECTION WITH AN EQUIPMENT LEASE/PURCHASE. WE WOULD APPRECIATE RECEIVING THE FOLLOWING INFORMATION AS A CREDIT REFERENCE ON THEIR ACCOUNT. ANY INFORMATION PROVIDED WILL BE HELD IN THE STRICTEST CONFIDENCE.

DATE OPENED: _____ June 1995 _____   HIGH CREDIT: $75,000

BALANCE? $19,000   CURRENT? (YES) NO   TERMS: _____ N30 _____

PAYMENT HISTORY: (PROMPT) SLOW   *If slow, how many days on average:* _____

GOODS / SERVICES YOU SUPPLY TO THEM: Structural Hardware

COMMENTS:
Always Current, Excellent Customer!
_____
_____

INFORMATION SUPPLIED BY: _____ Charlene _____
TITLE: _____ Accounts Receivable _____

AS A COURTESY TO OUR MUTUAL CUSTOMER, PLEASE REPLY BY FAX OR PHONE WITHIN **FOUR HOURS** FROM THE TIME YOU RECEIVE THIS REQUEST.

PLEASE FAX TO: (YOUR FAX NUMBER)   **OR**   **CALL** (YOUR PHONE NUMBER)

THANK YOU!

_____   _____   _____
CREDIT MANAGER   **DATE**   **TIME**

Scenario 1

Trade C

TRADE REFERENCE REQUEST

TO: __TRADE C_____   RE: ___COMPANY A_____

____FAX # (800) XXX-XXXX_____   _____

ATTN: Jason_____   _____

     ACCOUNT #: _____

CREDIT MANAGER,

THE ABOVE NAMED PARTY HAS APPLIED FOR CREDIT IN CONNECTION WITH AN EQUIPMENT LEASE/PURCHASE. WE WOULD APPRECIATE RECEIVING THE FOLLOWING INFORMATION AS A CREDIT REFERENCE ON THEIR ACCOUNT. ANY INFORMATION PROVIDED WILL BE HELD IN THE STRICTEST CONFIDENCE.

DATE OPENED: _5/7/99_____   HIGH CREDIT: _$155,000_____

BALANCE? _$35,106.00_____ CURRENT? (YES) NO TERMS: _Net 30 Days____

PAYMENT HISTORY: (PROMPT) SLOW   *If slow, how many days on average:* _____

GOODS / SERVICES YOU SUPPLY TO THEM: __Finishing Products_____

COMMENTS:
____Prompt_____

_____

_____

INFORMATION SUPPLIED BY: ___Jason_____
                       TITLE: __Credit Analyst_____

AS A COURTESY TO OUR MUTUAL CUSTOMER, PLEASE REPLY BY FAX OR PHONE WITHIN FOUR HOURS FROM THE TIME YOU RECEIVE THIS REQUEST.

PLEASE FAX TO: (YOUR FAX NUMBER)   **OR**   **CALL** (YOUR PHONE NUMBER)

THANK YOU!

_____   _____ _____
CREDIT MANAGER   **DATE**   **TIME**

Scenario 1

Lease Approval

LEASE APPROVAL

TO:	▓▓▓	FAX NO:	▓▓▓
ATTN:	▓▓▓	FROM:	▓▓▓
DECISION DATE:	06/05/2002	SENT:	0/5/02 11:20:32 AM
LEASE NUMBER:	▓▓▓		
LEGAL LESSEE NAME:	▓▓▓		
IS APPROVED FOR:	$43,500.00	DEPOSIT:	2
FACTOR:	CALL IF NEEDED	TERM:	60
PROGRAM:	$	COST W/O TAX:	$43,500.00
EQUIPMENT:	FORKLIFTS	MODEL:	
AUTHORIZED SIGNOR:	▓▓▓	TITLE:	▓▓▓

DOCUMENTS REQUIRED FOR FUNDING:

P.O. ▓

LEASE AGMT-PLAIN ENGLISH(FRONT
COPY OF SEC. DEPOSIT CHECK
INVOICE-VENDOR "W/ SERIAL #'S"
DELIVERY AND ACCEPTANCE
NORMAL ASSIGNMENT
P.O.C. & LIAB. INSURANCE VERIF
UCC-1
EQUIPMENT CONDITION REPORT

P.G. ▓

LEASE AGREEMENT P.ENG(BACK)
INVOICE-BROKER COMMISSION
VEHICLE DRIVERS LICENSE COPY
VERIFY TAX CALCULATION W/ DOCS
OPTION OF LESSEE $1.00 P.O.
PRICING
FEDERAL TAX ID NUMBER

NOTES:

▓▓▓ hanks for the deal. If the equipment is new then please disregard pricing & the condition report documents ▓▓▓

Credit approval is valid for 90 days from Decision date. If not acted upon, it will be withdrawn or cancelled.

If 10% funding variance exceeds $35,000, an account executive approval is required

Funding is contingent upon meeting pricing guidelines

Ucc-1 and fixture filings must be filed within 10 days of equipment delivery for transactions $15,000 and above

Approval is subject of the supplier being satisfactory

Physical audits are required on transactions $75,000+ Cost is split equally by broker and ▓▓▓

If ECL is granted, the additional takedowns must meet applicable criteria

For titled equipment, ▓▓▓ for specific state requirements

Invoice can not make reference to warranty or service

Pursuant to your Broker Agreement, you understand that we look to you to provide the applicant (on our behalf) written notification of this decision as required by law.

Scenario 1

Documentation Request

DOCUMENTATION REQUEST WORKSHEET

SALES REPRESENTATIVE: _____ Lucrative Leasing _____ DATE: _____

LESSEE INFORMATION

COMPLETE LESSEE NAME: COMPANY A

BILLING ADDRESS: 1234 Main Street

CITY, STATE, ZIP: Seattle, WA 98100   PHONE: (800) XXX-XXXX

EQUIPMENT LOCATION: Same

SIGNER: Joe Smith   TITLE: President   PG (YES) NO

SIGNER: _____   TITLE: _____   PG: YES NO

VENDOR AND EQUIPMENT INFORMATION

VENDOR NAME: Pacific Forklift Sales
STREET ADDRESS: 5000 Broadway, Seattle, WA 98110
PHONE: (800) XXX-XXXX   CONTACT PERSON: Jimbo

EQUIPMENT LEASE TERMS

LEASE AMOUNT: $ 47,197.50   SALES TAX INCLUDED: (YES) NO

LEASE TERM: 48 MONTHS   BUY-OUT (10% PUT) $1.00 OTHER_____

LEASE PAYMENT: $ 1,211.56   MONTHLY TAX (8.9%): $ _____

ADVANCED PAYMENTS: 1 ONLY (1+1)   10% SEC.   OTHER _____

FACTORS: *Buy Rate*: .02410   *Sell Rate*: .02567
GROSS COMMISSION   (6.5 %): $ 3,067.84

DOCUMENTATION SHIPPING INFORMATION

SEND DOCUMENTS TO:

(X) FED-X TO LESSEE AT LOCATION ABOVE

(   ) FED-X TO LESSEE AT FOLLOWING LOCATION: _____
_____
_____

Scenario 1

Documentation Cover Letter

LUCRATIVE LEASING

ATTN: **Joe Smith**
            COMPANY A
            1234 Main Street
            Seattle, WA 98100

Dear Mr. Smith,

Please pay close attention to the following requirements before returning the lease documents.

- Please sign and date each agreement for your equipment lease. **Make sure that all dates are the same throughout all the paperwork.**

- Make a check payable to <u>Lucrative Leasing</u> for the total amount of: **$2,573.12.**

    This amount equals 2 payments of $1,211.56 plus a $150.00 processing fee standard on all transactions.
    * * IMPORTANT: This check must be written from your business account.

- **Please provide your Federal Tax ID#:** _____

• COPY OF DRIVER'S LICENSE (Joe Smith)

<u>Overnight all original documentation to</u>: **Lucrative Leasing**
                                              Address
                                              City, State & Zip

OVERNIGHT ENVELOPE PROVIDED

Call me with any questions at (800-XXX-XXXX).

Sincerely,

Mr. Leasing

Scenario 1

Lease Agreement

MASTER LEASE / RENTAL AGREEMENT   Agreement Number   12002   Dealer No #

This document was written in "Plain English". The words YOU and YOUR refer to the customer. The words WE, US and OUR refer to the Lessor. Every attempt has been made to eliminate confusing language and create a simple, easy-to-read document

CUSTOMER INFORMATION

COMPANY A

FULL LEGAL NAME OF CUSTOMER   D/B/A

1234 MAIN STREET	SEATTLE	WA	98100	
STREET ADDRESS	CITY	STATE	ZIP	PHONE

COMPANY A   1234 MAIN STREET
BILLING NAME (IF DIFFERENT FROM ABOVE)   BILLING STREET ADDRESS

SEATTLE	WA	98100		
CITY	STATE	ZIP		PHONE

EQUIPMENT LOCATION (IF DIFFERENT FROM ABOVE)

SUPPLIER INFORMATION

See Schedule A
NAME OF SUPPLIER   STREET ADDRESS

CITY	STATE	ZIP	PHONE

QUANTITY	ITEM DESCRIPTION	MODEL NO.	SERIAL
	See Schedule A		

RENTAL TERMS	RENTAL PAYMENT AMOUNT	SECURITY DEPOSIT
Term in months **48** (MOS.) Rent Commencement Date:	48 Payments of $ __1211.56__ (Plus applicable taxes) Rental Payment Period is MONTHLY Unless Otherwise Indicated	$ 2423.12 RECEIVED

END OF LEASE OPTIONS: You will have the following options at the end of the original term, provided the lease has not terminated early and no event of default under the lease has occurred and is continuing.
1. Purchase the equipment for fair market value.   2. Renew the lease per Paragraph 1.   3. Return the equipment as provided in Paragraph 6 of this lease.

THIS IS A NONCANCELABLE/IRREVOCABLE LEASE. THIS LEASE CANNOT BE CANCELLED OR TERMINATED.

TERMS AND CONDITIONS (THIS LEASE AGREEMENT CONTAINS PROVISIONS SET FORTH ON THE REVERSE SIDE, ALL OF WHICH ARE MADE PART OF THIS LEASE AGREEMENT)
1. LEASE AGREEMENT: You agree to lease from us the personal property described under "ITEM DESCRIPTION" and as modified by supplements to this Master Agreement
(Continued on back)

LESSOR ACCEPTANCE	CUSTOMER ACCEPTANCE
DATED:	DATED:
LESSOR: Lucrative Leasing	CUSTOMER: COMPANY A
SIGNATURE: X	SIGNATURE: X JOE SMITH
TITLE:	TITLE: PRESIDENT

ACCEPTANCE OF DELIVERY

You certify that all the equipment listed above has been furnished, that delivery and installation has been fully completed and satisfactory. Further, all conditions and terms of this agreement have been reviewed and acknowledged. Upon your signing below, your promises herein will be irrevocable and unconditional in all respects. You understand and agree that we have purchased the equipment from the supplier, and you may contact the above supplier for your warranty rights, if any, which we transfer to you for the term of this lease. Your approval as indicated below of our purchase of the equipment from supplier is a condition precedent to effectiveness of this lease.

COMPANY A		X	PRESIDENT
Date of Delivery	Customer	Signature: JOE SMITH	Title

GUARANTY

As additional inducement for us to enter into the Agreement, the undersigned ("you"), jointly and severally, unconditionally personally guarantees that the customer will make all payments and meet all obligations required under this Agreement and any supplements fully and promptly. You agree that we may make other arrangements including compromise or settlement with the customer and you waive all defenses and notice of those changes and will remain responsible for the payment and obligations of this Agreement. We do not have to notify you if the customer is in default. If the customer defaults, you will immediately pay in accordance with the default provision of the Agreement all sums due under the terms of the Agreement and will perform all the obligations of the Agreement. If it is necessary for us to proceed legally to enforce this guaranty, you expressly consent to the jurisdiction of the court set out in paragraph 15 and agree to pay all costs, including attorneys fees incurred in enforcement of this guaranty. It is not necessary for us to proceed first against the customer or the Equipment before enforcing this guaranty. By signing this guaranty, you authorize us to obtain credit bureau reports for credit and collection purposes.

X	Joe Smith	
Signature	Print Name of Guarantor	Date

Scenario 1

Lease Agreement Page 2

from time to time signed by you and us (such property and any upgrades, replacements and additions referred to as "Equipment") for business purposes only. You agree to all of the terms and conditions contained in this Agreement and any supplement, which together are a complete statement of our Agreement regarding the listed equipment ("Agreement") and supersedes any purchase order or outstanding invoice. This Agreement may be modified only by written agreement and not by course of performance. This Agreement becomes valid upon execution by us and will begin on the rent commencement date shown and will continue from the first day of the following month for the number of consecutive months shown. You also agree to pay to Lessor interim rent. Interim rent shall be in an amount equal to 1/30th of the monthly rental, multiplied by the number of days between the rent commencement date and the first payment due date. The term will be extended automatically for successive 12 month terms unless you send us written notice you do not want it renewed at least thirty (30) days before the end of any term. If any provision of this Agreement is declared unenforceable in any jurisdiction, the other provisions herein shall remain in full force and effect in that jurisdiction and all others. THE BASE RENTAL PAYMENT SHALL BE ADJUSTED PROPORTIONATELY UPWARD OR DOWNWARD TO COMPLY WITH THE TAX LAWS OF THE STATE IN WHICH THE EQUIPMENT IS LOCATED. Equipment located in various states is subject to sales tax laws which require that tax be paid up front. You authorize us to advance tax and increase your monthly payment by an amount equal to the current tax percentage applied to the monthly rental shown above.

2. **RENT:** Rent will be payable in installments, each in the amount of the basic lease payment shown plus any applicable sales tax, use tax, plus 1/12th of the amount estimated by us to be personal property tax on the Equipment for each year of this Agreement. We will have the right to apply all sums, received from you, to any amounts due and owed to us under the terms of this Agreement. In the event this Agreement is not commenced, the security deposit will be retained by us to compensate us for our documentation, processing and other expenses. If for any reason, your check is returned for nonpayment, a $20.00 bad check charge will be assessed.

3. **COMPUTER SOFTWARE:** Not withstanding any other terms and conditions of the Agreement, you agree that as to software only; a) We have not had, do not have, nor will have any title to such software, b) You have executed or will execute a separate software license agreement and we are not a party to and have no responsibilities whatsoever in regards to such license agreement, c) You have selected such software and as per Agreement paragraph 5. WE MAKE NO WARRANTIES OF MERCHANTABILITY, DATA ACCURACY, YEAR 2000 COMPLIANCE, SYSTEM INTEGRATION OR FITNESS FOR USE AND TAKE ABSOLUTELY NO RESPONSIBILITY FOR THE FUNCTION OR DEFECTIVE NATURE OF SUCH SOFTWARE.

4. **OWNERSHIP OF EQUIPMENT:** We are the owner of the Equipment and have sole title to the Equipment (excluding software). You agree to keep the equipment free and clear of all liens and claims.

5. **WARRANTY DISCLAIMER:** WE MAKE NO WARRANTY EXPRESS OR IMPLIED, THAT THE EQUIPMENT IS FIT FOR A PARTICULAR PURPOSE OR THAT THE EQUIPMENT IS MERCHANTABLE. YOU AGREE THAT YOU HAVE SELECTED THE SUPPLIER AND EACH ITEM OF EQUIPMENT BASED UPON YOUR OWN JUDGMENT AND DISCLAIM ANY RELIANCE UPON ANY STATEMENTS OR REPRESENTATIONS MADE BY US OR ANY SUPPLIER. WE DO NOT TAKE RESPONSIBILITY FOR THE INSTALLATION OR PERFORMANCE OF THE EQUIPMENT. THE SUPPLIER IS NOT AN AGENT OF OURS AND NOTHING THE SUPPLIER STATES CAN AFFECT YOUR OBLIGATION UNDER THE LEASE. YOU WILL CONTINUE TO MAKE ALL PAYMENTS UNDER THIS AGREEMENT REGARDLESS OF ANY CLAIM OR COMPLAINT OF NON PERFORMANCE AGAINST SUPPLIER. WE HAVE NO RESPONSIBILITY FOR ANY MAINTENANCE OR SUPPORT TO BE SUPPLIED BY SUPPLIER.

6. **LOCATION OF EQUIPMENT:** You will keep and use the Equipment only at your address shown above and you agree not to move it unless we agree to it. At the end of the Agreement's term, you will return the Equipment to a location we specify at your expense, in retail resaleable condition, full working order, and in complete repair.

7. **LOSS OR DAMAGE:** You are responsible for the risk of loss or for any destruction of or damage to the Equipment. No such loss or damage relieves you from the payment obligations under this Agreement. You agree to promptly notify us in writing of any loss or damage and you will then pay to us the total of all unpaid lease payments for the full lease term plus the estimated fair market value of the Equipment at the end of the originally scheduled term, all discounted at six percent (6%) per year. Any proceeds of insurance will be paid to us and credited, at our option, against any loss or damage.

8. **COLLATERAL PROTECTION AND INSURANCE:** You agree to keep the equipment fully insured against loss with us as loss payee in an amount not less than the replacement cost until this Agreement is terminated. You also agree to obtain a general public liability insurance policy from anyone who is acceptable to us and to include us as an insured on the policy. You agree to provide us notification or other evidence of insurance acceptable to us, before this Agreement begins or, we will enroll you in our property damage coverage program and bill you a property damage surcharge as a result of our increased administrative costs and credit risk. As long as you are current at the time of the loss (excluding losses resulting from acts of god), the replacement value of the equipment will be applied against any loss or damage as per paragraph 7. You must be current to benefit from this program. NOTHING IN THIS PARAGRAPH WILL RELIEVE YOU OF YOUR RESPONSIBILITY FOR LIABILITY INSURANCE COVERAGE ON THIS EQUIPMENT.

9. **INDEMNITY:** We are not responsible for any loss or injuries caused by the installation or use of the Equipment. You agree to hold us harmless and reimburse us for loss and to defend us against any claim for losses or injury caused by the Equipment.

10. **TAXES AND FEES:** You agree to pay when due all taxes (including personal property tax, fines and penalties) and fees relating to this Agreement or the Equipment. If we pay any of these fees or taxes for you, you agree to reimburse us and to pay us a processing fee for each payment we make on your behalf. In addition, you agree to pay us any filing fees prescribed by the Uniform Commercial Code or other laws and reimburse us for all costs and expenses involved in documenting and servicing this transaction. You further agree to pay us up to $100.00 to facilitate the first lease payment is due to cover the expense of originating the Agreement.

11. **ASSIGNMENT:** YOU HAVE NO RIGHT TO SELL, TRANSFER, ASSIGN OR SUBLEASE THE EQUIPMENT OR THIS AGREEMENT. You understand that we, without prior notice, have the right to assign this Agreement to a financing source for financing purposes without your consent to such assignment. You understand that our assignee will have the same rights and benefits but they do not have to perform any of our obligations. You agree that the rights of assignee will not be subject to any claims, defenses, or setoffs that you may have against us.

12. **DEFAULT AND REMEDIES:** If you do not pay any lease payment or other sum due to us or other party when due or if you break any of your promises in the Agreement or any other Agreement with us, you will be in default. If any part of a payment is late, you agree to pay a late charge of 15% of the payment which is late or if less, the maximum charge allowed by law. If you are ever in default, we may retain your security deposit and at our option, we can terminate or cancel this Agreement and require that you pay (1) the unpaid balance of this Agreement (discounted at 6%); (2) the amount of any purchase option and if none is specified, 20% of the original equipment cost which represents our anticipated residual value in the equipment; (3) and return the equipment to us to a location designated by us. We may recover interest on any unpaid balance at the rate of 8% per annum. We may also use any of the remedies available to us under Article 2A of the Uniform Commercial Code as enacted in the State of Minnesota or any other law. If we refer this Agreement to an attorney for collection, you agree to pay our reasonable attorney's fees and actual court costs. If we have to take possession of the equipment, you agree to pay the cost of repossession. The net proceeds of the sale of any repossessed Equipment will be credited against what you owe us under this Agreement. YOU AGREE THAT WE WILL NOT BE RESPONSIBLE TO PAY YOU ANY CONSEQUENTIAL OR INCIDENTAL DAMAGES FOR ANY DEFAULT BY US UNDER THIS AGREEMENT. You agree that any delay or failure to enforce our rights under this Agreement does not prevent us from enforcing any rights at a later time. It is further agreed that your rights and remedies are governed exclusively by this Agreement and you waive lessee's rights under Article 2A (508-522) of the UCC.

13. **UCC FILINGS:** You grant us a security interest in the equipment if this agreement is deemed a secured transaction and you authorize us to record a UCC-1 financing statement or similar instrument, and appoint us your attorney-in-fact to execute and deliver such instrument, in order to show our interest in the Equipment.

14. **SECURITY DEPOSIT:** The security deposit is payable upon execution and is non interest bearing and is to secure your performance under this Agreement. Any security deposit made may be applied by us to satisfy any amount owed by you, in which event you will promptly restore the security deposit to its full amount as set forth above. If all conditions herein are fully complied with and provided you have not ever been in default of this Agreement per paragraph 12, the security deposit will be refunded to you after the return of the equipment in accordance with paragraph 6.

15. **LAW:** This Agreement shall be deemed fully executed and performed in the State of Minnesota or in the home state of whoever holds the Lessor's interest as it may be assigned from time to time per paragraph 11. This Agreement shall be governed by and construed in accordance with the laws of the State of Minnesota or the home state of Lessor's assignee. You expressly and unconditionally consent to the jurisdiction and venue of any court in the State of Minnesota and waive right to trial by jury for any claim or action arising out of or relating to this Agreement or the Equipment. Furthermore, you waive the defense of Forum Non Conveniens.

16. **LESSEE GUARANTY:** You agree to submit the original of the lease documents with the security deposit to Lessor or its assignee via overnight courier the same day of the facsimile transmission of the lease documents. Should we fail to receive these originals, you agree to be bound by the faxed copy of this agreement with appropriate signatures on the document. Lessee waives the right to challenge in court the authenticity of a faxed copy of this agreement and the faxed copy shall be considered the original and shall be the binding agreement for the purposes of any enforcement action under paragraph 12.

Signature ___JOE SMITH___   PRESIDENT
                              Title

Scenario 1
Lease Agreement – Guaranteed 10% Buyout

GUARANTEED 10% BUYOUT

Lease # _____12002_____ between ___Lucrative Leasing_____, Lessor,

and __COMPANY A_____, Lessee.

Provided the Lease has not terminated early and no event of default under the Lease has occurred and is continuing, THE LESSEE MUST AT THE END OF THE ORIGINAL TERM EXERCISE ONE OF THE FOLLOWING END OF LEASE AGREEMENTS:

BUY: Purchase the Equipment for 10% of the Lessors original cost of the equipment at the end of the original lease term.

OR

RENEW: Renew the Lease under the original terms and conditions for a minimum period of eight (8) months. At the expiration of such renewal period, this Lease shall automatically renew on a month to month basis unless Lessee notifies Lessor in writing of its intent either to purchase the Equipment for a price to be agreed upon by the Lessor and Lessee, or return the Equipment to a location specified by Lessor.

Failure to notify Lessor of which End of Lease Agreement is to be exercised shall constitute exercise of the renewal agreement.

The provisions in this Agreement supersede all others contained in the original Equipment Lease Agreement.

____LUCRATIVE LEASING_____   COMPANY A_____
Lessor   Lessee

_____   Signature JOE SMITH_____
Signature   Signature JOE SMITH

_____   PRESIDENT_____
Title   Title

_____   _____
Date   Date

Scenario 1

Lease Agreement – Schedule "A"

EQUIPMENT SCHEDULE "A"

LEASE # 12002

This Equipment Schedule "A" is to be attached to and become part of that Schedule of Leased Equipment dated

_____ , 20 _____ by and between the undersigned and

Lucrative Leasing   (Lessor).

QTY	DESCRIPTION	MODEL NO.	SERIAL NO.
	Vendor: PACIFIC FORKLIFT SALES		
	5000 BROADWAY		
	SEATTLE WA 98110		
1	GEHL 883 8,000LB FORKLIFT	883	

This Equipment Schedule "A" is hereby verified as correct by the undersigned Lessee, who acknowledges receipt of a copy.

Lessee: COMPANY A

Signature: X
          JOE SMITH

Title: PRESIDENT

Scenario 1
Insurance Request

Lessor: YOUR COMPANY NAME   Lease #: 12002
          YOUR COMPANY ADDRESS

INSURANCE AUTHORIZATION

To: ALL GOOD INSURANCE   Please input your insurance
                                              information on the left.
       _____

       Kari_____

Phone: (800) XXX-XXXX_____

Contact: _____

We have entered into an equipment lease agreement for the equipment shown on the attached Lease Copy. This equipment is located as stated on the Lease.

This is a net lease and we are responsible for the full equipment cost in the amount of $ 43,500.00.

Please see that we immediately have ALL RISK coverage for liability and full replacement cost of the equipment and that (FUNDING SOURCE)___ is shown as **LOSS PAYEE** and **ADDITIONAL INSURED** on the policy. Please forward a Certificate of Insurance and Loss Payable/Additional Insured Clause to:

               (FUNDING SOURCE)_____

               _____

               _____

Concurrent Certificates of Insurance, thirty (30) days notice in the event of cancellation or alteration, and general correspondence should be sent to the above addresses as well.

Sincerely,

               Lessee: COMPANY A_____

               X_____

               BY:_____Joe Smith, President_____

               DATE EXECUTED BY LESSEE_____

Scenario 1
Assignment Letter

ASSIGNMENT

RE: Lease No. _____12002_____, dated _____, _____

between _____COMPANY A_____

as Lessee and the undersigned as nominal Lessor (the "Lease").

The undersigned hereby sells, assigns, and transfers to The Manifest Group all of the undersigned's right, title, and interest in and to (a) the equipment covered by the Lease and (b) the undersigned's rights as Lessor under the Lease, including the right to receive rent thereunder.

_____Lucrative Leasing_____
(Name of Lessor)

_____
Signature

_____
Title

_____
Date

Scenario 1
Broker Fee Invoice

BROKER FEE INVOICE

LESSOR:..............................   LUCRATIVE LEASING

LESSEE NAME:.....................   COMPANY A

APPROVAL NUMBER:.............   12002

TOTAL LEASE AMOUNT:........... $ 47,197.50

MONTHLY PAYMENT:............... $ 1,211.56

RATE FACTORS:......................   Buy: .02410   Sell: .02567

OF ADVANCED PAYMENTS:....   2 Security

PURCHASE OPTION:.................   10% PUT

Broker Commission............	$ 3,067.84	Points: 6.5
+ Doc fees collected	$ 150.00	
- Docs fees required by bank	$ 77.50	
Sub-Total	$ 3,140.34	
Less Advanced Money Received	$ 2,573.12	

NET COMMISSION DUE........... $ 567.22

Please Standard Overnight BROKER & VENDOR checks via Federal Express or UPS.

Please send broker check to: LUCRATIVE LEASING

FedEx #: (Account #)

CONTACT: (Your Name) at (Your Phone) with any questions.

Scenario 1

Insurance Binder

CERTIFICATE OF LIABILITY INSURANCE

DATE (MM/DD/YY)
06/10/2002

PRODUCER	THIS CERTIFICATE IS ISSUED AS A MATTER OF INFORMATION ONLY AND CONFERS NO RIGHTS UPON THE CERTIFICATE HOLDER. THIS CERTIFICATE DOES NOT AMEND, EXTEND OR ALTER THE COVERAGE AFFORDED BY THE POLICIES BELOW.
ALL GOOD INSURANCE	**COMPANIES AFFORDING COVERAGE**
	COMPANY A — ALL GOOD INSURANCE
INSURED	COMPANY B
COMPANY A	COMPANY C
1234 Main Street	
Seattle, WA 98100	COMPANY D
JAV	

COVERAGES

THIS IS TO CERTIFY THAT THE POLICIES OF INSURANCE LISTED BELOW HAVE BEEN ISSUED TO THE INSURED NAMED ABOVE FOR THE POLICY PERIOD INDICATED. NOTWITHSTANDING ANY REQUIREMENT, TERM OR CONDITION OF ANY CONTRACT OR OTHER DOCUMENT WITH RESPECT TO WHICH THIS CERTIFICATE MAY BE ISSUED OR MAY PERTAIN, THE INSURANCE AFFORDED BY THE POLICIES DESCRIBED HEREIN IS SUBJECT TO ALL THE TERMS, EXCLUSIONS AND CONDITIONS OF SUCH POLICIES. LIMITS SHOWN MAY HAVE BEEN REDUCED BY PAID CLAIMS.

CO LTR	TYPE OF INSURANCE	POLICY NUMBER	POLICY EFFECTIVE DATE (MM/DD/YY)	POLICY EXPIRATION DATE (MM/DD/YY)	LIMITS	
A	**GENERAL LIABILITY**		02/10/02	02/10/03	GENERAL AGGREGATE	$ 2,000,000
	[X] COMMERCIAL GENERAL LIABILITY				PRODUCTS - COMP/OP AGG	$ 2,000,000
	[ ] CLAIMS MADE [X] OCCUR				PERSONAL & ADV INJURY	$ 1,000,000
	[ ] OWNER'S & CONTRACTOR'S PROT				EACH OCCURRENCE	$ 1,000,000
	[X] WA Stop Gap				FIRE DAMAGE (Any one fire)	$ 100,000
					MED EXP (Any one person)	$ 5,000
	AUTOMOBILE LIABILITY				COMBINED SINGLE LIMIT	$
	[ ] ANY AUTO					
	[ ] ALL OWNED AUTOS				BODILY INJURY (Per person)	$
	[ ] SCHEDULED AUTOS					
	[ ] HIRED AUTOS				BODILY INJURY (Per accident)	$
	[ ] NON-OWNED AUTOS					
					PROPERTY DAMAGE	$
	GARAGE LIABILITY				AUTO ONLY - EA ACCIDENT	$
	[ ] ANY AUTO				OTHER THAN AUTO ONLY:	
					EACH ACCIDENT	$
					AGGREGATE	$
	EXCESS LIABILITY				EACH OCCURRENCE	$
	[ ] UMBRELLA FORM				AGGREGATE	$
	[ ] OTHER THAN UMBRELLA FORM					$
	WORKERS COMPENSATION AND EMPLOYERS' LIABILITY				[ ] WC STATUTORY LIMITS [ ] OTH-ER	
	THE PROPRIETOR/ PARTNERS/EXECUTIVE OFFICERS ARE: [ ] INCL [ ] EXCL				EL EACH ACCIDENT	$
					EL DISEASE - POLICY LIMIT	$
					EL DISEASE - EA EMPLOYEE	$
A	**OTHER** Equipment Floater		02/10/02	02/10/03	Limit * - See Below Deductible $5,000	

DESCRIPTION OF OPERATIONS/LOCATIONS/VEHICLES/SPECIAL ITEMS
RE: GEHL FORKLIFT, ▮▮▮▮▮, $43,500.
CERTIFICATE HOLDER IS ADDED AS A LOSS PAYEE AND ADDITIONAL INSURED WITH RESPECT TO THE ABOVE.

CERTIFICATE HOLDER	CANCELLATION
	SHOULD ANY OF THE ABOVE DESCRIBED POLICIES BE CANCELLED BEFORE THE EXPIRATION DATE THEREOF, THE ISSUING COMPANY WILL ENDEAVOR TO MAIL __45__ DAYS WRITTEN NOTICE TO THE CERTIFICATE HOLDER NAMED TO THE LEFT, BUT FAILURE TO MAIL SUCH NOTICE SHALL IMPOSE NO OBLIGATION OR LIABILITY OF ANY KIND UPON THE ▮▮▮ OR REPRESENTATIVES.
	AUTHORIZED REPRESENTATIVE

25-S (1/95)

Scenario 1
Vendor Invoice

Invoice

PACIFIC FORKLIFT SALES
5000 Broadway Avenue
Seattle, WA 98110

DATE	INVOICE #
10/20/2002	1

BILL TO

LUCRATIVE LEASING

SHIP TO

COMPANY A
1234 Main Street
Seattle, WA 98100

P.O. NUMBER	TERMS	REP	SHIP	VIA	F.O.B.	PROJECT
12002	Lease		10/20/2002			

QUANTITY	ITEM CODE	DESCRIPTION	PRICE EACH	AMOUNT
1		GEHL 883 8,000 lb Forklift		$43,500.00
		Sales Tax	8.5%	3,697.50

| | | | | **Total** | $47,197.50 |

Scenario 2

A Lease that Required Tax Returns and a Little Extra Work

Scenario 2 examines a lease application that was not as easy as Scenario 1. In this scenario, the president's credit report showed some slow pay and a lot of debt. With the dollar amount being so high at $70,000 and risks being greater due to a questionable credit report, tax returns were required to get this deal done.

The fictitious companies for Scenario 2 are as follows:

Lease Broker:	Lucrative Leasing (Hereafter referred to as LL.)
Lessee:	Company B 4321 Main Street Sumner, WA 98390 Contact: John Jones, President
Vendor:	Perfect Packaging Machines 8000 Cherry Boulevard Spokane, WA 95000 Contact: Greg, Sales
Funding Source:	Funding Source
Insurance Company:	Incredible Insurance

Facts of Lease Scenario 2:

Equipment:	ZBT 900 Capsule Filling Machine
Dollar Amount:	$70,000.00
Terms:	60 Months
Residual:	$1.00 Buy Out

The application was received by LL from one of its valuable vendors. On the surface, everything appeared to be good, fourteen years in business, the application was complete, and the dollar amount was preferable (less than $75,000). However, once the credit bureau was pulled (see Scenario 2, Credit Report) things changed. The credit report shows a lot of debt, especially real estate (which isn't that bad) and $77,000 in revolving debt (credit cards, etc). Along with the high debt was a few thirty day late payments scattered around the gentleman's credit bureau (I put circles around the late payments). The combination of these factors made it difficult to ask for $70,000 without strengthening the package with tax returns.

While waiting for the tax returns, LL obtained a great bank rating (see Scenario 2, Bank A) dating back nine years with an average balance of $10,000. The bank reference was very helpful. LL next obtained the three loan references (see Scenario 2, Loan A, B & C), which were all very positive.

Just as LL completed work on the bank and loan references, the tax returns (see Scenario 2, 2001 Tax Return: S Corp., 2001 Tax Return: S Corp. (Page 2), 2000 Tax Return: Individual, 2000 Tax Return: Individual (Page 2), and 2000 Tax Return: Schedule C) arrived in the fax. They were a little confusing at first because LL received an S corporation return for 2001 and individual returns for 2000 along with a Schedule C showing that the company was a proprietorship the year before. It turns out that the company switched from a proprietorship in 2000 to an S corporation in 2001. The tax returns showed evidence of this, but some legal documentation showing business structure changes was required, requested and received to validate the change of business structure. It was important to prove to a funding source that this was the same company this year as it was last year so they do not classify it as a "New Business" and decline the applicant. Overall, the returns were great and showed an improvement from one year to the next. This company was on the up and up. A personal financial statement was also requested and received (I left this out of this scenario because of too much personal information).

With all of this information, the typed application, bank and loan references and tax returns, the deal was submitted to the first funding source. As you can see, the first funding source declined (see Scenario 2, Funding Source Decline) the transaction. Their reasoning was that the credit was too risky and there were too many inquiries from other banks. The funding source also found a tax lien (was later discovered to be a misprint on the company's business credit bureau) and were unwilling to reconsider the application. So, LL submitted the lease package to another source and received an approval (see Scenario 2, Funding Source Approval). It was just what LL was looking for. A lot of work went into getting this, now it was time to sell the payment and get documents to the lessee.

It was two months before the lessee was ready for documents. After all of their work, LL thought that there was not going to be a deal at all. The lessee kept stalling to proceed on the lease (probably waiting for a big order to come in; typical). After LL placed a number of follow up calls to the lessee, they were finally ready for documents. LL quoted the customer 60 months, $1.00 buy out and they accepted. The documentation request (see Scenario 2, Documentation Request) illustrates the details of the transaction. LL sold the payment with an 8 percent commission built in for themselves.

The documentation cover letter (see Scenario 2, Documentation Cover Letter) displays the check amount that the lessee needed to send back with the signed documents. Once again, you can see the documents that the customer had to sign (see Scenario 2, Lease Agreement Page 1, Lease Agreement Page 2, $1.00 Purchase Option, Equipment Schedule "A" and Insurance Request). The only difference in documents between this Scenario and Scenario 1 is the purchase option at the end of the lease. The previous scenario had a 10% Put, while this scenario has a $1.00 buyout. The reason this one is different is because the approval (see Scenario 2, Funding Source Approval) states that the deal was approved for $1.00 buyout only. The lessee had no choice regarding the buyout at the end of the lease.

Documentation was received and proof read. Everything was a go. LL completed the assignment of lease (see Scenario 2, Assignment of Lease) and broker fee invoice (see Scenario 2, Broker Fee Invoice) and forwarded them along with the documentation to the funding source overnight. In the meantime, LL received the original invoice (see Scenario 2, Vendor Invoice) and insurance binder (see Scenario 2, Insurance Binder). LL forwarded those to the funding source as well.

Delivery of the equipment took several weeks. The packaging machine was very big and had to be shipped by a large truck. Once the equipment was delivered, it had to be set up and operational before the funding source would call for a verbal.

Once the verbal was completed, LL received a commission check for $5,600.00 from the funding source. Company B was not charged a processing fee as an incentive for them to sign the documentation and return it quickly.

Scenario 2
Completed Lease Application

LUCRATIVE LEASING

Lease Application

VENDOR INFORMATION		
Vendor Name PERFECT PACKAGING MACHINES		Equipment Cost $70,000.00
Vendor Address 8000 Cherry Boulevard, Spokane, WA 95000		Initial Term 60 Months
Contact Person Greg	Telephone number (800)XXX-XXXX	Equipment Description

LESSEE COMPANY INFORMATION
Company Name COMPANY B

(1) ZBT 900 Capsule Filling
Machine

Company Address 4321 Main Street, Sumner, WA 98390		

Special Requirements

Signer John Jones, President	Title	Telephone number (800) XXX-XXXX
Nature of Business Packaging	Type of business _ Non-Profit _ Proprietorship _ Partnership X_ Corporation	No. of Years in Business 14 Years

PERSONAL INFORMATION ON OFFICERS, PARTNERS, OR GUARANTORS				
Name John Jones	Title President	Social Security Number XXX-XX-XXXX		Driver's License Number
Home Address NA	City	State	Zip	How Long? | Home Phone Number ( )
Previous Address	City	State	Zip	Own / Rent Present Home?
Name	Title	Social Security Number		Driver's License Number
Home Address	City	State	Zip	How Long? | Home Phone Number ( )
Previous Address	City	State	Zip	Own / Rent Present Home?

COMPANY BANK REFERENCES - TWO YEAR HISTORY				
Name of Bank/Branch BANK A	How Long?	Chkg. Acct. # Loan Acct. # XXX-XXX-XXX	Telephone No. (800) XXX-XXXX	Contact Officer Jerod
Name of Bank/Branch	How Long?	Chkg. Acct. # Loan Acct. #	Telephone No. ( )	Contact Officer
Name of Bank/Branch	How Long?	Chkg. Acct. # Loan Acct. #	Telephone No. ( )	Contact Officer

TRADE REFERENCES - TWO YEAR HISTORY			
Name of Supplier LOAN A	City/State Portland, OR	Telephone No. (800)XXX-XXXX	Contact Person Credit
Name of Supplier LOAN B	City/State Denver, CO	Telephone No. (800)XXX-XXXX	Contact Person Credit
Name of Supplier LOAN C	City/State AUBURN, WA	Telephone No. (800)XXX XXXX	Contact Person Credit

I/we hereby authorize you to whom this application is made, or your agents, to investigate my/our credit worthiness and will provide financial statements, tax returns, etc., as you deem necessary. I/we agree that the security deposit is not refundable unless the application is rejected by Lessor. By the execution of the lease agreement, I/we warrant that the information submitted herein is true and correct and hereby authorized references contained herein to release any necessary information. Further, I/we warrant it is understood that Lessor reserves the right to reverse any credit decision if the information contained herein is found to be incorrect, and I/we will indemnify Lessor for any and all costs incurred with this application for credit including any cost incurred in the placement or reservation of the intended leased equipment based on the information contained herein.

Signature X	Date:

Scenario 2
Credit Report Page 1

```
User ID :  ██████                        Date : 03/11/2002

Report Name : Bureau Data (Record ID # █████)        Page : 0001
-----------------------------------------------------------------------
██████████████████ : ██████
Record Number : ██████
Report Type : Credit - █████████████████████
Tracking:
S ....,....,HC
██████████████████████
████████████████████
████████████████████

              ██████████  CREDIT REPORT

<FOR>         <SUB NAME>      <MKT SUB> <INFILE> <DATE>    <TIME>
(████████████████████████     10 WA    12/87    03/11/02  13:00CT

<SUBJECT>                              <SSN>        <BIRTH DATE>
████████████████████          ████████████  12/53
                                                    <TELEPHONE>
                                                    ████████████

<CURRENT ADDRESS>                                   <DATE RPTD>
                                                    11/01
<FORMER ADDRESS>
████████████████████████████████████████
████████████████████████████████            4/01

<CURRENT EMPLOYER AND ADDRESS>         <VERF> <RPTD>
████████████████
                                       9/94V 11/94
-----------------------------------------------------------------------
S P E C I A L   M E S S A G E S
****HAWK-ALERT:INPUT SSN ISSUED: 1970 - 1971; STATE: WA
           :FILE SSN ISSUED: 1970 - 1971; STATE: WA; (EST. AGE OBTAINED:
            16 TO 18)***
-----------------------------------------------------------------------
M O D E L   P R O F I L E
***EMPIRICA 95 SCORE +658  : 005, 010, 002, 013 ***
-----------------------------------------------------------------------
C R E D I T   S U M M A R Y   * * *   T O T A L   F I L E   H I S T O R Y
PR=0  COL=0  NEG=0  HSTNEG=8-11  TRD=58 RVL=25 INST=21 MTG=12 OPN=0  INQ=12
          HIGH CRED  CRED LIM  BALANCE  PAST DUE  MNTHLY PAY AVAILABLE
REVOLVING:    $367K    $339K    $77.8K   $0        $1196      77%
INSTALLMENT:  $196K    $0       $99.9K   $0        $2766
MORTGAGE:     $865K    $        $810K    $0        $7153
TOTALS:       $1.4M    $339K    $987K    $0        $11.1K
-----------------------------------------------------------------------
T R A D E S
SUBNAME      SUBCODE    OPENED   HIGHCRED  TERMS     MAXDELQ  PAYPAT  1-12 MOP
ACCOUNT#                VERFIED  CREDLIM   PASTDUE   AMT-MOP  PAYPAT  13-24
ECOA COLLATRL/LOANTYPE  CLSD/PD  BALANCE   REMARKS            MO 30/60/90
███████████████████████ 7/93   $150K     360M1079           111111XX1111 M01
```

Scenario 2
Credit Report Page 2

```
User ID :  ██████████                      Date : 03/11/2002

Report Name : Bureau Data (Record ID # ██████████)      Page : 0002
- - - - - - - - - - - - - - - - - - - - - - - - - - - - - - - - - - - - -
              3/02A           $0              111111111111
C   ██████████               $134K               48    0/ 0/ 0

    ██████████   2/99  $35.5K   60M735       111111111111 I01
              3/02A            $0             111111111111
I   AUTOMOBILE              $16.7K               37    0/ 0/ 0

    ██████████   7/99  $8320    MIN142       111111111111 R01
              3/02A  $7000                   111111111111
I   CREDIT CARD           $2318                 31   (1/ 0/ 0)

    ██████████   2/00  $10.2K   MIN189       111111111111 R01
              3/02A  $10.0K    $0            111111
I   CREDIT CARD           $9489                 30    0/ 0/ 0

    ██████████   2/01  $16.8K   MIN269       111111111211 R01
              3/02A  $15.0K    $0
A   CREDIT CARD           $15.4K               13   (1/ 0/ 0)

    ██████████   1/02  $44.1K   60M854       1            I01
              3/02A            $0
C   AUTOMOBILE            $44.1K                 1    0/ 0/ 0

    ██████████   5/93  $540                  111111111111 R01
              2/02A  $800      $0            111111111111
C   CHARGE ACCOUNT  8/00P  $0                   48    0/ 0/ 0

    ██████████   1/94  $668            12/99  111111111111 R01
              2/02A  $300      $0      03   132111211111
C   CHARGE ACCOUNT  1/01P  $0                   48    2/ 1/ 0

    ██████████   4/94  $62.5K                111111111111 C01
              2/02A  $65.0K    $0            1X11111X11
P   HOME EQUITY LOAN 11/01P  $0                 48    0/ 0/ 0

    ██████████   8/94  $8020    MIN71        111111111111 R01
              2/02A  $13.5K    $0            11111XXXXX1
C   CREDIT CARD           $5545                 48    0/ 0/ 0

    ██████████   8/94  $35.7K   180M346      111111XXX111 I01
              2/02A            $0            111111111111
I   TLR ██████████         $23.2K               48    0/ 0/ 0

    ██████████  10/96  $25.0K                111111111111 R01
              2/02A  $25.0K    $0            12111111111
I   CREDIT CARD  10/97C  $0    ACCT CLSD BY CONSUMER 23   1/ 0/ 0

    ██████████   4/97  $36.8K   72M654       XX1X1X11X1X1 I01
              2/02A            $0            1XXXX1X11111
```

Scenario 2
Credit Report Page 3

C	AUTOMOBILE	2/02C	$0	CLOSED		48	0/ 0/ 0
	▒▒▒▒▒▒▒▒▒▒	5/98	$26.6K	60M514	111111111111 I01		
		2/02A		$0	111111111111		
I	AUTOMOBILE	1/02C	$0	CLOSED		44	0/ 0/ 0
	▒▒▒▒▒▒▒▒▒▒	11/98	$20.3K	60M426	111111111111 I01		
		2/02A		$0	111111X11111		
C	AUTOMOBILE		$8199			40	0/ 0/ 0
	▒▒▒▒▒▒▒▒▒▒	11/96	$25.0K		111111X1111X C01		
		2/02A	$25.0K	$0	111111111X11		
P	LINE OF CREDIT	11/01P	$0			32	0/ 0/ 0
	▒▒▒▒▒▒▒▒▒▒	10/98	$49.2K	MIN500	111111211111 C01		
		2/02A	$49.0K	$0	1111X11111X1		
I	LINE OF CREDIT		$20.3K			37	1/ 0/ 0
	▒▒▒▒▒▒▒▒▒▒	6/99	$64.9K		112211111111 C01		
		2/02A	$70.0K	$0	1X11111X1111		
P	HOME EQUITY LOAN	11/01P	$0			30	2/ 0/ 0
	▒▒▒▒▒▒▒▒▒▒	6/99	$224K	180M2302	111111111111 M01		
		2/02A		$0	111111111111		
C	CONVENTIONAL REAL		$198K			28	0/ 0/ 0
	▒▒▒▒▒▒▒▒▒▒	8/99	$26.2K	72M460	XX1X1X11X1X1 I01		
		2/02A		$0	1XXXX1X11111		
I	AUTOMOBILE	2/02C	$0	CLOSED		28	0/ 0/ 0
	▒▒▒▒▒▒▒▒▒▒	8/99	$43.5K	120M528	1X1X1X11X1X1 M01		
		2/02A		$0	1XXXX1X11111		
I	REAL ESTATE MORTG		$36.4K			28	0/ 0/ 0
	▒▒▒▒▒▒▒▒▒▒	7/91	$9201	MIN25	111111111111 R01		
		2/02A	$16.0K	$0	11111111		
C	CREDIT CARD		$79			48	0/ 0/ 0
	▒▒▒▒▒▒▒▒▒▒	10/00	$13.5K	36M405	1111XX11XXXX I01		
		2/02A		$0	11X1		
S	REVOLVING BUSINES		$7513	CNTIN LIAB-CORP DEFLT 16			0/ 0/ 0
	▒▒▒▒▒▒▒▒▒▒	2/99			1		R01
		2/02A	$1000	$0			
I	CREDIT CARD	11/99P	$0			1	0/ 0/ 0
	▒▒▒▒▒▒▒▒▒▒	3/00	$26.5K		1111		R01
		2/02A	$25.0K	$0			
I	CREDIT CARD		$24.5K			4	0/ 0/ 0

Scenario 2
Credit Report Page 4

```
User ID : ██████████                          Date : 03/11/2002

Report Name : Bureau Data (Record ID # ██████)          Page : 0004
--------------------------------------------------------------------

████████████████████  5/98   $1085                    111211111111 R01
                      1/02A  $1300    $0               11
I    CHARGE ACCOUNT    3/01P  $0                          32   1/ 0/ 0

████████████████████  12/99  $3779                    111111111111 R01
                      1/02A  $5500    $0               111111121111
A    CREDIT CARD       5/01P  $0                          25   1/ 0/ 0

████████████████████  9/99   $5006                    111111111111 R01
                      12/01A $6000    $0               111111111111
A    CREDIT CARD      12/01C  $0       ACCT CLSD BY CONSUMER 45  0/ 0/ 0

████████████████████  8/99   $152K    360M1290        X11111111111 M01
                      6/01A  $0        $0              1111
C    CONVENTIONAL REAL 5/01C  $0       CLOSED              16   0/ 0/ 0

████████████████████  5/93   $254                                 R01
                      12/00A $1000    $0
C    CHARGE ACCOUNT    9/00C  $0                          48   0/ 0/ 0

████████████████████  9/93   $2496                    211111111111 R01
                      10/00A $300     $0               111111111111
I    CREDIT CARD       9/00C  $0       CANC BY CRDT GRANTOR 48  1/ 0/ 0

████████████████████  9/94   $14.6K   72M255          X11111111111 I01
                      9/00A  $0        $0              11111111X111
I    NISSAN  KING CAB   9/00C  $0       ACCT CLSD BY CONSUMER 48  0/ 0/ 0

████████████████████  8/96   $671                     1XXXXXXXX111 R01
                      9/00A  $500     $0               111111111111
I    CREDIT CARD      10/98C  $0       ACCT CLSD BY CONSUMER 33  0/ 0/ 0

████████████████████  2/99                            1111111111   R01
                      6/00A  $10.0K    $0
I    CREDIT CARD      11/99P  $0                          10   0/ 0/ 0

████████████████████  1/95   $28.1K   72M516          X11XXX1X11X1 I01
                      7/99A             $0              1X1X1X1X1111
I    AUTOMOBILE        6/99C  $0        CLOSED              48   0/ 0/ 0

████████████████████  5/97   $214K    350M1896        X11111111111 M01
                      5/99A             $0              11111111
C    ████████          5/99C  $0        TRNSFRD: OTHER LENDER 20  0/ 0/ 0

████████████████████  6/94   $250                     111111111111 R01
                      1/99A  $300     $0               111111111111
C    CREDIT CARD       3/98C  $0        ACCT CLSD BY CONSUMER 34  0/ 0/ 0
```

Scenario 2
Credit Report Page 5

User ID : ▓▓▓▓   Date : 03/11/2002

Report Name : Bureau Data (Record ID # ▓▓▓)   Page : 0005

▓▓▓▓▓▓▓▓▓▓	5/97	$18.4K	60M383	1X11X11X1X1X I01
	12/98A		$0	1X11111
C AUTOMOBILE				19 0/ 0/ 0

▓▓▓▓▓▓▓▓▓▓	11/95	$24.0K	36M720	11X111111111 I01
	11/98A		$0	111111111111
I AUTO LEASE	10/98C	$0	CLOSED	35 0/ 0/ 0

▓▓▓▓▓▓▓▓▓	11/96	$25.0K		111111111111 C01
	5/98A	$25.0K	$0	11XXX1
M LINE OF CREDIT				18 0/ 0/ 0

▓▓▓▓▓▓▓▓▓	1/93	$86.1K	360M698	X11111111111 M01
	5/98A		$0	111X11X1111
C FRD713277769	5/98C	$0	CLOSED	23 0/ 0/ 0

▓▓▓▓▓▓▓▓▓	9/94	$212K	360M1721	X11X11X1111 M01
	5/97A		$0	
C CONVENTIONAL REAL	5/97C	$0	CLOSED	11 0/ 0/ 0

▓▓▓▓▓▓▓▓	7/93	$22.2K	60M441	1XXXXXXXXXXX I01
	1/97A		$0	XXXXXXX1
I AUTOMOBILE				20 0/ 0/ 0

▓▓▓▓▓▓▓▓	1/94	$16.0K	48M390	X11111X11111 I01
	9/96A	$0	$0	1111
C TOYOTA CAMRY	9/96P	$0		16 0/ 0/ 0

▓▓▓▓▓▓▓▓	11/93	$86.1K	360M678	X111111111 M01
	3/96A		$0	
C CONVENTIONAL REAL		$84.0K	TRANSFER	10 0/ 0/ 0

▓▓▓▓▓▓▓▓	9/94	$212K	348M1487	X111111111 M01
	3/96A		$0	
C CONVENTIONAL REAL		$209K	TRANSFER	10 0/ 0/ 0

▓▓▓▓▓▓▓▓	7/93	$150K	348M1079	X111111111 M01
	3/96A		$0	
C CONVENTIONAL REAL		$146K	TRANSFER	10 0/ 0/ 0

▓▓▓▓▓▓▓	4/95	$25.0K	M132	111111 I01
	2/96A		$0	
I BUSINESS	11/95C	$0		6 0/ 0/ 0

▓▓▓▓▓▓▓	12/93	$510B	24M231	I01
	9/94A	$0	$0	
C FORD RANGER	9/94P	$0		

| ▓▓▓▓▓▓▓ | 6/93 | $310B | 12M271 | I01 |

Scenario 2
Credit Report Page 6

```
User ID :  ████████                          Date : 03/11/2002

Report Name : Bureau Data (Record ID # ████)        Page : 0006
------------------------------------------------------------------
                          6/94A   $0      $0
C    BAYLINER LIBERTY     5/94P   $0

     ████████████████     6/91    $10.2K   42M293              I01
                          1/94A   $0       $0
C    LINCOLN  CONTINEN    1/94P   $0

     ████████████████     5/92    $35.7K                       R01
                          12/93A           $0
P                         12/93P  $0

     ████████████████     3/79    $61.5K   360X517             M01
                          11/93A           $0
C    V.A. LOAN            11/93C  $0

     ████████████████     2/91    $6890    36M227              I01
                          5/93A   $0       $0
C    OLDSMOBILE  DELTA

     ████████████████     12/87   $13.0K   60M279              I01
                          10/92A           $0
P    AUTOMOBILE           10/92C  $0

     ████████████████     1/92    $20.0K                       R01
                          5/92A            $0
P                         5/92P   $0

     ████████████████     1/94    $0                           IUR
                          9/00A            $0
C    INSTALLMENT SALES    6/00C   $0       TRANSFER      27   0/ 0/ 0

     ████████████████     5/97    $214K    360M               MUR
                          4/00A            $0
P    CONVENTIONAL REAL    6/99C   $0       CLOSED         1   0/ 0/ 0
------------------------------------------------------------------
I N Q U I R I E S
DATE       SUBCODE       SUBNAME        TYPE     AMOUNT
 3/11/02  ██████████████████████████G
11/19/01  ██████████████████████████
 8/07/01  ██████████████████████████3
 1/18/01  ██████████████████████████
12/15/00  ██████████████████████████
12/12/00  ██████████████████████████T
12/11/00  ██████████████████████████
10/03/00  ██████████████████████████S
10/02/00  ██████████████████████████
 9/25/00  ██████████████████████████
 9/18/00  ██████████████████████████
 7/10/00  ██████████████████████████
```

Scenario 2
Bank A

BANK RATING REQUEST

TO: ___BANK A_____   RE: ___COMPANY B_____

___FAX # (800) XXX-XXXX_____   _____

ATTN: Jerod_____   _____

                                   ACCOUNT #: ___XXX-XXX-XXX_____

CREDIT MANAGER,

THE ABOVE NAMED PARTY HAS APPLIED FOR CREDIT IN CONNECTION WITH AN EQUIPMENT LEASE/PURCHASE. WE WOULD APPRECIATE RECEIVING THE FOLLOWING INFORMATION AS A CREDIT REFERENCE ON THEIR ACCOUNT. ANY INFORMATION PROVIDED WILL BE HELD IN THE STRICTEST CONFIDENCE.

DATE OPENED: __10/28/93_____   AVERAGE BALANCE: __$10,000___

OF NSF'S: __N/A___   # OF OD'S: __N/A___ IF CLOSED, WHEN? _____
            (within last 6 months)   (within last 6 months)

RATING AND/OR COMMENTS: _____Good Account_____

NAME EXACTLY AS IT APPEARS ON THE ACCOUNT: _____

_____

ARE THERE ANY LOANS/NOTES/LINES OF CREDIT?   (YES)   NO
IF YES, PLEASE DETAIL BELOW:

TYPE	OPEN DATE	HIGH CREDIT	BALANCE	(UN)SECURED?	RATING
Credit Line	10/28/93	$10,000	$3,000		Good

_____

INFORMATION SUPPLIED BY: _____Jerod_____
TITLE: _____Banker_____

AS A COURTESY TO OUR MUTUAL CUSTOMER, PLEASE REPLY BY FAX OR PHONE WITHIN FOUR HOURS FROM THE TIME YOU RECEIVE THIS REQUEST.
PLEASE FAX TO: (YOUR FAX #)   **OR   CALL** (YOUR PHONE #)

THANK YOU!

_____   _____   _____
CREDIT MANAGER   **DATE**   **TIME**

Scenario 2

Loan A

LOAN REFERENCE REQUEST

TO: LOAN A   RE: COMPANY B
      FAX # (800) XXX-XXXX

ATTN: Credit

                                          ACCOUNT #: _____

CREDIT MANAGER,

THE ABOVE NAMED PARTY HAS APPLIED FOR A CREDIT ACCOUNT WITH OUR COMPANY. WE WOULD APPRECIATE RECEIVING THE FOLLOWING INFORMATION AS A CREDIT REFERENCE ON THEIR ACCOUNT. ANY INFORMATION PROVIDED WILL BE HELD IN THE STRICTEST CONFIDENCE.

DATE OPENED: 3/08/01   TERM: 60 Months

ORIGINAL BALANCE: $67,851.60

CURRENT BALANCE: $53,150.42   # LATES: 1   x 30 0   X 60 0   x 90

RATING AND/OR COMMENTS: Good Customer

INFORMATION SUPPLIED BY: Michael
                    TITLE: Accts. Rec.

AS A COURTESY TO OUR MUTUAL CUSTOMER, PLEASE REPLY BY FAX OR PHONE WITHIN **FOUR HOURS** FROM THE TIME YOU RECEIVE THIS REQUEST.
PLEASE FAX TO: (YOUR FAX NUMBER HERE)   **OR**   **CALL** (YOUR PHONE NUMBER HERE)

THANK YOU!

_____   _____   _____ PST
CREDIT MANAGER   **DATE**   **TIME**

Scenario 2
Loan B

LOAN REFERENCE REQUEST

TO: <u>LOAN B</u>   RE: <u>COMPANY B</u>
<u>FAX # (800) XXX-XXXX</u>

ATTN: <u>Heather</u>

ACCOUNT #: _____

CREDIT MANAGER,

THE ABOVE NAMED PARTY HAS APPLIED FOR A CREDIT ACCOUNT WITH OUR COMPANY. WE WOULD APPRECIATE RECEIVING THE FOLLOWING INFORMATION AS A CREDIT REFERENCE ON THEIR ACCOUNT. ANY INFORMATION PROVIDED WILL BE HELD IN THE STRICTEST CONFIDENCE.

DATE OPENED: <u>10/12/00</u>   TERM: <u>36 Months, 18/36 made</u>

ORIGINAL BALANCE: <u>$13,524.84</u>

CURRENT BALANCE: <u>$6,762.42</u>   # LATES: <u>1</u> x 30 <u>0</u> X 60 <u>0</u> x 90

RATING AND/OR COMMENTS: _____

INFORMATION SUPPLIED BY: <u>Heather</u>
          TITLE: <u>Customer Service</u>

AS A COURTESY TO OUR MUTUAL CUSTOMER, PLEASE REPLY BY FAX OR PHONE WITHIN FOUR HOURS FROM THE TIME YOU RECEIVE THIS REQUEST.
PLEASE FAX TO: (YOUR FAX NUMBER HERE)   **OR**   **CALL** (YOUR PHONE NUMBER HERE)

THANK YOU!

_____   _____ _____ PST
CREDIT MANAGER   **DATE**   **TIME**

Scenario 2
Loan C

LOAN REFERENCE REQUEST

TO: <u>LOAN C</u>   RE: <u>COMPANY B</u>
     <u>FAX # (800) XXX XXXX</u>

ATTN: <u>Credit</u>

ACCOUNT #: _____

CREDIT MANAGER,

THE ABOVE NAMED PARTY HAS APPLIED FOR A CREDIT ACCOUNT WITH OUR COMPANY. WE WOULD APPRECIATE RECEIVING THE FOLLOWING INFORMATION AS A CREDIT REFERENCE ON THEIR ACCOUNT. ANY INFORMATION PROVIDED WILL BE HELD IN THE STRICTEST CONFIDENCE.

DATE OPENED: <u>4/15/01</u>   TERM: <u>60 Months</u>

ORIGINAL BALANCE: <u>$114,753.60</u>

CURRENT BALANCE: <u>$91,802.88</u>   # LATES: ___0 x 30 ___0 X 60 ___0 x 90

RATING AND/OR COMMENTS: <u>Paid As Agreed</u>

INFORMATION SUPPLIED BY: <u>Kate</u>
                    TITLE: <u>Customer Service Manager</u>

AS A COURTESY TO OUR MUTUAL CUSTOMER, PLEASE REPLY BY FAX OR PHONE WITHIN **FOUR HOURS** FROM THE TIME YOU RECEIVE THIS REQUEST.
PLEASE FAX TO: (YOUR FAX NUMBER HERE)   **OR**   **CALL** (YOUR PHONE NUMBER HERE)

THANK YOU!

_____   _____ _____ PST
CREDIT MANAGER   **DATE**   **TIME**

Scenario 2

2001 Tax Return: S Corp.

Form **1120S**	**U.S. Income Tax Return for an S Corporation**	OMB No. 1545-0130
Department of the Treasury Internal Revenue Service	▶ Do not file this form unless the corporation has timely filed Form 2553 to elect to be an S corporation. ▶ See separate instructions.	**2001**

For calendar year 2001, or tax year beginning **January 2, 2001**, 2001, and ending **December 31, 2001**

A Effective date of election as an S corporation **01/01/2001**	Use IRS label. Other- wise, print or type.	Name **COMPANY B**	C Employer Identification number **XX-XXXXXXX**
B Business code no. (see pages 29 - 31)		Number, street, and room or suite no. (if a P.O. box, see page 11 of the instructions.) **4321 Main Street**	D Date incorporated **01/02/2001**
		City or town, state, and ZIP code **Sumner, WA 98390**	E Total assets (see page 11) $ **666,751**

F Check applicable boxes: (1) [X] Initial return   (2) [ ] Final return   (3) [ ] Name change   (4) [ ] Address change   (5) [ ] Amended return

G Enter number of shareholders in the corporation at end of the tax year . . . . ▶

Caution: *Include only trade or business income and expenses on lines 1a through 21. See page 11 of the instructions for more information.*

Income	1a	Gross receipts or sales **$1,835,138.** b Less returns and allowances [ ] c Bal ▶	1c	1,835,138.
	2	Cost of goods sold (Schedule A, line 8)	2	1,127,887.
	3	Gross profit. Subtract line 2 from line 1c	3	707,251.
	4	Net gain (loss) from Form 4797, Part II, line 18 (attach Form 4797)	4	
	5	Other income (loss) (attach schedule)	5	
	6	Total income (loss). Combine lines 3 through 5 . . . . ▶	6	707,251.
Deductions (see page 12 of the instructions for limitations)	7	Compensation of officers . . . . **Statement 1**	7	
	8	Salaries and wages (less employment credits)	8	
	9	Repairs and maintenance	9	
	10	Bad debts	10	6,514.
	11	Rents	11	31,513.
	12	Taxes and licenses . . . . **Statement 2**	12	7,897.
	13	Interest	13	60,278.
	14a	Depreciation (if required, attach Form 4562) 14a	39,884.		
	b	Depreciation claimed on Schedule A and elsewhere on return 14b			
	c	Subtract line 14b from line 14a	14c	39,884.
	15	Depletion (Do not deduct oil and gas depletion.)	15	
	16	Advertising	16	48,215.
	17	Pension, profit-sharing, etc., plans	17	
	18	Employee benefit programs	18	
	19	Other deductions (attach schedule) . . . . **Statement 3**	19	387,555.
	20	Total deductions. Add the amounts shown in the far right column for lines 7 through 19 . . . . . . ▶	20	581,856.
	21	Ordinary income (loss) from trade or business activities. Subtract line 20 from line 6	21	125,395.
Tax and Payments	22	Tax: a Excess net passive income tax (attach schedule) 22a			
	b	Tax from Schedule D (Form 1120S) 22b			
	c	Add lines 22a and 22b (see page 16 of the instructions for additional taxes)	22c	
	23	Payments: a 2001 estimated tax payments and amount applied from 2000 return 23a			
	b	Tax deposited with Form 7004 . . . . 23b			
	c	Credit for Federal tax paid on fuels (attach Form 4136) 23c			
	d	Add lines 23a through 23c	23d	
	24	Estimated tax penalty. Check if Form 2220 is attached . . . . ▶ [ ]	24	
	25	Tax due. If the total of lines 22c and 24 is larger than line 23d, enter amount owed. See page 4 of the instructions for depository method of payment . . . . ▶	25	
	26	Overpayment. If line 23d is larger than the total of lines 22c and 24, enter amount overpaid . . . . ▶	26	
	27	Enter amount of line 26 you want: Credited to 2002 estimated tax ▶ [ ] Refunded ▶	27	

Sign Here	Under penalties of perjury, I declare that I have examined this return, including accompanying schedules and statements, and to the best of my knowledge and belief, it is true, correct, and complete. Declaration of preparer (other than taxpayer) is based on all information of which preparer has any knowledge.	May the IRS discuss this return with the preparer shown below (see instructions)? [ ] Yes [ ] No
	▶ Signature of officer Date ▶ Title	

Paid Preparer's Use Only	Preparer's signature ▶	Date	Check if self-employed [ ]	Preparer's SSN or PTIN
	Firm's name (or yours if self-employed), address, and ZIP code ▶		EIN	
			Phone no.	

For Paperwork Reduction Act Notice, see the separate instructions.

Form **1120S** (2001)

ISA
STF FED4210F.1

Scenario 2

2001 Tax Return: S Corp. (Page 2)

Form 1120S (2001) COMPANY B XX-XXXXXXX Page 2

Schedule A **Cost of Goods Sold** (see page 16 of the instructions)

1	Inventory at beginning of year	1	228,018.
2	Purchases	2	563,593.
3	Cost of labor	3	386,802.
4	Additional section 263A costs *(attach schedule)*	4	
5	Other costs *(attach schedule)* See Statement 4	5	206,255.
6	Total. Add lines 1 through 5	6	1,384,668.
7	Inventory at end of year	7	256,781.
8	**Cost of goods sold.** Subtract line 7 from line 6. Enter here and on page 1, line 2	8	1,127,887.

9a Check all methods used for valuing closing inventory:
(i) [X] Cost as described in Regulations section 1.471-3
(ii) [ ] Lower of cost or market as described in Regulations section 1.471-4
(iii) [ ] Other (specify method used and attach explanation) ▶

b Check if there was a writedown of "subnormal" goods as described in Regulations section 1.471-2(c) ▶ [ ]

c Check if the LIFO inventory method was adopted this tax year for any goods *(if checked, attach Form 970)* ▶ [ ]

d If the LIFO inventory method was used for this tax year, enter percentage (or amounts) of closing inventory computed under LIFO | 9d |

e Do the rules of section 263A (for property produced or acquired for resale) apply to the corporation? [ ] Yes [X] No

f Was there any change in determining quantities, cost, or valuations between opening and closing inventory? [ ] Yes [X] No
If "Yes," attach explanation.

Schedule B **Other Information**

		Yes	No
1	Check method of accounting: (a) [ ] Cash (b) [ ] Accrual (c) [ ] Other (specify) ▶		
2	Refer to the list on pages 29 through 31 of the instructions and state the corporation's principal: (a) Business activity ▶ Wholesaling (b) Product or service ▶ Vitamins		
3	Did the corporation at the end of the tax year own, directly or indirectly, 50% or more of the voting stock of a domestic corporation? (For rules of attribution, see section 267(c).) If "Yes," attach a schedule showing: (a) name, address, and employer identification number and (b) percentage owned.		X
4	Was the corporation a member of a controlled group subject to the provisions of section 1561?		X
5	Check this box if the corporation has filed or is required to file **Form 8264**, Application for Registration of a Tax Shelter ▶ [ ]		
6	Check this box if the corporation issued publicly offered debt instruments with original issue discount ▶ [ ] If so, the corporation may have to file **Form 8281**, Information Return for Publicly Offered Original Issue Discount Instruments.		
7	If the corporation: (a) filed its election to be an S corporation after 1986, (b) was a C corporation before it elected to be an S corporation or the corporation acquired an asset with a basis determined by reference to its basis (or the basis of any other property) in the hands of a C corporation, and (c) has net unrealized built-in gain (defined in section 1374(d)(1)) in excess of the net recognized built-in gain from prior years, enter the net unrealized built-in gain reduced by net recognized built-in gain from prior years (see page 17 of the instructions) ▶ $		
8	Check this box if the corporation had accumulated earnings and profits at the close of the tax year (see page 17 of the instructions) ▶ [ ]		

Note: *If the corporation had assets or operated a business in a foreign country or U.S. possession, it may be required to attach* ***Schedule N (Form 1120),*** *Foreign Operations of U.S. Corporations, to this return. See Schedule N for details.*

Schedule K **Shareholders' Shares of Income, Credits, Deductions, etc.**

		(a) Pro rata share items		(b) Total amount
Income (Loss)	1	Ordinary income (loss) from trade or business activities (page 1, line 21)	1	125,395.
	2	Net income (loss) from rental real estate activities *(attach Form 8825)*	2	
	3a	Gross income from other rental activities | 3a |		
	b	Expenses from other rental activities *(attach schedule)* | 3b |		
	c	Net income (loss) from other rental activities. Subtract line 3b from line 3a	3c	
	4	Portfolio income (loss):		
	a	Interest income	4a	
	b	Ordinary dividends	4b	
	c	Royalty income	4c	
	d	Net short-term capital gain (loss) *(attach Schedule D (Form 1120S))*	4d	
	e	(1) Net long-term capital gain (loss) *(attach Schedule D (Form 1120S))*	4e(1)	
		(2) 28% rate gain (loss) ▶ (3) Qualified 5-year gain ▶		
	f	Other portfolio income (loss) *(attach schedule)*	4f	
	5	Net section 1231 gain (loss) (other than due to casualty or theft) *(attach Form 4797)*	5	
	6	Other income (loss) *(attach schedule)*	6	

Form **1120S** (2001)

STF FED4219F.2

Scenario 2

2000 Tax Return: Individual

1040	Department of the Treasury – Internal Revenue Service **U.S. Individual Income Tax Return**	**2000**	(99) IRS Use Only – Do not write or staple in this space.

For the year Jan. 1 – Dec. 31, 2000, or other tax year beginning , 2000, ending , 20   OMB No. 1545-0074

Label
(See instructions on page 19.)
Use the IRS label. Otherwise, please print or type.

John Jones
1000 Old Barn Road
Olympia, WA 98000

Your social security number
XXX–XX–XXXX
Spouse's social security number

▲ **IMPORTANT!** ▲
You must enter your SSN(s) above.

Presidential Election Campaign (See page 19.)
Note. Checking "Yes" will not change your tax or reduce your refund.
Do you, or your spouse if filing a joint return, want $3 to go to this fund? ▶

	You	Spouse
	☐ Yes ☒ No	☐ Yes ☐ No

Filing Status
Check only one box.

1 X Single
2 ☐ Married filing joint return (even if only one had income)
3 ☐ Married filing separate return. Enter spouse's soc. sec. no. above & full name here ▶
4 ☐ Head of household (with qualifying person). (See page 19.) If the qualifying person is a child but not your dependent, enter this child's name here ▶
5 ☐ Qualifying widow(er) with dependent child (year spouse died ▶   ). (See page 19.)

Exemptions

6a ☒ Yourself. If your parent (or someone else) can claim you as a dependent on his or her tax return, do not check box 6a.

No. of boxes checked on 6a and 6b   1

b ☐ Spouse

c Dependents:

(1) First Name Last name	(2) Dependent's social security number	(3) Dependent's relationship to you	(4) ✓ if qualifying child for child tax credit (see page 20)

If more than six dependents, see page 20.

No. of your children on 6c who:
● lived with you
● did not live with you due to divorce or separation (see page 20)
Dependents on 6c not entered above
Add numbers entered on lines above ▶

d Total number of exemptions claimed

Income

Attach Forms W-2 and W-2G here. Also attach Form 1099-R if tax was withheld.

If you did not get a W-2, see page 21.

Enclose, but do not attach, any payment. Also, please use Form 1040-V.

7	Wages, salaries, tips, etc. Attach Form(s) W-2	7	
8a	Taxable interest. Attach Schedule B if required	8a	3,470.
b	Tax-exempt interest. Do not include on line 8a ... 8b		
9	Ordinary dividends. Attach Schedule B if required	9	
10	Taxable refunds, credits, or offsets of state and local income taxes (see page 22)	10	
11	Alimony received	11	
12	Business income or (loss). Attach Schedule C or C-EZ	12	-38,493.
13	Capital gain or (loss). Attach Schedule D if required. If not required, check here ▶ ☐	13	-3,000.
14	Other gains or (losses). Attach Form 4797	14	
15a	Total IRA distributions ... 15a b Taxable amount (see pg. 23)	15b	
16a	Total pensions and annuities 16a b Taxable amount (see pg. 23)	16b	
17	Rental real estate, royalties, partnerships, S corporations, trusts, etc. Attach Schedule E	17	-16,589.
18	Farm income or (loss). Attach Schedule F	18	
19	Unemployment compensation	19	
20a	Social security benefits ... 20a b Taxable amount (see pg. 25)	20b	
21	Other income.	21	
22	Add the amounts in the far right column for lines 7 through 21. This is your total income ▶	22	-54,612.

Adjusted Gross Income

23	IRA deduction (see page 27)	23	
24	Student loan interest deduction (see page 27)	24	
25	Medical savings account deduction. Attach Form 8853	25	
26	Moving expenses. Attach Form 3903	26	
27	One-half of self-employment tax. Attach Schedule SE	27	
28	Self-employed health insurance deduction (see page 29)	28	
29	Self-employed SEP, SIMPLE, and qualified plans	29	
30	Penalty on early withdrawal of savings	30	
31a	Alimony paid. b Recipient's SSN ▶	31a	
32	Add lines 23 through 31a	32	
33	Subtract line 32 from line 22. This is your adjusted gross income ▶	33	-54,612.

KFA For Disclosure, Privacy Act, and Paperwork Reduction Act Notice, see page 56.   IF0U91X 11/07/00   Form **1040** (20

Scenario 2

2000 Tax Return: Individual (Page 2)

Form 1040 (2000)

Tax and Credits	34	Amount from line 33 (adjusted gross income)	34
	35a	Check if: ☐ You were 65 or older, ☐ Blind; ☐ Spouse was 65 or older, ☐ Blind. Add the number of boxes checked above and enter the total here . . . . ▶ 35a	
Standard Deduction for Most People	b	If you are married filing separately and your spouse itemizes deductions, or you were a dual-status alien, see page 31 and check here . . . . ▶ 35b ☐	
Single: $4,400	36	Enter your **itemized deductions** from Schedule A, line 28, **or standard deduction** shown on the left. But see page 31 to find your standard deduction if you checked any box on line 35a or 35b or if someone can claim you as a dependent	36
Head of household: $6,450	37	Subtract line 36 from line 34	37
Married filing jointly or Qualifying widow(er): $7,350	38	If line 34 is $96,700 or less, multiply $2,800 by the total number of exemptions claimed on line 6d. If line 34 is over $96,700, see the worksheet on page 32 for the amount to enter.	38
	39	**Taxable income.** Subtract line 38 from line 37. If line 38 is more than line 37, enter -0-	39
Married filing separately: $3,675	40	**Tax** (see page 32). Check if any tax is from a ☐ Form(s) 8814 b ☐ Form 4972 .	40
	41	Alternative minimum tax. Attach Form 6251	41
	42	Add lines 40 and 41 . . . . ▶	42
	43	Foreign tax credit. Attach Form 1116 if required	43	
	44	Credit for child and dependent care expenses. Att. Form 2441	44	
	45	Credit for the elderly or the disabled. Attach Schedule R . . .	45	
	46	Education credits. Attach Form 8863	46	
	47	Child tax credit (see page 36)	47	
	48	Adoption credit. Attach Form 8839	48	
	49	Other. Check if from a ☐ Form 3800 b ☐ Form 8396 c ☐ Form 8801 d ☐ Form (specify)	49	
	50	Add lines 43 through 49. These are your **total credits**	50
	51	Subtract line 50 from line 42. If line 50 is more than line 42, enter -0- . . . . . . ▶	51
Other Taxes	52	Self-employment tax. Att. Sch. SE	52
	53	Social security and Medicare tax on tip income not reported to employer. Attach Form 4137 . . .	53
	54	Tax on IRAs, other retirement plans, and MSAs. Attach Form 5329 if required	54
	55	Advance earned income credit payments from Form(s) W-2	55
	56	Household employment taxes. Attach Schedule H	56
	57	Add lines 51 through 56. This is your **total tax** . . . . ▶	57
Payments	58	Federal income tax withheld from Forms W-2 and 1099 . .	58	
If you have a qualifying child, attach Schedule EIC.	59	2000 estimated tax payments and amount applied from 1999 return .	59	
	60a	Earned income credit (EIC)	60a	
	b	Nontaxable earned income: amt. ▶ and type▶	NO	
	61	Excess social security and RRTA tax withheld (see page 50)	61	
	62	Additional child tax credit. Attach Form 8812	62	
	63	Amount paid with request for extension to file (see page 50)	63	
	64	Other payments. Check if from a ☐ Form 2439 b ☐ Form 4136 . .	64	
	65	Add lines 58, 59, 60a, and 61 through 64. These are your **total payments** . . . . ▶	65
Refund Have it directly deposited! See page 50 and fill in 67b, 67c, and 67d.	66	If line 65 is more than line 57, subtract line 57 from line 65. This is the amount you **overpaid**	66
	67a	Amount of line 66 you want **refunded to you** . . . . ▶	67a
	b	Routing number ☐ ▶ c Type: ☐ Checking ☐ Savings	
	d	Account number ☐	
	68	Amount of line 66 you want applied to your 2001 estimated tax ▶	68	
Amount You Owe	69	If line 57 is more than line 65, subtract line 65 from line 57. This is the **amount you owe.** For details on how to pay, see page 51 . . . . ▶	69
	70	Estimated tax penalty. Also include on line 69	70	

Sign Here
Joint return? See page 18.
Keep a copy for your records.

Under penalties of perjury, I declare that I have examined this return and accompanying schedules and statements, and to the best of my knowledge and belief, they are true, correct, and complete. Declaration of preparer (other than taxpayer) is based on all information of which preparer has any knowledge.

▶ Your signature	Date	Your occupation	Daytime phone number
▶ Spouse's signature. If a joint return, both must sign.	Date	Spouse's occupation	May the IRS discuss this return with the preparer shown below? (see page 52)? ☒ Yes ☐ No

Paid Preparer's Use Only

Preparer's signature ▶		Date	Check if self-employed ☐	Preparer's SSN or PTIN
Firm's name (or yours if self-employed), address, and ZIP code ▶			EIN	
			Phone no.	

IRS151A 11/22/00

Form 1040 (2000)

Scenario 2
2000 Tax Return: Schedule C

SCHEDULE C (Form 1040) Department of the Treasury Internal Revenue Service (99)	**Profit or Loss From Business** **(Sole Proprietorship)** ▶ Partnerships, joint ventures, etc., must file Form 1065 or Form 1065-B. ▶ Attach to Form 1040 or Form 1041. ▶ See Instructions for Schedule C (Form 1040).	OMB No. 1545-0074 **2000** Attachment Sequence No. 09

Name of proprietor: **John Jones**   Social security number (SSN): **XXX-XX-XXXX**

A Principal business or profession, including product or service (see page C-1 of the Instructions)
Vitamins – Wholesale

B Enter code from pages C-7 & 8 ▶

C Business name. If no separate business name, leave blank.
COMPANY B

D Employer ID number (EIN), if any

E Business address (including suite or room no.) ▶
City, town or post office, state, and ZIP code

F Accounting method: (1) ☒ Cash   (2) ☐ Accrual   (3) ☐ Other (specify) ▶

G Did you "materially participate" in the operation of this business during 2000? If "No," see page C-2 for limit on losses . . . . ☒ Yes ☐ No

H If you started or acquired this business during 2000, check here . . . . ▶ ☒

Part I Income

1	Gross receipts or sales. Caution: If this income was reported to you on Form W-2 and the "Statutory employee" box on that form was checked, see page C-2 and check here ▶ ☐	1 438,917.
2	Returns and allowances	2 1,538.
3	Subtract line 2 from line 1	3 437,379.
4	Cost of goods sold (from line 42 on page 2)	4 60,444.
5	Gross profit. Subtract line 4 from line 3	5 376,935.
6	Other income, including Federal and state gasoline or fuel tax credit or refund (see page C-2)	6
7	Gross income. Add lines 5 and 6 . . . . ▶	7 376,935.

Part II Expenses. Enter expenses for business use of your home only on line 30.

8	Advertising	8 37,217.	19	Pension and profit-sharing plans . . .	19
9	Bad debts from sales or services (see page C-3)	9 1,240.	20	Rent or lease (see page C-4):	
10	Car and truck expenses (see page C-3)	10 195.	a	Vehicles, machinery & equipment . . .	20a 31,513.
11	Commissions and fees	11	b	Other business property	20b 19,862.
12	Depletion	12	21	Repairs and maintenance	21 8,188.
13	Depreciation and section 179 expense deduction (not included in Part III) (see page C-3) . . .	13 28,072.	22	Supplies (not included in Part III) . . .	22
			23	Taxes and licenses	23 9,568.
			24	Travel, meals, and entertainment:	
			a	Travel	24a 789.
14	Employee benefit programs (other than on line 19) . .	14	b	Meals and entertainment . . . . 40.	
15	Insurance (other than health) . .	15 4,457.	c	Enter nondeductible amount included on line 24b (see page C-5) . . . . 20.	
16	Interest:		d	Subtract line 24c from line 24b . . .	24d 20.
a	Mortgage (paid to banks, etc.) . .	16a 21,991.	25	Utilities	25 3,501.
b	Other	16b 1,837.	26	Wages (less employment credits) . . .	26 107,913.
17	Legal and professional services . .	17 4,150.	27	Other expenses (from line 48 on page 2)	27 13,317.
18	Office expense	18 19,319.			

28	Total expenses before expenses for business use of home. Add lines 8 through 27 in columns . . . . ▶	28 313,149.
29	Tentative profit (loss). Subtract line 28 from line 7	29 63,786.
30	Expenses for business use of your home. Attach Form 8829	30
31	Net profit or (loss). Subtract line 30 from line 29. • If a profit, enter on Form 1040, line 12, and also on Schedule SE, line 2 (statutory employees, see page C-5). Estates and trusts, enter on Form 1041, line 3. • If a loss, you must go to line 32.	31 63,786.
32	If you have a loss, check the box that describes your investment in this activity (see page C-5). • If you checked 32a, enter the loss on Form 1040, line 12, and also on Schedule SE, line 2 (statutory employees, see page C-6). Estates and trusts, enter on Form 1041, line 3. • If you checked 32b, you must attach Form 6198.	32a ☐ All investment is at risk. 32b ☐ Some investment is not at risk.

For Paperwork Reduction Act Notice, see Form 1040 Instructions.   Schedule C (Form 1040) 2000

KFA   IF0US4 11/08/00

Scenario 2
Funding Source Decline

TO: ████████████████

ATTN: ████████████████

LEASE NUMBER: ██████████

LESSEE NAME: ██████████████

FAX NO: ████████████

DECISION DATE: 3/12/02 11:21:12 AM

HAS BEEN DECLINED.

REASONS FOR DECLINING APPLICATION:

████ Thanks for the deal. Unfortunately I can't help you out on this one. D&b is reporting the ████████ took over this business in 2001. Technically we have less than 1 year time in business. They also have a $6060.00 state tax lien that is pending from 7-5-2001. I have concerns with the personal credit for ████████ My bureau is scoring high due to alot of slowness in the past year on installment and bank cards ████████ Inquiries. There have been many banks and financing sources looking at this customer. Sorry I can't help you out. Please call me if you'd like to discuss. Thanks, ████████

THANK YOU FOR THE SUBMITTAL.
PLEASE CALL WITH ANY QUESTIONS.

████████████████

Equal Credit Opportunity Notice

The federal equal credit opportunity act prohibits creditors from discriminating against credit applicants on the basis of race, color, religion, national origin, sex, marital status, age (provided that the applicant has the capacity to enter into a binding contract), because all or part of the applicant's income derived from any public assistance program, or because the applicant has in good faith exercised any right under the consumer credit protection act. The federal agency that administers compliance with this law concerning this creditor is Office of ██

Pursuant to your Broker Agreement, you understand that we look to you to provide this applicant (on our behalf) written notification of this decision as required by law.

Scenario 2
Funding Source Approval

Phone   **Fax**

Credit Approval –

TO:
FAX: on file
Date: 03/27/02

Lessee:
Amount $70,000.00
Equipment: Filling Equipment
Term: 60 months
Advance Payments: First & last payment
Buy Rate: .002258
Purchase option: 1.00
*Maximum Commission (10) points Max

- ❖ Lease Agreement and supporting documents
- ❖ Delivery & Acceptance
- ❖ Copy of Driver's License of all signors
- ❖ Insurance ---
- Personal Guarantee:

Landlord Waiver
ACH Required

APROVAL VALID FOR Ninety (90) days

Approval based on the information that was given on the application. If there is any material change in the credit or financial position of this lessee it will be subject to review.

Thanks for your Business and Our Relationship

Scenario 2
Documentation Request

DOCUMENTATION REQUEST WORKSHEET

SALES REPRESENTATIVE: Lucrative Leasing   **DATE:** _____

LESSEE INFORMATION

COMPLETE LESSEE NAME: COMPANY B

BILLING ADDRESS: 4321 Main Street

CITY, STATE, ZIP: Sumner, WA 98390   PHONE: (800)XXX-XXXX

EQUIPMENT LOCATION: Same

SIGNER: John Jones   TITLE: President   PG: YES NO

SIGNER: _____   TITLE: _____   PG: YES NO

VENDOR AND EQUIPMENT INFORMATION

VENDOR NAME: Perfect Packaging Machines
STREET ADDRESS: 8000 Cherry Boulevard, Spokane, WA 95000
PHONE: (800) XXX-XXXX   CONTACT PERSON: Greg

EQUIPMENT LEASE TERMS

LEASE AMOUNT: $ 70,000.00   SALES TAX INCLUDED: YES   NO

LEASE TERM: 60 MONTHS   BUY-OUT: 10%PUT $1.00 OTHER_____

LEASE PAYMENT: $ 1,707.30   MONTHLY TAX (%): $_____

ADVANCED PAYMENTS: 1 ONLY   1+1   10% SEC.   OTHER _____

FACTORS: *Buy Rate:* .02258   *Sell Rate:* .02439
GROSS COMMISSION (8 %): $ 5,600.00

DOCUMENTATION SHIPPING INFORMATION

SEND DOCUMENTS TO:

(X) FED-X TO LESSEE AT LOCATION ABOVE

(   ) FED-X TO LESSEE AT FOLLOWING LOCATION: _____
                                                  _____
                                                  _____

Scenario 2
Documentation Cover Letter

LUCRATIVE LEASING

ATTN: **John Jones**
          COMPANY B
          4321 Main Street
          Sumner, WA 98390

Dear Mr. Jones,

Please pay close attention to the following requirements before returning the lease documents.

- Please sign and date each agreement for your equipment lease. **Make sure that all dates are the same throughout all the paperwork.**

- Make a check payable to <u>Lucrative Leasing</u> for the total amount of: **$3,414.60.**

     This amount equals 2 payments of $1,707.30 (Processing Fee Waived).
          * * IMPORTANT: This check must be written from your business account.

- **Please provide your Federal Tax ID#:** _____

• COPY OF DRIVER'S LICENSE (John Jones)

<u>**Overnight all original documentation to**</u>: **Lucrative Leasing**
                                          Address
┌─────────────────────────┐   **City, State & Zip**
│   **OVERNIGHT**   │
│ **ENVELOPE PROVIDED**   │
└─────────────────────────┘

Call me with any questions at (800-XXX-XXXX).

Sincerely,

Mr. Leasing

Scenario 2

Lease Agreement Page 1

EQUIPMENT LEASE AGREEMENT   Agreement Number 22002

This document was written in "Plain English". The words YOU and YOUR refer to the customer. The words WE, US and OUR refer to the Lessor. Every attempt has been made to eliminate confusing language and create a simple, easy-to-read document

CUSTOMER INFORMATION

COMPANY B				
FULL LEGAL NAME OF CUSTOMER		D/B/A		

4321 MAIN STREET	SUMNER	WA	98390	
STREET ADDRESS	CITY	STATE	ZIP	PHONE

COMPANY B		4321 MAIN STREET	
BILLING NAME (IF DIFFERENT FROM ABOVE)		BILLING STREET ADDRESS	

SUMNER	WA	98390	
CITY	STATE	ZIP	PHONE

EQUIPMENT LOCATION (IF DIFFERENT FROM ABOVE)

SUPPLIER INFORMATION

See Schedule A	
NAME OF SUPPLIER	STREET ADDRESS

CITY	STATE	ZIP	PHONE

QUANTITY	ITEM DESCRIPTION	MODEL NO.	SERIAL
	See Schedule A		

RENTAL TERMS	RENTAL PAYMENT AMOUNT	SECURITY DEPOSIT
Term in months 60 (MOS.) Rent Commencement Date:	60 Payments of $ 1707.30 (Plus applicable taxes) Rental Payment Period is MONTHLY Unless Otherwise indicated	$ 3414.60 RECEIVED

END OF LEASE OPTIONS: You will have the following options at the end of the original term, provided the lease has not terminated early and no event of default under this lease has occurred and is continuing.
1. Purchase the equipment for fair market value.   2. Renew the lease per Paragraph 1.   3. Return the equipment as provided in Paragraph 6 of this lease.

THIS IS A NONCANCELABLE/IRREVOCABLE LEASE, THIS LEASE CANNOT BE CANCELLED OR TERMINATED.

TERMS AND CONDITIONS THIS LEASE AGREEMENT CONTAINS PROVISIONS SET FORTH ON THE REVERSE SIDE, ALL OF WHICH ARE MADE PART OF THIS LEASE AGREEMENT)
1. LEASE AGREEMENT: You agree to lease from us the personal property described under "ITEM DESCRIPTION" and as modified by supplements to this Master Agreement
(Continued on back)

LESSOR ACCEPTANCE	CUSTOMER ACCEPTANCE
DATED:	DATED:
LESSOR: Lucrative Leasing	CUSTOMER: COMPANY B
SIGNATURE: X	SIGNATURE: X __JOHN JONES__
TITLE:	TITLE: PRESIDENT

ACCEPTANCE OF DELIVERY

You certify that all the equipment listed above has been furnished, that delivery and installation has been fully completed and satisfactory. Further, all conditions and terms of this agreement have been reviewed and acknowledged. Upon your signing below, your promises herein will be irrevocable and unconditional in all respects. You understand and agree that we have purchased the equipment from the supplier, and you may contact the above supplier for your warranty rights, if any, which we transfer to you for the term of this lease. Your approval as indicated below of our purchase of the equipment from supplier is a condition precedent to effectiveness of this lease.

COMPANY B		X	PRESIDENT
Date of Delivery	Customer	Signature: JOHN JONES	Title

GUARANTY

As additional inducement for us to enter into the Agreement, the undersigned ("you"), jointly and severally, unconditionally personally guarantees that the customer will make all payments and meet all obligations required under this Agreement and any supplements fully and promptly. You agree that we may make other arrangements including compromise or settlement with the customer and you waive all defenses and notice of those changes and will remain responsible for the payment and obligations of this Agreement. We do not have to notify you if the customer is in default. If the customer defaults, you will immediately pay in accordance with the default provision of the Agreement all sums due under the terms of the Agreement and will perform all the obligations of the Agreement. If it is necessary for us to proceed legally to enforce this guaranty, you expressly consent to the jurisdiction of the court set out in paragraph 15 and agree to pay all costs, including attorneys fees incurred in enforcement of this guaranty. It is not necessary for us to proceed first against the customer or the Equipment before enforcing this guaranty. By signing this guaranty, you authorize us to obtain credit bureau reports for credit and collection purposes.

X		John Jones	
Signature 0326		Print Name of Guarantor	Date

Scenario 2

Lease Agreement Page 2

from time to time signed by you and us (such property and any upgrades, replacements and additions referred to as "Equipment") for business purposes only. You agree to all of the terms and conditions contained in this Agreement and any supplement, which together are a complete statement of our Agreement regarding the listed equipment ("Agreement") and supersedes any purchase order or outstanding invoice. This Agreement may be modified only by written agreement and not by course of performance. This Agreement becomes valid upon execution by us and will begin on the rent commencement date shown and will continue from the first day of the following month for the number of consecutive months shown. You also agree to pay to Lessor interim rent. Interim rent shall be in an amount equal to 1/30th of the monthly rental, multiplied by the number of days between the rent commencement date and the first payment due date. The term will be extended automatically for successive 12 month terms unless you send us written notice you do not want it renewed at least thirty (30) days before the end of any term. If any provision of this Agreement is declared unenforceable in any jurisdiction, the other provisions herein shall remain in full force and effect in that jurisdiction and all others. THE BASE RENTAL PAYMENT SHALL BE ADJUSTED PROPORTIONATELY UPWARD OR DOWNWARD TO COMPLY WITH THE TAX LAWS OF THE STATE IN WHICH THE EQUIPMENT IS LOCATED. Equipment located in various states is subject to sales tax laws which require that tax be paid up front. You authorize us to advance tax and increase your monthly payment by an amount equal to the current tax percentage applied to the monthly rental shown above.

2. RENT: Rent will be payable in installments, each in the amount of the basic lease payment shown plus any applicable sales tax, use tax, plus 1/12th of the amount estimated by us to be personal property tax on the Equipment for each year of this Agreement. We will have the right to apply all sums received from you, in any amounts due and owed to us under the terms of this Agreement. In the event this Agreement is not commenced, the security deposit will be retained by us to compensate us for our documentation, processing, and other expenses. If for any reason, your check is returned for nonpayment, a $20.00 bad check charge will be assessed.

3. COMPUTER SOFTWARE: Notwithstanding any other terms and conditions of the Agreement, you agree that as to software only: a) We have not had, do not have, nor will have any title to such software, b) You have executed or will execute a separate software license agreement and we are not a party to and have no responsibilities whatsoever in regards to such license agreement, c) You have selected such software and as per Agreement paragraph 5, WE MAKE NO WARRANTIES OF MERCHANTABILITY, DATA ACCURACY, YEAR 2000 COMPLIANCE, SYSTEM INTEGRATION OR FITNESS FOR USE AND TAKE ABSOLUTELY NO RESPONSIBILITY FOR THE FUNCTION OR DEFECTIVE NATURE OF SUCH SOFTWARE.

4. OWNERSHIP OF EQUIPMENT: We are the owner of the Equipment and have sole title to the Equipment (excluding software). You agree to keep the equipment free and clear of all liens and claims.

5. WARRANTY DISCLAIMER: WE MAKE NO WARRANTY, EXPRESS OR IMPLIED, THAT THE EQUIPMENT IS FIT FOR A PARTICULAR PURPOSE OR THAT THE EQUIPMENT IS MERCHANTABLE. YOU AGREE THAT YOU HAVE SELECTED THIS SUPPLIER AND EACH ITEM OF EQUIPMENT BASED UPON YOUR OWN JUDGMENT AND DISCLAIM ANY RELIANCE UPON ANY STATEMENTS OR REPRESENTATIONS MADE BY US OR ANY SUPPLIER. WE DO NOT TAKE RESPONSIBILITY FOR THE INSTALLATION OR PERFORMANCE OF THE EQUIPMENT. THE SUPPLIER IS NOT AN AGENT OF OURS AND NOTHING THE SUPPLIER STATES CAN AFFECT YOUR OBLIGATION UNDER THE LEASE. YOU WILL CONTINUE TO MAKE ALL PAYMENTS UNDER THIS AGREEMENT REGARDLESS OF ANY CLAIM OR COMPLAINT OF NON PERFORMANCE AGAINST SUPPLIER. WE HAVE NO RESPONSIBILITY FOR ANY MAINTENANCE OR SUPPORT TO BE SUPPLIED BY SUPPLIER.

6. LOCATION OF EQUIPMENT: You will keep and use the Equipment only at your address shown above and you agree not to move it unless we agree to it. At the end of the Agreement's term, you will return the Equipment to a location we specify at your expense, in retail resaleable condition, full working order, and in complete repair.

7. LOSS OR DAMAGE: You are responsible for the risk of loss or for any destruction of or damage to the Equipment. No such loss or damage relieves you from the payment obligations under this Agreement. You agree to promptly notify us in writing of any loss or damage and you will then pay to us the total of all unpaid lease payments for the full lease term plus the estimated fair market value of the Equipment at the end of the originally scheduled term, all discounted at six percent (6%) per year. Any proceeds of insurance will be paid to us and credited, at our option, against any loss or damage.

8. COLLATERAL PROTECTION AND INSURANCE: You agree to keep the equipment fully insured against loss with us as loss payee in an amount not less than the replacement cost until this Agreement is terminated. You also agree to obtain a general public liability insurance policy from anyone who is acceptable to us and to include us as an insured on the policy. You agree to provide us certificates or other evidence of insurance acceptable to us, before this Agreement begins or, we will enroll you in our property damage coverage program and bill you a property damage surcharge as a result of our increased administrative costs and increased credit risk. As long as you are current at the time of the loss (excluding losses resulting from acts of god), the replacement value of the equipment will be applied against any actual damage as per paragraph 7. You must be current to benefit from this program. NOTHING IN THIS PARAGRAPH WILL RELIEVE YOU OF YOUR RESPONSIBILITY FOR LIABILITY INSURANCE COVERAGE ON THIS EQUIPMENT.

9. INDEMNITY: We are not responsible for any loss or injuries caused by the installation or use of the Equipment. You agree to hold us harmless and reimburse us for loss and to defend us against any claim for losses or injury caused by the Equipment.

10. TAXES AND FEES: You agree to pay when due all taxes (including personal property tax, fines and penalties) and fees relating to this Agreement or the Equipment. If we pay any of these fees or taxes for you, you agree to reimburse us and to pay us a processing fee for such payment we make on your behalf. In addition, you agree to pay us any filing fees prescribed by the Uniform Commercial Code or other law and reimburse us for all costs and expenses involved in documenting and servicing this transaction. You further agree to pay us up to $100.00 on the date the first lease payment is due to cover the expense of originating the Agreement.

11. ASSIGNMENT: YOU HAVE NO RIGHT TO SELL, TRANSFER, ASSIGN OR SUBLEASE THE EQUIPMENT OR THIS AGREEMENT. You understand that we, without prior notice, have the right to assign this Agreement to a financing source for financing purposes without your consent to such assignment. You understand that our assignee will have the same rights and benefits but they do not have to perform any of our obligations. You agree that the rights of assignee will not be subject to any claims, defenses, or setoffs that you may have against us.

12. DEFAULT AND REMEDIES: If you do not pay any lease payment or other sum due to us or other party when due or if you break any of your promises in this Agreement or any other Agreement with us, you will be in default. If any part of a payment is late, you agree to pay a late charge of 15% of the payment which is late or if less, the maximum charge allowed by law. If you are ever in default, we may retain your security deposit and at our option, we can terminate or cancel this Agreement and require that you pay (1) the unpaid balance of this Agreement (discounted at 6%); (2) the amount of any purchase option and if none is specified, 20% of the original equipment cost which represents our anticipated residual value in the equipment; (3) and return the equipment to us to a location designated by us. We may recover interest on any unpaid balance at the rate of 8% per annum. We may also use any of the remedies available to us under Article 2A of the Uniform Commercial Code as enacted in the State of Minnesota or any other law. If we refer this Agreement to an attorney for collection, you agree to pay our reasonable attorney's fees and actual court costs. If we have to take possession of the equipment, you agree to pay the cost of repossession. The net proceeds of the sale of any repossessed Equipment will be credited against what you owe us under this Agreement. YOU AGREE THAT WE WILL NOT BE RESPONSIBLE TO PAY YOU ANY CONSEQUENTIAL OR INCIDENTAL DAMAGES FOR ANY DEFAULT BY US UNDER THIS AGREEMENT. You agree that any delay or failure to enforce our rights under this Agreement does not prevent us from enforcing any rights at a later time. It is further agreed that your rights and remedies are governed exclusively by this Agreement and you waive Lessee's rights under Article 2A (508-522) of the UCC.

13. UCC FILINGS: You grant us a security interest in the equipment if this agreement is deemed a secured transaction and you authorize us to record a UCC-1 financing statement or similar instruments, and appoint us your attorney-in-fact to execute and deliver such instrument, in order to show our interest in the Equipment.

14. SECURITY DEPOSIT: The security deposit is payable upon execution and is non interest bearing and is to secure your performance under this Agreement. Any security deposit made may be applied by us to satisfy any amount owed by you, in which event you will promptly restore the security deposit to its full amount as set forth above. If all conditions herein are fully complied with and provided you have not ever been in default of this Agreement per paragraph 12, the security deposit will be refunded to you after the return of the equipment in accordance with paragraph 6.

15. LAW: This Agreement shall be deemed fully executed and performed in the State of Minnesota or in the home state of whoever holds the Lessor's interest as it may be assigned from time to time per paragraph 11. This Agreement shall be governed by and construed in accordance with the laws of the State of Minnesota or the laws of the home state of Lessor's assignee. You expressly and unconditionally consent to the jurisdiction and venue of any court in the State of Minnesota and waive right to trial by jury for any claim or action arising out of or relating to this Agreement or the Equipment. Furthermore, you waive the defense of Forum Non Conveniens.

16. LESSEE GUARANTY: You agree to submit the original master lease documents with the security deposit to Lessor or its assignee via overnight courier the same day of the facsimile transmission of the lease documents. Should we fail to receive these originals, you agree to be bound by the faxed copy of this agreement with appropriate signatures on the document. Lessee waives the right to challenge in court the authenticity of a faxed copy of this agreement and the faxed copy shall be considered the original and shall be the binding agreement for the purposes of any enforcement action under paragraph 12.

X		PRESIDENT
Signature JOHN JONES		Title

0272

Scenario 2

Lease Agreement – $1.00 Purchase Option

OPTION OF LESSEE
$1.00 PURCHASE OPTIONS

Lease # ___22002_____ between _____ , Lessor,
_____Lucrative Leasing_____ _____

and ____COMPANY B_____ _____ , Lessee.
                (Full Legal Name of Lessee)

Provided the lease has not terminated early and no event of default under the lease has occurred and is continuing, Lessee shall have the following options:

PURCHASE EQUIPMENT FOR $1.00

     OR

RETURN EQUIPMENT TO LESSOR

LESSOR: Lucrative Leasing _____   LESSEE: _____COMPANY B_____
                                                              (Full Legal Name)

_____   _____
Signature   Signature   JOHN JONES

_____   _____
Title   Title   PRESIDENT

NOTE: SIGNATURE MUST BE SAME AS ON LEASE

0305

Scenario 2

Lease Agreement – Schedule A

EQUIPMENT SCHEDULE "A"

LEASE # 22002

This Equipment Schedule "A" is to be attached to and become part of that Schedule of Leased Equipment dated

_____ , 20 _____ by and between the undersigned and

Lucrative Leasing   (Lessor).

QTY	DESCRIPTION	MODEL NO.	SERIAL NO.
	Vendor: PERFECT PACKAGING MACHINES		
	8000 CHERRY BOULEVARD		
	SPOKANE WA 95000		
I	ZBT 900 CAPSULE FILLING MACHINE	ZBT 900	

This Equipment Schedule "A" is hereby verified as correct by the undersigned Lessee, who acknowledges receipt of a copy.

Lessee: COMPANY B

Signature: X

JOHN JONES

Title: PRESIDENT

Scenario 2
Insurance Request

Lessor: YOUR COMPANY NAME   Lease #: _22002_
           YOUR COMPANY ADDRESS

INSURANCE AUTHORIZATION

To: _INCREDIBLE INSURANCE_   **Please input your insurance**
                                             information on the left.
       _____

       _____

Phone: (_800_) XXX-XXXX
Contact: _Kathy_

We have entered into an equipment lease agreement for the equipment shown on the attached Lease Copy. This equipment is located as stated on the Lease.

This is a net lease and we are responsible for the full equipment cost in the amount of $_70,000_.00.

Please see that we immediately have ALL RISK coverage for liability and full replacement cost of the equipment and that _(Funding Source)_ is shown as **LOSS PAYEE** and **ADDITIONAL INSURED** on the policy. Please forward a Certificate of Insurance and Loss Payable/Additional Insured Clause to:

       (Funding Source)

       _____

       _____

Concurrent Certificates of Insurance, thirty (30) days notice in the event of cancellation or alteration, and general correspondence should be sent to the above addresses as well.

Sincerely,

                    Lessee: _COMPANY B_

                    X _____

                    BY: _____John Jones, President_

                    DATE EXECUTED BY LESSEE _____

Scenario 2
Assignment of Lease

ASSIGNMENT

RE: Lease No. ___ 22002 _____, dated _____, _____

between _____ COMPANY B _____ _____

as Lessee and the undersigned as nominal Lessor (the "Lease").

The undersigned hereby sells, assigns, and transfers to The Manifest Group all of the undersigned's right, title, and interest in and to (a) the equipment covered by the Lease and (b) the undersigned's rights as Lessor under the Lease, including the right to receive rent thereunder.

_____ Lucrative Leasing _____
                  (Name of Lessor)

_____
Signature

_____
Title

_____
Date

(033

Scenario 2
Broker Fee Invoice

BROKER FEE INVOICE

LESSOR:..............................   Lucrative Leasing

LESSEE NAME:.......................   COMPANY B

APPROVAL NUMBER:.............   22002

TOTAL LEASE AMOUNT:.......... $ 70,000.00

MONTHLY PAYMENT:.............. $ 1,707.30

RATE FACTORS:.....................   Buy: .02258   Sell: .02439

OF ADVANCED PAYMENTS:....   1 + 1

PURCHASE OPTION:................. $1.00
    Broker Commission........... $ 5,600.00   Points: 8
    + Doc fees collected .... $ 0
    - Docs fees required by bank $ 0
          Sub-Total $ 5,600.00
Less Advanced Money Received . . . . $ 0

NET COMMISSION DUE.......... $ 5,600.00

Please Standard Overnight BROKER & VENDOR checks via Federal Express or UPS.

Please send broker check to: LUCRATIVE LEASING

FedEx #: (Account #)

Scenario 2

Insurance Binder

CERTIFICATE OF LIABILITY INSURANCE		DATE (MM/DD/YY) 07/19/2002

PRODUCER FAX	THIS CERTIFICATE IS ISSUED AS A MATTER OF INFORMATION ONLY AND CONFERS NO RIGHTS UPON THE CERTIFICATE HOLDER. THIS CERTIFICATE DOES NOT AMEND, EXTEND OR ALTER THE COVERAGE AFFORDED BY THE POLICIES BELOW.
Incredible Insurance	
	INSURERS AFFORDING COVERAGE
INSURED	INSURER A: Incredible Insurance
COMPANY B	INSURER B:
4321 Main Street	INSURER C:
Sumner, WA 98390	INSURER D:
	INSURER E:

COVERAGES

THE POLICIES OF INSURANCE LISTED BELOW HAVE BEEN ISSUED TO THE INSURED NAMED ABOVE FOR THE POLICY PERIOD INDICATED. NOTWITHSTANDING ANY REQUIREMENT, TERM OR CONDITION OF ANY CONTRACT OR OTHER DOCUMENT WITH RESPECT TO WHICH THIS CERTIFICATE MAY BE ISSUED OR MAY PERTAIN, THE INSURANCE AFFORDED BY THE POLICIES DESCRIBED HEREIN IS SUBJECT TO ALL THE TERMS, EXCLUSIONS AND CONDITIONS OF SUCH POLICIES. AGGREGATE LIMITS SHOWN MAY HAVE BEEN REDUCED BY PAID CLAIMS.

INSR LTR	TYPE OF INSURANCE	POLICY NUMBER	POLICY EFFECTIVE DATE (MM/DD/YY)	POLICY EXPIRATION DATE (MM/DD/YY)	LIMITS	
A	GENERAL LIABILITY	GL300006083	02/04/2002	02/04/2003	EACH OCCURRENCE	$ 1,000,000
	COMMERCIAL GENERAL LIABILITY				FIRE DAMAGE (Any one fire)	$ 200,000
	☐ CLAIMS MADE ☐ OCCUR				MED EXP (Any one person)	$ 5,000
					PERSONAL & ADV INJURY	$ 1,000,000
					GENERAL AGGREGATE	$ 2,000,000
	GEN'L AGGREGATE LIMIT APPLIES PER:				PRODUCTS - COMP/OP AGG	$ Excluded
	☒ POLICY ☐ PRO-JECT ☐ LOC					
	AUTOMOBILE LIABILITY				COMBINED SINGLE LIMIT (Ea accident)	$
	☐ ANY AUTO					
	☐ ALL OWNED AUTOS				BODILY INJURY (Per person)	$
	☐ SCHEDULED AUTOS					
	☐ HIRED AUTOS				BODILY INJURY (Per accident)	$
	☐ NON-OWNED AUTOS					
					PROPERTY DAMAGE (Per accident)	$
	GARAGE LIABILITY				AUTO ONLY - EA ACCIDENT	$
	☐ ANY AUTO				OTHER THAN EA ACC AUTO ONLY: AGG	$
	EXCESS LIABILITY				EACH OCCURRENCE	$
	☐ OCCUR ☐ CLAIMS MADE				AGGREGATE	$
						$
	☐ DEDUCTIBLE					$
	☐ RETENTION $					$
	WORKERS COMPENSATION AND EMPLOYERS' LIABILITY				☐ WC STATU-TORY LIMITS ☐ OTH-ER	
					E.L. EACH ACCIDENT	$
					E.L. DISEASE - EA EMPLOYEE	$
					E.L. DISEASE - POLICY LIMIT	$
	OTHER					

DESCRIPTION OF OPERATIONS/LOCATIONS/VEHICLES/EXCLUSIONS ADDED BY ENDORSEMENT/SPECIAL PROVISIONS
Certificate holder is named Additional Insured with respects to leased equipment, ZBT 900 Capsule Filling Machine

CERTIFICATE HOLDER	ADDITIONAL INSURED; INSURER LETTER:	CANCELLATION
		SHOULD ANY OF THE ABOVE DESCRIBED POLICIES BE CANCELLED BEFORE THE EXPIRATION DATE THEREOF, THE ISSUING COMPANY WILL ENDEAVOR TO MAIL ___30___ DAYS WRITTEN NOTICE TO THE CERTIFICATE HOLDER NAMED TO THE LEFT, BUT FAILURE TO MAIL SUCH NOTICE SHALL IMPOSE NO OBLIGATION OR LIABILITY OF ANY KIND UPON THE COMPANY, ITS AGENTS OR REPRESENTATIVES.
		AUTHORIZED REPRESENTATIVE

Scenario 2

Vendor Invoice

Invoice

PERFECT PACKAGING MACHINES
8000 Cherry Boulevard
Spokane, WA 95000

DATE	INVOICE #
10/20/2002	2

BILL TO	SHIP TO
LUCRATIVE LEASING	COMPANY B 4321 Main Street Sumner, WA 98390

P.O. NUMBER	TERMS	REP	SHIP	VIA	F.O.B.	PROJECT
22002	Lease		10/20/2002			

QUANTITY	ITEM CODE	DESCRIPTION	PRICE EACH	AMOUNT
1		ZBT 900 Capsule Filling Machine		$70,000.00
			Total	$70,000.00

Scenario 3

A Tough lease That Required Determination

While Scenario 1 & 2 examined leases funded at competitively priced banks, Scenario 3 examines a tougher deal that had to go to a more expensive lender because it was a very risky lease. This was considered a risky lease is primarily because this gentleman's business bank account had an average monthly balance of $400 to $700, which would barely cover his lease payments. The credit report and tax returns showed just enough income to help the applicant barely get an approval at a high interest rate.

The fictitious companies for Scenario 3 are as follows:

Lease Broker:	Lucrative Leasing (Hereafter referred to as LL)
Lessee:	Company C 600 Accord Street Grandview, WA 98880 Contact: William Kent, (Sole Proprietor)
Vendor:	Super Trucks 905 North Lake Way Yakima, WA 98901 Contact: Jack, Sales
Funding Source:	Funding Source
Insurance Company:	AAAAA Insurance

Facts of Lease Scenario 3:

Equipment:	1993 Utility Reefer (Trailer) Model 48102
Dollar Amount:	$13,953.75
Terms:	48 Months
Residual:	FMV – Fair Market Value

The lease application (see Scenario 3, Completed Lease Application) was received by fax from a preferred LL's vendor. If you haven't noticed yet, all of the applications in the scenarios have come from vendors. Vendors are your bread and butter; the more you have, the more business you will have.

The application was semi-complete, and the applicant, William Kent, had to be reached by phone to fill in the missing information on the application. Once the application was complete, with a signature, LL obtained a credit report (see Scenario 3, Credit Report). The credit report seemed okay; however, it scored low due to a lot of new unpaid debt and recent inquiries (per page 3 of Scenario 3 Credit Report). LL knew that with the credit report scoring so low, this was going to be a tough lease to approve. Another thing that made this very tough was the equipment. Not all funding sources will approve titled vehicles. Since this was a titled trailer, and the credit was thin, LL had a challenge ahead of them.

LL obtained the bank reference (see Scenario 3, Bank A) and trade reference (see Scenario 3, Trade A) to find that the customer had an extremely low average bank account balance. Normally, a leasing company might stop at this point and decline the deal before putting anymore work into it. LL decided to take a look at the applicant's tax returns before walking away from the potential lease.

Because Company C was a sole proprietorship, LL requested 2 years of William's personal tax returns (see Scenario 3, 2001 Individual Tax Return, 2001 Individual Tax Return (Page 2), 2000 Individual Tax Return, and 2000 Individual Tax Return (Page 2). Also required were the last two years Schedule C's (see Scenario 3, 2001 Schedule C and 2000 Schedule C) showing income from business activity. The results of the tax returns were not stellar, but LL could tell that if you put some of the "intangible" write-offs (like depreciation) back into the net profit, that the company actually makes money at the end of each year. LL was confident that they could get an approval and submitted it to the appropriate source that considers both tough credits and titled vehicles.

The lease application was approved (see Scenario 3, Funding Source Approval). Per the funding source approval, the lessee, William, had to put up a 20 percent security deposit and a large processing fee to get the lease.

William agreed to the terms of the lease, which were: 48 months, fair market value (residual), 20 percent security deposit and a $350 processing fee.

Once William agreed to the terms, LL immediately completed a documentation request worksheet (see Scenario 3, Documentation Request) to outline the important details of the transaction.

The documents (see Scenario 3, Documentation Cover Letter, Lease Agreement Page 1, Lease Agreement Page 2, ACH, Schedule A, Photo ID, and Insurance Request) were overnighted to Company C. The documentation is different than the last two scenarios because the funding source is different. The documentation is stricter with an ACH form which authorizes the funding source to automatically withdraw the monthly payments from the lessee's bank account every month. The Documentation Cover Letter and Lease Agreement Page 1 illustrate the dollar amount needed to start the lease.

The documents were received a couple of days later. The lessee was in a hurry and the trailer was not too far from him waiting to be picked up. LL overnighted the completed documents along with an assignment of lease (see Scenario 3, Assignment of Lease) and broker invoice (see Scenario 3, Broker Invoice) to the funding source for funding. The insurance binder (see Scenario 3, Insurance Binder) came in, along with the vendor invoice (see Scenario 3, Vendor Invoice) and condition report (see Scenario 3, Condition Report).

RE: Condition Report

The condition report was required by the funding source because the equipment was used. Anytime you work with used equipment, a condition report will be expected. The funding source will usually provide a blank one for you to use. If not, I have provided you with one (see Example W).

RE: Broker Invoice

Lucrative Leasing had to send a check for $982.69 to the funding source because they received a larger amount of money with the lessee's first payment than their commission (see Broker Fee Invoice). So, as soon as LL received documents with the lessee's check, they were already paid. (This will happen often. NOTE: That money is not yours to spend until the funding source funds the vendor. Some times, even after the checks are in, the lessee changes his/her mind. If this happens, you better be able to send that person's money back, or you could get into legal trouble).

LL sent the remaining documentation to the funding source and a couple days later the vendor, Super Trucks, received their money. LL earned $2,158.06 on a deal that most lease brokers would have walked away from. Do not be afraid to put a little extra effort into your deals. It is easy to get spoiled by easy lease transactions like Scenario 1, and you won't want to work hard when a Scenario 3 comes your way. Experience will guide you as to which hard deals actually have a chance.

Scenario 3
Completed Lease Application

LUCRATIVE LEASING

Lease Application

VENDOR INFORMATION		
Vendor Name SUPER TRUCKS		Equipment Cost **$13,953.75**
Vendor Address 905 North Lake Way, **City** Yakima, **State** WA **Zip** 98901		Initial Term **48 Months**
Contact Person JACK	**Telephone number** (800) XXX-XXXX	Equipment Description

Equipment Description:
(1) 1993 Utility Reefer Model 48102

Special Requirements

LESSEE COMPANY INFORMATION			
Company Name COMPANY C			
Company Address 600 Accord Street, **City** Grandview, **County** **State** WA **Zip** 98880			
Signer William Kent, **Title** Proprietor	**Telephone number** (800 XXX-XXXX		
Nature of Business Trucking	**Type of business** _ Non-Profit XProprietorship ...Partnership _ Corporation	**No. of Years in Business** 40 Years	

PERSONAL INFORMATION ON OFFICERS, PARTNERS, OR GUARANTORS

Name	Title	Social Security Number		Driver's License Number
William Kent	Owner	XXX-XX-XXXX		
Home Address 600 Accord Street, Grandview, WA 98880	**City**	**State** **Zip**	**How Long?** **Home Phone Number** ( )	**Own/Rent Present Home?**
Previous Address	**City**	**State** **Zip**	**Own/Rent Present Home?**	
Name	Title	Social Security Number		Driver's License Number
Home Address	**City**	**State** **Zip**	**How Long?** **Home Phone Number** ( )	**Own/Rent Present Home?**
Previous Address	**City**	**State** **Zip**		

COMPANY BANK REFERENCES - TWO YEAR HISTORY

Name of Bank/Branch	How Long?	Chkg. Acct. # / Loan Acct. #	Telephone No.	Contact Officer
Bank A	7 yr	XXXX-XXXX	(800) XXX-XXXX	Credit
			( )	
			( )	

TRADE REFERENCES - TWO YEAR HISTORY

Name of Supplier	City/State	Telephone No.	Contact Person
Trade A	Grandview, WA	(800) XXX-XXXX	Chris
Loan A	Grandview, WA	(800) XXX_XXXX	Credit
		( )	

I/we hereby authorize you to whom this application is made, or your agents, to investigate my/our credit worthiness and will provide financial statements, tax returns, etc., as you deem necessary. I/we agree that the security deposit is not refundable unless the application is rejected by Lessor. By the execution of the lease agreement, I/we warrant that the information submitted herein is true and correct and hereby authorized references contained herein to release any necessary information. Further, I/we warrant it is understood that Lessor reserves the right to reverse any credit decision if the information contained herein is found to be incorrect, and I/we will indemnify Lessor for any and all costs incurred with this application for credit including any cost incurred in the placement or reservation of the intended leased equipment based on the information contained herein.

Signature X	Date:

Scenario 3
Credit Report Page 1

User ID :   Date : 05/20/2002

Report Name : Bureau Data (Record ID # ▮▮▮▮)   Page : 0001

▮▮▮▮▮▮▮▮epartment :
Record Number : ▮▮▮▮▮
Report Type : Credit – ▮▮▮▮▮▮▮▮▮▮▮▮▮
Tracking:
S ....,....,HC
I ▮▮▮▮▮▮▮▮▮▮▮▮▮
▮▮▮▮▮▮▮

<FOR>	<SUB NAME>	<MKT SUB>	<INFILE>	<DATE>	<TIME>
(I) ▮▮▮▮▮▮▮		10 TC	1/82	05/20/02	13:38CT

<SUBJECT>   <SSN>   <BIRTH DATE>
▮▮▮▮▮▮▮▮   ▮▮▮▮▮▮   6/44
                                                           <TELEPHONE>
                                                           ▮▮▮▮▮▮

<CURRENT ADDRESS>   <DATE RPTD>
▮▮▮▮▮▮▮▮▮▮▮▮▮▮   12/93

<FORMER ADDRESS>
▮▮▮▮▮▮▮▮▮▮▮▮▮▮   8/93

                                       <POSITION>
<CURRENT EMPLOYER AND ADDRESS>   <RPTD>
▮▮▮▮▮▮   TRUCK DRIVER   9/93

<FORMER EMPLOYER AND ADDRESS>
▮▮▮▮▮▮   7/93

S P E C I A L   M E S S A G E S
****HAWK-ALERT: INPUT SSN ISSUED: 1959 - 1961; STATE: ▮▮▮▮
:FILE SSN ISSUED: 1959 - 1961; STATE: ▮▮▮ (EST. AGE OBTAINED:
14 TO 17)***

M O D E L   P R O F I L E   * * * A L E R T * * *
***EMPIRICA 95 ALERT: SCORE +605 : 022, 018, 010, 014 ***

C R E D I T   S U M M A R Y   * * *   T O T A L   F I L E   H I S T O R Y
PR=0 COL=0   NEG=2 HSTNEG=4-32   TRD=17 RVL=10 INST=6 MTG=1 OPN=0 INQ=11

	HIGH CRED	CRED LIM	BALANCE	PAST DUE	MNTHLY PAY	AVAILABLE
REVOLVING:	$4475	$4700	$731	$0	$22	84%
INSTALLMENT:	$50.4K	$	$44.0K	$0	$909	
MORTGAGE:	$55.0K	$	$54.1K	$0	$523	
TOTALS:	$109K	$4700	$98.8K	$0	$1454	

T R A D E S

Scenario 3
Credit Report Page 2

Date : 05/20/2002

Report Name : Bureau Data (Record ID #█████)   Page : 0002

```
---------------------------------------------------------------------------------
SUBNAME        SUBCODE    OPENED   HIGHCRED  TERMS      MAXDELQ   PAYPAT  1-12 MOP
ACCOUNT#                  VERFIED  CREDLIM   PASTDUE    AMT-MOP   PAYPAT 13-24
ECOA COLLATRL/LOANTYPE    CLSD/PD  BALANCE   REMARKS                  MO 30/60/90
████████████████         3/93     $788                                      R09
                         10/99A
C    CHARGE ACCOUNT       9/99P   $0         P AND L WRITEOFF

████████████████         5/97     $337                                      R9P
                         8/02A
P    CREDIT CARD          2/01F   $0         PAID PROFIT AND LOSS

████████████████         1/92     $492                  111111111111 R01
                         4/02A    $600       $0          112121111111
C    CHARGE ACCOUNT       3/99P   $0                        44  2/ 0/ 0

████████████████         1/01     $16.4K    96M322        111111111111 I01
                         4/02A               $0          1111
C    PARTLY SECURED                $15.4K                    16  0/ 0/ 0

████████████████         8/01     $30.4K    72M587        1111111      I01
                         4/02A               $0
I    AUTOMOBILE                    $28.6K                     7  0/ 0/ 0

████████████████         11/01    $792      MIN22         11111        R01
                         4/02A    $800       $0
I    CREDIT CARD                   $731                      28  0/ 0/ 0

████████████████         12/98    $55.0K    360M523       111111111111 M01
                         3/02A               $0           111111X11111
C    CONVENTIONAL REAL             $54.1K                    38  0/ 0/ 0

████████████████         3/92     $1031               8/99 11111111321l R01
                         2/02A    $0         $0       03 111111111111
P    CHARGE ACCOUNT       4/00P   $0         CLOSED          29  2/ 2/ 0

████████████████         8/92     $1739                   112111111111 R01
                         7/01A    $1300      $0           111111111111
C    CREDIT CARD          6/01C   $0         ACCT CLSD BY CONSUMER 48 0/ 0/ 0

████████████████         6/99     $5637     60M157        X11111111X11 I01
                         1/01A               $0           11111111
C    PARTLY SECURED       1/01C   $0         CLOSED          20  0/ 0/ 0

████████████████         6/89     $1130                   111X11111    R01
                         11/99A   $500       $0
I    CHARGE ACCOUNT       8/99C   $0                         48  0/ 0/ 0

████████████████         3/95     $3770     48M125   7/97 X11111111115 I01
                         1/99A               $0      $532 05 555554544333
```

Scenario 3
Credit Report Page 3

Date :　▆▆▆▆▆▆▆▆

Report Name : Bureau Data (Record ID #▆▆▆▆)   Page : 0003

C	SECURED BY HSHLD	1/99C	$0	CLOSED		42	0/ 3/10
▆▆▆▆▆▆▆▆▆▆		7/93	$3600		11/95	11111114X444 I01	
		5/97A		$0	04	4444444333	
C	SECURED					32	0/ 3/11
▆▆▆▆▆▆▆▆		8/92	$558			111111XX11X1 R01	
		2/97A	$2000	$0		1111111	
P						19	0/ 0/ 0
▆▆▆▆B▆▆▆		8/93	$1602			1111111 R01	
		3/96A	$1300	$0			
C						8	0/ 0/ 0
▆▆▆▆▆▆		1/93	$4521	48M149			I01
		3/95A		$0			
C	HOUSEHOLD GOODS	3/95C	$0	REFINANCED			
▆▆▆▆▆▆		12/91	$500				R01
		7/93A	$500	$0			
I		10/92C	$0	CLOSED			

I N Q U I R I E S

DATE	SUBCODE	SUBNAME	TYPE	AMOUNT
5/20/02	▆▆▆▆▆▆▆▆	▆▆▆▆▆▆▆		
3/29/02	▆▆▆▆▆▆▆▆	▆▆▆▆▆▆▆		
3/04/02	▆▆▆▆▆▆▆▆	▆▆▆▆▆▆▆		
2/25/02	▆▆▆▆▆▆▆▆	▆▆▆▆▆▆▆		
2/20/02	▆▆▆▆▆▆▆▆	▆▆▆▆▆▆		
12/13/01	▆▆▆▆▆▆▆▆	▆▆▆▆▆▆		
11/13/01	▆▆▆▆▆▆▆▆	▆▆▆▆▆K		
8/14/01	▆▆▆▆▆▆▆▆	▆▆▆▆▆D		
8/11/01	▆▆▆▆▆▆▆▆	▆▆▆▆▆L		
3/21/01	▆▆▆▆▆B)	▆▆▆▆▆▆		
12/30/00	▆▆▆▆▆▆▆▆	▆▆▆▆▆▆		

E N D   O F   C R E D I T   R E P O R T   -   S E R V I C E D   B Y :
▆▆▆▆▆▆ CONSUMER RELATIONS   ▆▆▆▆▆▆

TOTAL P.04

Scenario 3
Bank A

BANK RATING REQUEST

TO: BANK A _____   RE: _____ COMPANY C _____

    FAX # (800) XXX-XXXX _____   _____

ATTN: ___CREDIT_____   _____

                                  ACCOUNT #: ___XXXX-XXXX_____

CREDIT MANAGER,

THE ABOVE NAMED PARTY HAS APPLIED FOR CREDIT IN CONNECTION WITH AN EQUIPMENT LEASE/PURCHASE. WE WOULD APPRECIATE RECEIVING THE FOLLOWING INFORMATION AS A CREDIT REFERENCE ON THEIR ACCOUNT. ANY INFORMATION PROVIDED WILL BE HELD IN THE STRICTEST CONFIDENCE.

DATE OPENED: ___4/94_____   AVERAGE BALANCE: Moderate 3 _____

OF NSF'S: _____   # OF OD'S: _____ IF CLOSED, WHEN? _____
          (within last 6 months)   (within last 6 months)

RATING AND/OR COMMENTS: _____

NAME EXACTLY AS IT APPEARS ON THE ACCOUNT: _____

_____ COMPANY C _____

ARE THERE ANY LOANS/NOTES/LINES OF CREDIT?   YES   (NO)
IF YES, PLEASE DETAIL BELOW:

TYPE	OPEN DATE	HIGH CREDIT	BALANCE	(UN) SECURED?	RATING

INFORMATION SUPPLIED BY: _____ Susan _____
               TITLE: _____ Credit Inquiry Specialist _____

AS A COURTESY TO OUR MUTUAL CUSTOMER, PLEASE REPLY BY FAX OR PHONE WITHIN FOUR HOURS FROM THE TIME YOU RECEIVE THIS REQUEST.
PLEASE FAX TO: (YOUR FAX #)   **OR**   **CALL** (YOUR PHONE #)

THANK YOU!

_____   _____   _____
CREDIT MANAGER   **DATE**   **TIME**

Scenario 3
Trade A

TRADE REFERENCE REQUEST

TO: _____TRADE A_____   RE: _____COMPANY C_____

_____FAX # (800) XXX-XXXX_____   _____

ATTN: _____Chris_____   _____

ACCOUNT #: _____NA_____

CREDIT MANAGER,

THE ABOVE NAMED PARTY HAS APPLIED FOR CREDIT IN CONNECTION WITH AN EQUIPMENT LEASE/PURCHASE. WE WOULD APPRECIATE RECEIVING THE FOLLOWING INFORMATION AS A CREDIT REFERENCE ON THEIR ACCOUNT. ANY INFORMATION PROVIDED WILL BE HELD IN THE STRICTEST CONFIDENCE.

DATE OPENED: ___6/2001___   HIGH CREDIT: ___$1,360.00___

BALANCE? _None_   CURRENT? YES NO   TERMS: Commercial Account 1/3 balance due net 30

PAYMENT HISTORY: PROMPT   SLOW   *If slow, how many days on average:* _____

GOODS / SERVICES YOU SUPPLY TO THEM: ___Tires, Batteries___

COMMENTS:
___Good Customer___
_____
_____

INFORMATION SUPPLIED BY: ___Chris___
          TITLE: ___Customer Service___

AS A COURTESY TO OUR MUTUAL CUSTOMER, PLEASE REPLY BY FAX OR PHONE WITHIN FOUR HOURS FROM THE TIME YOU RECEIVE THIS REQUEST.

PLEASE FAX TO: (YOUR FAX NUMBER)   **OR**   **CALL** (YOUR PHONE NUMBER)

THANK YOU!

_____   _____   _____
CREDIT MANAGER   **DATE**   **TIME**

Scenario 3

2001 Individual Tax Return

Form **1040**	Department of the Treasury — Internal Revenue Service **U.S. Individual Income Tax Return**	**2001**	(99)	IRS Use Only — Do not write or staple in this space.

For the year Jan. 1 - Dec. 31, 2001, or other tax year beginning _____, 2001, ending _____, 20___   OMB No. 1545-0074

Label (See instructions on page 19.) Use the IRS label. Otherwise, please print or type.	Your first name and initial **William**	Last name **Kent**	Your social security number **XXX-XX-XXXX**
	If a joint return, spouse's first name and initial	Last name	Spouse's social security number
	Home address (number and street). If you have a P.O. box, see page 19. **600 Accord Street** Apt. no.		**Important!** You must enter your SSN(s) above.
	City, town or post office, state, and ZIP code. If you have a foreign address, see page 19. **Grandview, WA 98880**		

Presidential Election Campaign (See page 19.)   Note. Checking "Yes" will not change your tax or reduce your refund.
Do you, or your spouse if filing a joint return, want $3 to go to this fund? ▶ You ☐Yes ☐No Spouse ☐Yes ☐No

Filing Status

Check only one box.

1. [X] Single
2. ☐ Married filing joint return (even if only one had income)
3. ☐ Married filing separate return. Enter spouse's social security no. above and full name here. ▶ _____
4. ☐ Head of household (with qualifying person). (See page 19.) If the qualifying person is a child but not your dependent, enter this child's name here. ▶ _____
5. ☐ Qualifying widow(er) with dependent child (year spouse died ▶ _____). (See page 19.)

Exemptions

If more than six dependents, see page 20.

6a ☐ Yourself. If your parent (or someone else) can claim you as a dependent on his or her tax return, **do not** check box 6a.
b ☐ Spouse
c Dependents:

(1) First name Last name	(2) Dependent's social security number	(3) Dependent's relationship to you	(4) ✔ if qualifying child for child tax credit (see page 20)
			☐
			☐
			☐
			☐
			☐
			☐

No. of boxes checked on 6a and 6b ___
No. of your children on 6c who:
• lived with you ___
• did not live with you due to divorce or separation (see page 20) ___
Dependents on 6c not entered above ___
Add numbers entered on lines above ▶ ___

d Total number of exemptions claimed ....

Income

Attach Forms W-2 and W-2G here. Also attach Form(s) 1099-R if tax was withheld.

If you did not get a W-2, see page 21.

Enclose, but do not attach, any payment. Also, please use Form 1040-V.

7	Wages, salaries, tips, etc. Attach Form(s) W-2	7	14,721
8a	Taxable interest. Attach Schedule B if required	8a	
b	Tax-exempt interest. Do not include on line 8a	8b	
9	Ordinary dividends. Attach Schedule B if required	9	
10	Taxable refunds, credits, or offsets of state and local income taxes (see page 22)	10	
11	Alimony received	11	
12	Business income or (loss). Attach Schedule C or C-EZ	12	−212
13	Capital gain or (loss). Attach Schedule D if required. If not required, check here ▶ ☐	13	
14	Other gains or (losses). Attach Form 4797	14	
15a	Total IRA distributions ... 15a ___ b Taxable amount (see page 23)	15b	
16a	Total pensions and annuities ... 16a ___ b Taxable amount (see page 23)	16b	
17	Rental real estate, royalties, partnerships, S corporations, trusts, etc. Attach Schedule E	17	
18	Farm income or (loss). Attach Schedule F	18	
19	Unemployment compensation	19	
20a	Social security benefits .. 20a ___ b Taxable amount (see page 25)	20b	
21	Other income. List type and amount (see page 27)	21	
22	Add the amounts in the far right column for lines 7 through 21. This is your total income ▶	22	14,509

Adjusted Gross Income

23	IRA deduction (see page 27)	23	
24	Student loan interest deduction (see page 28)	24	
25	Archer MSA deduction. Attach Form 8853	25	
26	Moving expenses. Attach Form 3903	26	
27	One-half of self-employment tax. Attach Schedule SE	27	
28	Self-employed health insurance deduction (see page 30)	28	
29	Self-employed SEP, SIMPLE, and qualified plans	29	
30	Penalty on early withdrawal of savings	30	
31a	Alimony paid b Recipient's SSN ▶ _____	31a	
32	Add lines 23 through 31a	32	14,509
33	Subtract line 32 from line 22. This is your **adjusted gross income** ▶	33	14,509

For Disclosure, Privacy Act, and Paperwork Reduction Act Notice, see page 72.
ISA
STF FED2011F.1

Form **1040** (2001)

Scenario 3

2001 Individual Tax Return (Page 2)

Form 1040 (2001)   William Kent   XXX-XX-XXXX   Page 2

Tax and Credits	34	Amount from line 33 (adjusted gross income)	34	14,509
	35a	Check if: ☐ You were 65 or older. ☐ Blind; ☐ Spouse was 65 or older, ☐ Blind. Add the number of boxes checked above and enter the total here . . . . ▶ 35a		
Standard Deduction for —	b	If you are married filing separately and your spouse itemizes deductions, or you were a dual-status alien, see page 31 and check here . . . . ▶ 35b ☐		
● People who checked any box on line 35a or 35b or who can be claimed as a dependent, see page 31.	36	Itemized deductions (from Schedule A) or your standard deduction (see left margin)	36	7,600
	37	Subtract line 36 from line 34	37	6,909
	38	If line 34 is $99,725 or less, multiply $2,900 by the total number of exemptions claimed on line 6d. If line 34 is over $99,725, see the worksheet on page 32	38	5,800
● All others:	39	Taxable income. Subtract line 38 from line 37. If line 38 is more than line 37, enter -0-	39	1,109
Single, $4,550	40	Tax (see page 33). Check if any tax is from a ☐ Form(s) 8814 b ☐ Form 4972	40	167
Head of household, $6,650	41	Alternative minimum tax (see page 34). Attach Form 6251	41	
	42	Add lines 40 and 41 . . . . ▶	42	167
Married filing jointly or Qualifying widow(er), $7,600	43	Foreign tax credit. Attach Form 1116 if required	43		
	44	Credit for child and dependent care expenses. Attach Form 2441 .	44		
	45	Credit for the elderly or the disabled. Attach Schedule R	45		
Married filing separately, $3,800	46	Education credits. Attach Form 8863	46		
	47	Rate reduction credit. See the worksheet on page 36	47		
	48	Child tax credit (see page 37)	48		
	49	Adoption credit. Attach Form 8839	49		
	50	Other credits from: a ☐ Form 3800 b ☐ Form 8396 c ☐ Form 8801 d ☐ Form (specify) _____	50		
	51	Add lines 43 through 50. These are your total credits	51	
	52	Subtract line 51 from line 42. If line 51 is more than line 42, enter -0- . . . . ▶	52	167
Other Taxes	53	Self-employment tax. Attach Schedule SE	53	
	54	Social security and Medicare tax on tip income not reported to employer. Attach Form 4137	54	
	55	Tax on qualified plans, including IRAs, and other tax-favored accounts. Attach Form 5329 if required	55	
	56	Advance earned income credit payments from Form(s) W-2	56	
	57	Household employment taxes. Attach Schedule H	57	
	58	Add lines 52 through 57. This is your total tax . . . . ▶	58	167
Payments	59	Federal income tax withheld from Forms W-2 and 1099	59	1,267	
	60	2001 estimated tax payments and amount applied from 2000 return	60		
If you have a qualifying child, attach Schedule EIC.	61a	Earned income credit (EIC)	61a		
	b	Nontaxable earned income 61b			
	62	Excess social security and RRTA tax withheld (see page 51)	62		
	63	Additional child tax credit. Attach Form 8812	63		
	64	Amount paid with request for extension to file (see page 51)	64		
	65	Other payments. Check if from a ☐ Form 2439 b ☐ Form 4136	65		
	66	Add lines 59, 60, 61a, and 62 through 65. These are your total payments . . . . ▶	66	1,267
Refund	67	If line 66 is more than line 58, subtract line 58 from line 66. This is the amount you overpaid	67	1,100
Direct deposit? See page 51 and fill in 68b, 68c, and 68d.	68a	Amount of line 67 you want refunded to you . . . . ▶	68a	1,100
	▶ b	Routing number ☐☐☐☐☐☐☐☐☐ ▶ c Type: ☐ Checking ☐ Savings		
	▶ d	Account number ☐☐☐☐☐☐☐☐☐☐☐☐☐☐☐☐☐		
	69	Amount of line 67 you want applied to your 2002 estimated tax . . . . ▶	69	
Amount You Owe	70	Amount you owe. Subtract line 66 from line 58. For details on how to pay, see page 52 . . . . . ▶	70	
	71	Estimated tax penalty. Also include on line 70	71		

Third Party Designee   Do you want to allow another person to discuss this return with the IRS (see page 53)? ☐ Yes. Complete the following.   ☒ No

Designee's name ▶ _____   Phone no. ▶ _____   Personal identification number (PIN) ▶ _____

Sign Here   Under penalties of perjury, I declare that I have examined this return and accompanying schedules and statements, and to the best of my knowledge and belief, they are true, correct, and complete. Declaration of preparer (other than taxpayer) is based on all information of which preparer has any knowledge.

Joint return? See page 19.
Keep a copy for your records.

Your signature _____   Date _____   Your occupation TRUCKER   Daytime phone number _____

Spouse's signature. If a joint return, both must sign. _____   Date _____   Spouse's occupation _____

Paid Preparer's Use Only

Preparer's signature _____   Date _____   Check if self-employed ☐   Preparer's SSN or PTIN _____

Firm's name (or yours if self-employed), address, and ZIP code ▶ _____   EIN _____   Phone no. _____

Form 1040 (2001)

Scenario 3
2001 Schedule C

SCHEDULE C (Form 1040)	Profit or Loss From Business	OMB No. 1545-0074
Department of the Treasury Internal Revenue Service (99)	(Sole Proprietorship) ▶ Partnerships, joint ventures, etc., must file Form 1065 or Form 1065-B. ▶ Attach to Form 1040 or Form 1041. ▶ See Instructions for Schedule C (Form 1040).	**2001** Attachment Sequence No. **09**

Name of proprietor William Kent

Social security number (SSN) XXX-XX-XXXX

A Principal business or profession, including product or service (see page C-1 of the instructions)
Short Haul Trucking

B Enter code from pages C-7 & 8

C Business name. If no separate business name, leave blank.
COMPANY C

D Employer ID number (EIN), if any

E Business address (including suite or room no.) ▶ 600 Accord Street
City, town or post office, state, and ZIP code Grandview, WA 98880

F Accounting method: (1) ☒ Cash (2) ☐ Accrual (3) ☐ Other (specify) ▶ ....

G Did you "materially participate" in the operation of this business during 2001? If "No," see page C-2 for limit on losses .... ☒ Yes ☐ No

H If you started or acquired this business during 2001, check here ...... ▶ ☐

Part I Income

1	Gross receipts or sales. Caution. If this income was reported to you on Form W-2 and the "Statutory employee" box on that form was checked, see page C-2 and check here .... ▶ ☐	1	110,572
2	Returns and allowances	2	
3	Subtract line 2 from line 1	3	110,572
4	Cost of goods sold (from line 42 on page 2)	4	
5	Gross profit. Subtract line 4 from line 3	5	110,572
6	Other income, including Federal and state gasoline or fuel tax credit or refund (see page C-3)	6	
7	Gross income. Add lines 5 and 6 .... ▶	7	110,572

Part II Expenses. Enter expenses for business use of your home only on line 30.

8	Advertising	8		19 Pension and profit-sharing plans	19	
9	Bad debts from sales or services (see page C-3)	9		20 Rent or lease (see page C-4):		
				a Vehicles, machinery, and equipment	20a	
10	Car and truck expenses (see page C-3)	10	638	b Other business property	20b	
11	Commissions and fees	11	11,057	21 Repairs and maintenance	21	22,350
12	Depletion	12		22 Supplies (not included in Part III)	22	680
13	Depreciation and section 179 expense deduction (not included in Part III) (see page C-3)	13	11,145	23 Taxes and licenses	23	5,208
				24 Travel, meals, and entertainment:		
14	Employee benefit programs (other than on line 19)	14		a Travel	24a	
15	Insurance (other than health) ...	15	6,905	b Meals and entertainment .		
16	Interest:			c Enter nondeductible amount included on line 24b (see page C-5)		
a	Mortgage (paid to banks, etc.) ...	16a		d Subtract line 24c from line 24b ...	24d	3,996
b	Other	16b	5,348	25 Utilities	25	1,681
17	Legal and professional services .	17	75	26 Wages (less employment credits)	26	
18	Office expense	18	1,908	27 Other expenses (from line 48 on page 2)	27	39,793
28	Total expenses before expenses for business use of home. Add lines 8 through 27 in columns .... ▶				28	110,784

29	Tentative profit (loss). Subtract line 28 from line 7	29	-212
30	Expenses for business use of your home. Attach Form 8829	30	
31	Net profit or (loss). Subtract line 30 from line 29. • If a profit, enter on Form 1040, line 12, and also on Schedule SE, line 2 (statutory employees, see page C-5). Estates and trusts, enter on Form 1041, line 3. • If a loss, you must go on to line 32.	31	-212
32	If you have a loss, check the box that describes your investment in this activity (see page C-6). • If you checked 32a, enter the loss on Form 1040, line 12, and also on Schedule SE, line 2 (statutory employees, see page C-5). Estates and trusts, enter on Form 1041, line 3. • If you checked 32b, you must attach Form 6198.	32a ☐ All investment is at risk. 32b ☐ Some investment is not at risk.	

For Paperwork Reduction Act Notice, see Form 1040 Instructions.

ISA
STF FED2615F 1

Schedule C (Form 1040) 2001

Scenario 3

2000 Individual Tax Return

FORM 1040	Department of the Treasury – Internal Revenue Service **U.S. Individual Income Tax Return**	2000	(99)	IRS Use Only – Do not write or staple in this space.

For the year Jan. 1 – Dec. 31, 2000, or other tax year beginning ____, 2000, ending ____, 20____   OMB No. 1545-0074

Label
(See instructions on page 19.)

Use the IRS label. Otherwise, please print or type.

```
William Kent
600 Accord Street
Grandview, WA   98880
```

Your social security number: XXX–XX–XXXX
Spouse's social security number

▲ **IMPORTANT!** ▲
You must enter your SSN(s) above.

Presidential Election Campaign (See page 19.)
Note. Checking "Yes" will not change your tax or reduce your refund.
Do you, or your spouse if filing a joint return, want $3 to go to this fund? ....▶ ☐ Yes ☒ No | ☐ Yes ☐ No
You | Spouse

Filing Status

Check only one box.

1. ☒ Single
2. ☐ Married filing joint return (even if only one had income)
3. ☐ Married filing separate return. Enter spouse's soc. sec. no. above & full name here ▶
4. ☐ Head of household (with qualifying person). (See page 19.) If the qualifying person is a child but not your dependent, enter this child's name here ▶
5. ☐ Qualifying widow(er) with dependent child (year spouse died ▶ ____). (See page 19.)

Exemptions

6a ☒ **Yourself.** If your parent (or someone else) can claim you as a dependent on his or her tax return, **do not** check box 6a ....

b ☐ **Spouse** ....

c **Dependents:**

(1) First Name Last name	(2) Dependent's social security number	(3) Dependent's relationship to you	(4) Chk if qualifying child for child tax credit (see page 20)

If more than six dependents, see page 20.

No. of boxes checked on 6a and 6b: 1

No. of your children on 6c who:
● lived with you
● did not live with you due to divorce or separation (see page 20)
Dependents on 6c not entered above
Add numbers entered on lines above ▶ [1]

d Total number of exemptions claimed .... [1]

Income

Attach Forms W-2 and W-2G here. Also attach Form 1099-R if tax was withheld.

If you did not get a W-2, see page 21.

Enclose, but do not attach, any payment. Also, please use Form 1040-V.

7	Wages, salaries, tips, etc. Attach Form(s) W-2	7	18,412
8a	Taxable interest. Attach Schedule B if required	8a	
b	Tax-exempt interest. Do not include on line 8a	8b	
9	Ordinary dividends. Attach Schedule B if required	9	
10	Taxable refunds, credits, or offsets of state and local income taxes (see page 22)	10	
11	Alimony received	11	
12	Business income or (loss). Attach Schedule C or C-EZ	12	–4,286
13	Capital gain or (loss). Attach Schedule D if required. If not required, check here ▶ ☐	13	
14	Other gains or (losses). Attach Form 4797	14	
15a	Total IRA distributions .... 15a ____ b Taxable amount (see pg. 23)	15b	
16a	Total pensions and annuities 16a ____ b Taxable amount (see pg. 23)	16b	
17	Rental real estate, royalties, partnerships, S corporations, trusts, etc. Attach Schedule E	17	
18	Farm income or (loss). Attach Schedule F	18	
19	Unemployment compensation	19	
20a	Social security benefits .... 20a ____ b Taxable amount (see pg. 25)	20b	
21	Other income	21	
22	Add the amounts in the far right column for lines 7 through 21. This is your **total income** ....▶	22	14,126

Adjusted Gross Income

23	IRA deduction (see page 27)	23	
24	Student loan interest deduction (see page 27)	24	
25	Medical savings account deduction. Attach Form 8853	25	
26	Moving expenses. Attach Form 3903	26	
27	One-half of self-employment tax. Attach Schedule SE	27	
28	Self-employed health insurance deduction (see page 29)	28	
29	Self-employed SEP, SIMPLE, and qualified plans	29	
30	Penalty on early withdrawal of savings	30	
31a	Alimony paid. b Recipient's SSN ▶ ____	31a	
32	Add lines 23 through 31a	32	
33	Subtract line 32 from line 22. This is your **adjusted gross income** ....▶	33	14,126

KFA For Disclosure, Privacy Act, and Paperwork Reduction Act Notice, see page 56.   IFoUS1X 11/07/00   Form **1040** (2000)

Scenario 3

2000 Individual Tax Return (Page 2)

Form 1040 (2000)   William Kent   XXX-XX-XXXX   Page **2**

Tax and Credits	34	Amount from line 33 (adjusted gross income)	**34** 14,126
	35a	Check if: ☐ You were 65 or older, ☐ Blind; ☐ Spouse was 65 or older, ☐ Blind. Add the number of boxes checked above and enter the total here ▶ 35a	
Standard Deduction for Most People	b	If you are married filing separately and your spouse itemizes deductions, or you were a dual-status alien, see page 31 and check here ▶ 35b ☐	
Single: $4,400	36	Enter your **itemized deductions** from Schedule A, line 28, or **standard deduction** shown on the left. But see page 31 to find your standard deduction if you checked any box on line 35a or 35b **or** if someone can claim you as a dependent	**36** 7,350
Head of household: $6,450	37	Subtract line 36 from line 34	**37** 6,776
Married filing jointly or Qualifying widow(er): $7,350	38	If line 34 is $96,700 or less, multiply $2,800 by the total number of exemptions claimed on line 6d. If line 34 is over $96,700, see the worksheet on page 32 for the amount to enter	**38** 5,600
	39	**Taxable income.** Subtract line 38 from line 37. If line 38 is more than line 37, enter -0-	**39** 1,176
Married filing separately: $3,675.	40	Tax (see page 32). Check if any tax is from a ☐ Form(s) 8814 b ☐ Form 4972	**40** 178
	41	Alternative minimum tax. Attach Form 6251	**41**
	42	Add lines 40 and 41 ▶	**42** 178
	43	Foreign tax credit. Attach Form 1116 if required	43	
	44	Credit for child and dependent care expenses. Att. Form 2441	44	
	45	Credit for the elderly or the disabled. Attach Schedule R	45	
	46	Education credits. Attach Form 8863	46	
	47	Child tax credit (see page 36)	47	
	48	Adoption credit. Attach Form 8839	48	
	49	Other. Check if from a ☐ Form 3800 b ☐ Form 8396 c ☐ Form 8801 d ☐ Form (specify)	49	
	50	Add lines 43 through 49. These are your **total credits**	**50**
	51	Subtract line 50 from line 42. If line 50 is more than line 42, enter -0- ▶	**51** 178
Other Taxes	52	Self-employment tax. Att. Sch. SE	**52**
	53	Social security and Medicare tax on tip income not reported to employer. Attach Form 4137	**53**
	54	Tax on IRAs, other retirement plans, and MSAs. Attach Form 5329 if required	**54**
	55	Advance earned income credit payments from Form(s) W-2	**55**
	56	Household employment taxes. Attach Schedule H	**56**
	57	Add lines 51 through 56. This is your **total tax** ▶	**57** 178
Payments	58	Federal income tax withheld from Forms W-2 and 1099	58 1,794	
If you have a qualifying child, attach Schedule EIC.	59	2000 estimated tax payments and amount applied from 1999 return	59	
	60a	Earned income credit (EIC)	60a	
	b	Nontaxable earned income: amt. ▶ [ ] and type ▶ NO		
	61	Excess social security and RRTA tax withheld (see page 50)	61	
	62	Additional child tax credit. Attach Form 8812	62	
	63	Amount paid with request for extension to file (see page 50)	63	
	64	Other payments. Check if from a ☐ Form 2439 b ☐ Form 4136	64	
	65	Add lines 58, 59, 60a, and 61 through 64. These are your **total payments** ▶	**65** 1,794
Refund	66	If line 65 is more than line 57, subtract line 57 from line 65. This is the amount you **overpaid**	**66** 1,616
Have it directly deposited! See page 50 and fill in 67b, 67c, and 67d.	67a	Amount of line 66 you want **refunded to you** ▶	**67a** 1,616
	b	Routing number [ ] ▶ c Type: ☐ Checking ☐ Savings	
	d	Account number [ ]	
	68	Amount of line 66 you want applied to your 2001 estimated tax ▶ 68	
Amount You Owe	69	If line 57 is more than line 65, subtract line 65 from line 57. This is the **amount you owe**. For details on how to pay, see page 51 ▶	**69**
	70	Estimated tax penalty. Also include on line 69	70	

Sign Here

Joint return? See page 19. Keep a copy for your records.

Under penalties of perjury, I declare that I have examined this return and accompanying schedules and statements, and to the best of my knowledge and belief, they are true, correct, and complete. Declaration of preparer (other than taxpayer) is based on all information of which preparer has any knowledge.

Your signature	Date	Your occupation Trucker	Daytime phone number
Spouse's signature. If a joint return, both must sign.	Date	Spouse's occupation	May the IRS discuss this return with the preparer shown below? (see page 52)? ☒ Yes ☐ No

Paid Preparer's Use Only

Preparer's signature ▶ Self Prepared	Date	Check if self-employed ☐	Preparer's SSN or PTIN
Firm's name (or yours if self-employed), address, and ZIP code ▶		EIN	
		Phone no.	

IFCUS1A 11/22/00   Form 1040 (2000)

Scenario 3

2000 Schedule C

SCHEDULE C (Form 1040) Department of the Treasury Internal Revenue Service (99)	**Profit or Loss From Business** (Sole Proprietorship) ▶ Partnerships, joint ventures, etc., must file Form 1065 or Form 1065-B. ▶ Attach to Form 1040 or Form 1041. ▶ See Instructions for Schedule C (Form 1040).	OMB No. 1545-0074 **2000** Attachment Sequence No. 09

Name of proprietor	Social security number (SSN)
William Kent	XXX-XX-XXXX

A Principal business or profession, including product or service (see page C-1 of the instructions)   **B** Enter code from pages C-7 & 8

  Short Haul Trucking   ▶

C Business name. If no separate business name, leave blank.   **D** Employer ID number (EIN), if any

  COMPANY C

E Business address (including suite or room no.) ▶   600 Accord Street
  City, town or post office, state, and ZIP code   Grandview, WA 98880

F Accounting method: (1) ☒ Cash   (2) ☐ Accrual   (3) ☐ Other (specify)   ▶

G Did you "materially participate" in the operation of this business during 2000? If "No," see page C-2 for limit on losses . . . . ☒ Yes   ☐ No

H If you started or acquired this business during 2000, check here . . . . ▶ ☒

Part I   Income

1	Gross receipts or sales. Caution: If this income was reported to you on Form W-2 and the "Statutory employee" box on that form was checked, see page C-2 and check here . . . . ▶ ☐	1	102,262
2	Returns and allowances	2	
3	Subtract line 2 from line 1	3	102,262
4	Cost of goods sold (from line 42 on page 2)	4	
5	Gross profit. Subtract line 4 from line 3	5	102,262
6	Other income, including Federal and state gasoline or fuel tax credit or refund (see page C-2)	6	
7	Gross income. Add lines 5 and 6 . . . . ▶	7	102,262

Part II   Expenses.   Enter expenses for business use of your home only on line 30.

8	Advertising	8		19 Pension and profit-sharing plans	19	
9	Bad debts from sales or services (see page C-3) . . .	9		20 Rent or lease (see page C-4):		
10	Car and truck expenses (see page C-3)	10		a Vehicles, machinery & equipment . . .	20a	
				b Other business property	20b	
11	Commissions and fees	11	10,006	21 Repairs and maintenance	21	13,026
12	Depletion	12		22 Supplies (not included in Part III)	22	2,912
13	Depreciation and section 179 expense deduction (not included in Part III) (see page C-3)	13	16,324	23 Taxes and licenses	23	6,681
				24 Travel, meals, and entertainment:		
				a Travel	24a	
14	Employee benefit programs (other than on line 19) . . .	14		b Meals and entertainment 7,884		
15	Insurance (other than health) . . .	15	5,987	c Enter nondeductible amount included on line 24b (see page C-5) 3,942		
16	Interest:			d Subtract line 24c from line 24b	24d	3,942
a	Mortgage (paid to banks, etc.) . . .	16a		25 Utilities	25	1,062
b	Other	16b		26 Wages (less employment credits)	26	
17	Legal and professional services . .	17	75	27 Other expenses (from line 48 on page 2)	27	44,472
18	Office expense	18	2,061			

28	Total expenses before expenses for business use of home. Add lines 8 through 27 in columns . . . . ▶	28	106,548
29	Tentative profit (loss). Subtract line 28 from line 7	29	-4,286
30	Expenses for business use of your home. Attach Form 8829	30	
31	Net profit or (loss). Subtract line 30 from line 29. • If a profit, enter on Form 1040, line 12, and also on Schedule SE, line 2 (statutory employees, see page C-5). Estates and trusts, enter on Form 1041, line 3. • If a loss, you must go to line 32.	31	-4,286
32	If you have a loss, check the box that describes your investment in this activity (see page C-5). • If you checked 32a, enter the loss on Form 1040, line 12, and also on Schedule SE, line 2 (statutory employees, see page C-5). Estates and trusts, enter on Form 1041, line 3. • If you checked 32b, you must attach Form 6198.	32a ☐ All investment is at risk. 32b ☐ Some investment is not at risk.	

For Paperwork Reduction Act Notice, see Form 1040 Instructions.   Schedule C (Form 1040) 2000

Scenario 3
Funding Source Approval

LEASING CORPORATION

TEL:
FAX:
EMAIL:

BROKER:
LESSEE:
APPROVAL EXPIRES: 45 days

DATE: JUN 13, 2002   7:44:26
APPLICATION NO:
CREDIT OFFICER:

CONDITIONAL APPROVAL

LEASE AMOUNT:	$13,900.00	PURCHASE OPTION:	FMV OR DOLLAR
SECURITY DEPOSIT:	20%	BUY RATE CHART:	B
TERM:	60 MONTHS	ADMINISTRATION FEE:	$125.00
		NEW/USED CODE:	U

REQUIRED CONDITIONS

(X) Site inspection $160/24hr—$125/72hr or cost if more
(X) Require vendor approval PRIOR to docing
(X) Confirmed telephone directory assistance
(X) Advise of any other lease financing prior to docs

(X) Commercial bank rating prior to signing docs
(X) Invoice/equipment approved PRIOR to signing docs
(X) Condition report (if used equipment)
(X) Security Deposits over $3,000 must have certified funds

(X) Additional Comments:

REQUIRED WEBSITE DOCUMENTS

All document preparation must be completed on our new on—line system @
effective 4/1/2001

(X) Lease agreement/equipment lease guaranty
(X) Security deposit from lessee's business account
(X) Vendor's invoice with serial numbers
(X) Proof of loss insurance
(X) All insurance requirements met prior to funding
(X) Copy of title (front/back) or MSO
(X) Broker to sign "Guaranty of Title" form
(X) Personal Guarantees of All Owners, Including:

(X) Authorization for automatic withdrawal/required
(X) Copy of driver's license of all guarantors
(X) Broker invoice
(X) Proof of liability insurance
(X) Additional $50 doc fee for each titled piece
(X) Broker responsibile for titling
(X) 50% commission hold for original title w/Pawnee

(X) Legal Name To Read:

BROKER'S WARRANTY

By submitting this transaction for funding, broker warrants that the transaction DOES NOT INVOLVE a Sale—Leaseback, Cash Back To Lessee, Private Party Sale, or an undisclosed Split Transaction.

Scenario 3
Documentation Request

DOCUMENTATION REQUEST WORKSHEET

SALES REPRESENTATIVE: __Lucrative Leasing__   DATE: _____

LESSEE INFORMATION

COMPLETE LESSEE NAME: __COMPANY C__

BILLING ADDRESS: __600 Accord Street__

CITY, STATE, ZIP: __Grandview, WA   98880__   PHONE: (800) XXX-XXXX

EQUIPMENT LOCATION: __Same__

SIGNER: __William Kent__   TITLE: __Owner__   PG: (YES) NO

SIGNER: _____   TITLE: _____   PG: YES NO

VENDOR AND EQUIPMENT INFORMATION

VENDOR NAME: __SUPER TRUCKS__
STREET ADDRESS: __905 North Lake Way, Yakima, WA   98901__
PHONE: (800) XXX-XXXX   CONTACT PERSON: JACK

EQUIPMENT LEASE TERMS

LEASE AMOUNT: $ 13,953.75   SALES TAX INCLUDED: YES (NO)

LEASE TERM: __48__ MONTHS   BUY-OUT: 10% PUT $1.00 OTHER FMV

LEASE PAYMENT: $481.68   MONTHLY TAX (7.6%): $36.61

ADVANCED PAYMENTS: 1 ONLY   1+1   10% SEC.   OTHER __20% S.D.__

FACTORS: *Buy Rate:* .03002   *Sell Rate:* .03452
GROSS COMMISSION (15 %): $ 2,093.06

DOCUMENTATION SHIPPING INFORMATION

SEND DOCUMENTS TO:

(X) FED-X TO LESSEE AT LOCATION ABOVE

(   ) FED-X TO LESSEE AT FOLLOWING LOCATION: _____

Scenario 3
Documentation Cover Letter

LUCRATIVE LEASING

ATTN: **William Kent**
          COMPANY C
          600 Accord Street
          Grandview, WA 98880

Dear Mr. Kent,

Please pay close attention to the following requirements before returning the lease documents.

- Please sign and date each agreement for your equipment lease. **Make sure that all dates are the same throughout all the paperwork.**

- Make a check payable to <u>Lucrative Leasing</u> for the total amount of: **<u>$3,140.75.</u>**

    This amount equals 1 20% Security Deposit of $2,790.75, plus a $350.00 processing fee to cover cost of documentation, postage and site inspection. .
    * * IMPORTANT: This check must be written from your business account.

- **Please provide your Federal Tax ID#:** _____

• COPY OF DRIVER'S LICENSE (William Kent)

<u>Overnight all original documentation to</u>: **Lucrative Leasing**
                                        Address
                                        City, State & Zip

OVERNIGHT ENVELOPE PROVIDED

Call me with any questions at (800-XXX-XXXX).

Sincerely,

Mr. Leasing

Scenario 3
Lease Agreement Page 1

LESSOR: LUCRATIVE LEASING

LEASE AGREEMENT

NOTICE: THIS IS A NON-CANCELABLE, BINDING CONTRACT CONSISTING OF ALL TERMS ON BOTH PAGES, IT CONTAINS IMPORTANT TERMS AND CONDITIONS AND HAS LEGAL AND FINANCIAL CONSEQUENCES TO YOU. PLEASE READ CAREFULLY.

Leasing Customer (Lessee): Complete with Full Legal Name, if a corporation, sign exact registered corporate name.

Company Name   Company C

Billing Address	Supplier of Equipment
600 Accord Street Grandview WA 98880	**See Attached Schedule "A"**
County: Phone:	Phone: Salesperson:

EQUIPMENT DESCRIPTION (Include Quantity, Make, Model, Serial Models)

See Attached Schedule "A"

Equipment Location: Same as Lessee		Equipment Cost:	$13,953.75
SCHEDULE OF LEASE PAYMENTS		Payment	$481.68
Term of Lease (in months)	48	Payment with Tax (Tax Rate 7.8 %)	$518.29
Total Number of Rental Payments	48	Security Deposit (# of payments w/ tax or %)	$2,790.75
Administration Fee	$350.00	Total Initial Payment (Security Deposit + Doc Fee)	$3,140.75

1. LEASE: LESSOR hereby leases to the LESSEE the above Equipment (hereinafter called "Equipment") for the number of months and the lease payments as set forth above and on the terms and conditions stated herein AND ON PAGE 2. LESSEE agrees that if there are any inconsistencies between the Terms and Conditions of this Lease and of any of the LESSEE'S written purchase orders, the terms of this Lease will govern. The lease payments shall commence when the Lessee has received Equipment which is equal to fifty percent of the value at the cost of LESSOR of all the Equipment to be leased hereunder and shall continue thereafter to be paid on the first day of each succeeding month in the amount specified and for the total number of payments as provided in the Schedule of Lease Payments as set forth above. Lessor may charge Lessee a partial payment for the time between the delivery date and the date the first regular payment is due. All lease payments by LESSEE shall be payable at the office of LESSOR or at such other places LESSOR may from time to time appoint. LESSEE hereby authorizes LESSOR the use of the Security Deposit made by LESSEE under this Lease. Such Security Deposit to be returned in Escrow at the expiration of this Lease, less any outstanding charges or expense in taking the equipment to good working order and repair.

2. DISCLAIMER OF WARRANTIES AND CLAIMS; LIMITATION OF REMEDIES: THERE ARE NO WARRANTIES BY OR ON BEHALF OF LESSOR. Lessee acknowledges and agrees by their signature below as follows:
(a) LESSOR MAKES NO WARRANTIES EITHER EXPRESS OR IMPLIED AS TO THE CONDITION OF THE EQUIPMENT, ITS MERCHANTABILITY, ITS FITNESS OR SUITABILITY FOR ANY PARTICULAR PURPOSE, ITS DESIGN, ITS CAPACITY, ITS QUALITY, OR WITH RESPECT TO ANY CHARACTERISTICS OF THE EQUIPMENT;
(b) Lessee has fully inspected the Equipment which it has requested Lessor to acquire and lease to Lessee, and the Equipment is in good condition and to the Lessee's complete satisfaction;
(c) Lessee leases the Equipment "as is" and with all faults;
(d) Lessee specifically acknowledges that the Equipment is leased to the Lessee solely for commercial or business purposes and not for personal, family, household, or agricultural purposes;
(e) If the Equipment is not properly installed, does not operate as represented or warranted by the supplier or manufacturer, or is unsatisfactory for any reason, regardless of cause or consequence, Lessee's only remedy, if ANY, shall be against the supplier or manufacturer of the Equipment and not against the Lessor;
(f) Provided Lessee is not in default under this Lease, Lessor assigns to Lessee any warranties made by the supplier or the manufacturer of the Equipment;
(g) LESSEE SHALL HAVE NO REMEDY FOR CONSEQUENTIAL OR INCIDENTAL DAMAGES AGAINST LESSOR, AND
(h) NO DEFECT, DAMAGE, OR UNFITNESS OF THE EQUIPMENT FOR ANY PURPOSE SHALL RELIEVE LESSEE OF THE OBLIGATION TO PAY RENT OR RELIEVE LESSEE OF ANY OTHER OBLIGATION UNDER THIS LEASE. The parties have specifically negotiated and agreed to the foregoing paragraph.

3. DELIVERY AND ACCEPTANCE: The equipment shall be shipped directly to the LESSEE by the SUPPLIER. LESSEE agreed to accept such delivery of the Equipment. LESSEE further agrees that the validity of this Lease shall not be affected by any delay in the shipment of the Equipment by the SUPPLIER. In the event that LESSEE does not execute and deliver to LESSOR, a submitted Delivery and Acceptance receipt upon installation of the Equipment then it shall be conclusively presumed, as between LESSOR and LESSEE, that the Equipment is acknowledged to be in good working order and condition and that Lessee has accepted and is satisfied that the Equipment constitutes the Equipment specified in this Lease. By execution hereof, the signer hereby certifies that he has read this Lease consisting of the foregoing and INCLUDING THE REVERSE SIDE HEREOF, and that he is duly authorized to execute this Lease on behalf of the LESSEE and hereby acknowledges receipt of a copy of this Lease. LESSEE UNDERSTANDS AND AGREES THAT NEITHER THE SUPPLIER NOR ANY SALESMAN OR OTHER AGENT OF THE SUPPLIER IS AN AGENT OF LESSOR. NO SALESMAN OR AGENT OF THE SUPPLIER IS AUTHORIZED TO WAIVE OR ALTER ANY TERM OR CONDITION OF THIS LEASE, AND NO REPRESENTATION AS TO THE EQUIPMENT OR ANY OTHER MATTER BY THE SUPPLIER SHALL IN ANY WAY AFFECT THE LESSEE'S OBLIGATION TO PERFORM INCLUDING THE PAYMENT OF THE LEASE PAYMENTS SET FORTH IN THIS LEASE. LESSEE REPRESENTS AND WARRANTS THAT THIS IS A COMMERCIAL AND BUSINESS TRANSACTION AND NOT A CONSUMER TRANSACTION. ANY OFFICER/OWNER/PARTNER EXECUTING THIS DOCUMENT HEREBY AFFIRMS THAT ALL SHAREHOLDERS / OWNERS / PARTNERS OF LESSEE HAVE BEEN IDENTIFIED AND SUBMITTED TO LESSOR IN WRITING.

SEE PAGE 2 FOR LEASE TERMS

LESSEE: Company C

Owner

Signature William Kent	Title	Date	Signature	Title	Date

EQUIPMENT LEASE GUARANTY

To induce the above LESSOR to make it's Lease and purchase the equipment for the above leasing customer ("Lessee"), knowing that the LESSOR is relying on the Guaranty as a precondition to making this Lease, the undersigned "Guarantor", jointly and severally, INDIVIDUALLY, PERSONALLY, ABSOLUTELY AND UNCONDITIONALLY GUARANTY to the LESSOR (and any person or firm the LESSOR may transfer its interest to) all payments and other obligations owned by the Lessee to the LESSOR under this Lease and any add-on leases and future leases between LESSOR and Lessee, including but not limited to the LESSOR's attorney fees and legal costs incurred in enforcing this Lease. Guarantor(s) has an interest, financial or otherwise, in Lessee and will also pay all costs and fees incurred by the LESSOR in enforcing this Guaranty. Accounts settled between the LESSOR and the Lessee will bind Guarantor(s). Guarantor(s) waive notice of default and agree that the LESSOR may proceed directly against Guarantor(s) without first proceeding against the Lessee or the security (including equipment). This Guaranty shall be governed by the laws of Colorado. GUARANTOR(S) FREELY CONSENT TO PERSONAL JURISDICTION IN THE COLORADO COURTS AND WAIVE TRIAL BY JURY. This guaranty will bind my heirs, representatives and successors. Guarantor(s) further agree to, understands and gives permission for LESSOR, to report Guarantor(s) to a national credit bureau as past due or otherwise delinquent should Guarantor(s) fail to timely make any payment to LESSOR due or payable under this agreement. LESSOR may apply all proceeds received from Lessee or others to such part of Lessee's indebtedness as LESSOR may deem appropriate without consulting Guarantor(s) and without prejudice to or in any way limiting or lessening the liability of Guarantor(s) under this Guaranty. If Lessee is a Corporation, the undersigned warrant and represent that they are stockholders, directors or officers and/or are financially or otherwise interested in Lessee, and if married their marital communities are so interested. IMPORTANT: THIS AGREEMENT CREATES SPECIFIC LEGAL OBLIGATIONS, DO NOT SIGN UNTIL YOU HAVE FULLY READ IT. BY SIGNING YOU COMPLETELY AGREE TO ITS TERMS.

GUARANTOR: William Kent		GUARANTOR:	
Signature (Individually; No Title)	Social Security Number	Signature (Individually; No Title)	Social Security Number
Home Address 600 Accord Street		Home Address	
Grandview WA 98880			
City State Zip Home Phone		City State Zip Home Phone	

Scenario 3

Lease Agreement Page 2

4. Statutory Finance Lease: Lessee agrees and acknowledges that it is the intent of both parties to this Lease that it qualify as a statutory finance lease under Article 2A of the Uniform Commercial Code. Lessee acknowledges and agrees that Lessee has selected both (1) the Equipment; and (2) the supplier from whom Lessor is to purchase the Equipment. Lessee acknowledges that Lessor has not participated in any way in Lessee's selection of the Equipment or of the supplier, and Lessor has not selected, manufactured, or supplied the Equipment. Lessee is advised that it may have rights under the contract evidencing the Lessor's purchase of the equipment from the supplier chosen by Lessee and that Lessee should contact the supplier of the Equipment for a description of any such rights. Lessee hereby waives its right under Section 508 (5) of Article 2A of the UCC to assume a security interest in the Equipment in the event of a default by the Lessor.

5. Use/Assignment: Lessee shall use the equipment only in the conduct of its business in a careful and proper manner. Lessee, at its sole expense, shall keep the equipment in good order and repair and any alterations are expressly prohibited without written consent of Lessor. All additions, replacements, parts, or accessories immediately become the property of the Lessor and shall be deemed to be incorporated in this lease. Equipment is located at the address on the front of the lease and cannot be removed without the written consent of Lessor. Lessor reserves the right to inspect the equipment during normal business hours. Lessee shall not assign this Lease or any of the rights hereunder, including use of the equipment, without written permission of Lessor. Lessor may assign their rights, including rights to payments, without notice, and the transferee or assignee shall have all of the rights, remedies, powers and privileges of the Lessor under this Lease and Lessee's obligation under this lease shall not be subject to any defense, offset, or counterclaim available to Lessee against Lessor.

6. Late Payment/Other Charges: Should the Lessee fail to pay any rent, or other sum required by Lessee to be paid to Lessor, within ten (10) days after the due date, Lessee agrees to pay Lessor a late payment fee equal to 10% of the delinquent lease payment and Lessee further agrees to pay to Lessor the sum of $10 for each collection telephone call made to Lessee because of Lessee's failure to make payments in a timely manner. In addition, Lessee shall pay Lessor interest on any sums past due, calculated from the due date, at the rate of 24% percent per annum or the maximum interest rate permitted by Colorado law, whichever is highest. Lessee further agrees to, understands, and gives permission to Lessor, to report to any national credit bureau as past due or otherwise delinquent should Lessee fail to timely make any payment due under this lease agreement. If for any reason a check or ACH payment is returned unpaid to Lessor then Lessee shall pay Lessor a fee of $25 for each time the check or ACH is returned. In addition, Lessee agrees to notify Lessor 15 business days prior to changing Lessee ACH bank and Lessor is entitled to an additional fee of $100 for failure of Lessee to give timely notification. If for any reason, Lessor must make or contact agents, to make a collection visit at the Lessees address, Lessee agrees to pay reasonable collection fees.

7. Loss or Damage: Risk of loss shall pass to the Lessee upon shipment to the Lessee of the Equipment. In the event any item shall become lost, stolen, destroyed, damaged beyond repair, or otherwise rendered permanently unfit for use. Lessee shall promptly pay Lessor the remaining payments, plus tax, discounted at 8% plus the residual value of the equipment. Upon payment of the above sum, title shall pass to Lessee.

8. Taxes and Fees: Lessee shall comply with all laws and regulations relating to the lease of this equipment. Lessee shall promptly pay when due all license fees, registrations fees, assessments, charges and taxes, municipal, state, and federal (excluding taxes on Lessor's income), which now or hereafter be imposed on the ownership, leasing, renting, possession of, control, use, maintenance, delivery and/or return of the equipment, and shall save Lessor harmless against actual or asserted violations and shall pay all expenses and costs of every character in connection herewith or arising therefrom. Should Lessee fail to file any required tax return the Lessor may do so to protect their interest and Lessee hereby agrees to pay to Lessor a tax filing fee, for each such tax return filed on behalf of the Lessee.

9. Insurance: Lessee shall obtain, at its own expense, insurance on the equipment as follows: (a) Liability insurance for bodily injury and property damage with a minimum limit of $300,000 combined single limit naming Lessor as "additional insured", (b) physical damage insurance for the amount of equipment cost or replacement value, whichever is higher, naming Lessor as "Loss Payee". Each such policy shall be with an insurer and such form satisfactory to Lessor including clauses requiring insurer to give at least 30 days written notice to Lessor of any alteration or cancelation and specifying that no action or misrepresentation by Lessee shall invalidate the policy. Lessor shall be under no obligation to inspect the policy or inform the Lessee if the policy does not conform to the requirements hereof. In the event Lessee fails to deliver to Lessor a certificate evidencing physical damage insurance, Lessee shall pay Lessor an amount equal to 1% of the equipment cost as compensation for additional risk for each month, or fraction thereof, Lessee fails to deliver such certificate.

10. Title/UCC/Power of Attorney: Lessee understands that Lessor will have sole title to the Equipment during the entire Lease Term, and Lessee agrees this is a "true Lease" and not one intended as security for purposes of Section 1-201 (37) of the Uniform Commercial Code. The Lessee shall keep the equipment free and clear from levies, attachments, liens, encumbrances, or other judicial processes of any kind and shall save Lessor harmless from and damage or loss thereby. Lessee hereby appoints Lessor as Lessee's attorney-in-fact to file financing statements to protect Lessor's interest hereunder in accordance with the Uniform Commercial Code, or other applicable law, Lessee hereby agrees that Lessor may make any adjustment in payments due to the actual cost of the equipment, a change in the sales or use tax rate, corrected description of the equipment, or proper allocation of any advance payments or security deposits, to date this lease, or fill in any blank spaces, and all such changes shall become incorporated herein.

11. Renewal: Unless Lessee notifies Lessor in writing sixty (60) days prior to the expiration of the lease, then this Lease shall automatically renew on a month to month basis and shall continue from month to month thereafter under the same terms and conditions with the exception that lease payment shall be 50% of the lease payment set forth herein, until terminated.

12. Default: Any of the following conditions shall constitute an event of default: (a) Lessee's failure to pay rent or any sum due Lessor or other party, on the due date; (b) Lessee's failure to observe, keep, or perform any other term, covenant, or condition of this lease or any other agreement with Lessor and such failure continues after the due date; (c) Lessee or any partner of Lessee if Lessee is a partnership, or any guarantor, dies, becomes insolvent or unable to pay debts when due, stops doing business as a going concern, merges, consolidates, makes an assignment for the benefit of creditors, or suffers a deterioration of financial health; (d) Lessee, any guarantor of Lessee, or partner if Lessee is a partnership, shall file or have filed against it, a petition for reorganization, liquidation, or similar relief under the federal bankruptcy laws, or if any trustee or receiver is appointed over it or over any part of its assets; (e) breach of any representation or warranty made by Lessee, or guarantor or any officer, partner, or member of Lessee in any document delivered to Lessor, failure of Lessee to fully identify any shareholder, partner, or member that owns or controls more than a 10% ownership interest in the Lessee, any misrepresentation or withholding of information by Lessee in any dealing with the Lessor that would cause Lessor to extend credit based on false or misleading information or financial data, fraudulent claims of ownership, or other acts by Lessee that might cause Lessor to misconstrue the credit worthiness or ownership of Lessee or of any guarantor of Lessee; (f) any levy, attachment, or seizure of the equipment. Remedies: Lessor and Lessee agree that Lessors damages suffered by reason of a default are uncertain and not capable of exact measurement at the time this lease is executed because the value of the equipment at the expiration of this lease is uncertain, therefore they agree that Lessor's loss as of any date shall be the sum of the following: (a) the amount of all rent and other amounts payable by Lessee with respect to items due but unpaid at the date of calculation, plus; (b) the amount of all unpaid rent for the balance of this lease agreement discounted from the respective date the payment becomes due at the rate of 8% per annum, plus; (c) the end of lease purchase option, if one was specified, otherwise 20% of the original amount of the equipment cost which represents Lessor's anticipated end of lease residual value. Upon occurrence of an event of default, and at any time thereafter, Lessor may terminate this lease and declare an amount equal to the Lessor's Loss as of the date of such notice to be immediately due and payable and Lessee agrees to immediately pay such sum. Lessor may recover interest on the unpaid balance of Lessor's Loss from the date it becomes payable until fully paid at the maximum rate permitted by Colorado law. If such amount is not paid upon demand by Lessee, Lessor may proceed by appropriate court action to enforce performance by Lessee of the applicable covenants of this agreement or to recover, for breach of this lease, Lessor's Loss as of the date the Lessor's Loss is declared due and payable, plus interest as set forth above. Lessor may recover all costs and expenses, including legal fees, collection fees or commissions, travel, or any other cost incurred by Lessor in enforcing the remedies herein. Upon termination of the lease by this paragraph, all rights of Lessee to use the equipment shall terminate but Lessee shall remain liable as provided herein. Lessee shall, at its expense, promptly deliver the equipment to Lessor at a location or locations specified by Lessor, or Lessor, or Lessor's agents may enter upon the premises where the equipment is located and take immediate possession of and remove the same without instituting legal proceedings. Damages occasioned by Lessor's taking possession of the equipment are hereby waived by Lessee. Upon repossession or surrender, and without the necessity of notice to Lessee, Lessor may retain the equipment in full satisfaction of Lessee's obligation hereunder, or sell or lease each item of equipment in such manner and upon such terms as Lessor in its sole discretion determines. The proceeds of such sale or lease shall first be applied to reimburse Lessor for expenses of repossession, storage, repair, transportation, and disposition of the equipment and then for Lessor's Loss and any additional amounts due under this paragraph. Lessee shall remain liable for any deficiency. Lessor may exercise any other right or remedy. Lessor shall recover legal costs and fees and all other expenses incurred by reason thereof. No remedy given in this paragraph is intended to be exclusive, and each shall be cumulative, but only to the extent necessary to permit Lessor to recover amounts for which Lessee is liable hereunder. No express or implied waiver by Lessor of any event of default shall constitute a waiver of any other event of default.

13. Security Deposit & Termination: To secure this lease, Lessee agrees to pay to Lessor the Security Deposit on page 1 at the time this lease is submitted to Lessor. If for any reason this lease is not finalized, it is specifically agreed that Lessor may retain the Security Deposit and such amount is fully earned by Lessor. Upon termination Lessor shall be entitled to a fee of 2% of the original cost of Equipment plus $50.00.

14. Consent to Colorado law, Jurisdiction, and Venue: This lease shall be deemed fully executed and performed in the State of Colorado and shall be governed and construed in accordance with the laws thereof, and Lessee hereby irrevocably submits generally and unconditionally to the exclusive jurisdiction of the District Court of County Court for the County of Larimer, Colorado. In the event either Lessor or Lessee brings any judicial proceedings in relation to any matter arising under this Lease Agreement, the parties further agree that such matters shall be adjudged or determined by the District or County Court for the County of Larimer, Colorado. Lessee further agrees that service of process in any such action shall be sufficient if made by certified mail, return receipt requested, to the address of the Lessee set forth herein.

15. Return of Equipment: On termination or expiration of this lease, or upon Lessee's default, Lessee shall, at its own cost and expense, return the equipment to Lessor at an address specified by Lessor in the same condition as originally received by Lessee, reasonable wear and tear excepted. The Lessee shall, in addition to all other payments due Lessor, pay to Lessor 3 (Three) times the amount as may be necessary to provide for replacement, whether repaired or replaced by Lessor or not, for all damaged, broken, or missing parts of the equipment or the operating and instruction manuals for the equipment.

16. Amounts Due: In the event this lease is construed to involve a loan of money and any amounts due herein are deemed to constitute interest, then without waiving any claim or defense to the contrary, no such amount shall exceed the maximum lawful interest rate for the State of Colorado or the state where venue is located. In the event Lessor ever collects or applies as interest any such amounts in excess of the maximum lawful rate for the state of venue, such amounts shall be deemed a prepayment of principal and if such principal is paid in full then any excess payments by Lessee shall immediately be refunded to Lessee.

17. Credit Information: Lessee hereby authorizes Lessor, or their assigns, to access business and consumer credit bureau reports as Lessor deems necessary and to report to any credit bureau of Lessor's choice any delinquency of payments due hereunder.

18. Miscellaneous: Captions are intended for convenience or reference only and shall not alter the text. This lease contains the entire agreement between the parties and with the exception of the agreements contained in paragraph 10, may not be altered, amended, or terminated except in writing by an executive officer of Lessor. This lease shall be enforceable only when signed by an executive officer of Lessor. Lessee agrees to defend Lessor against and indemnify (reimburse) Lessor for all claims, liabilities, costs and legal fees arising out of the leasing, use or possession of the equipment, including claims of property damage or injury to persons. This promise will continue after the end of the lease term.

19. Facsimile Statement: If this document is executed by you and thereafter sent to us by facsimile transmission, then until such time as we have received this document with your manual signature thereon, such facsimile transmission shall constitute, upon acceptance and execution by us in our offices, the original document and chattel paper and shall be admissible for all purposes as the original document. You agree to promptly forward to us the document with your manual signature thereon and upon receipt by us this document with your manual signature thereon shall constitute the chattel paper in lieu of such facsimile transmission.

5/2011 language

Accepted by Lessor: Lucrative Leasing			
By:	Title:	Date:	Lease #:

Scenario 3
Lease Agreement - ACH

Authorization Agreement for Automatic Withdrawals

LESSOR:_____(FUNDING SOURCE)_____

I (we)hereby authorize the above referenced LESSOR to initiate, on the **1st of each month**, debit entries and to initiate, if necessary, credit entries and adjustments for any debit entries in error to my (our) account indicated below and the bank named below.

Name on
Account: Company 3 _____

Bank
Name: Bank of Business _____ Ph:_____

Commercial Checking Account Number:_____ Lease Payment: $518.29_____

Transit / ABA Number (lower left corner of check, 9 digits):_____

This authority is to remain in full force and effect until LESSOR has received written notification from me(us)of its termination in such time and in such manner as to afford LESSOR and the bank a reasonable opportunity to act on it. We understand that our withdrawal of this authority without the express written consent of LESSOR shall constitute a default of the lease agreement for which this payment is being made.

If this Agreement is executed by you and thereafter sent to us by facsimile transmission, then until such time as we have received this Agreement with your manual signature thereon, such facsimile transmission shall constitute, upon acceptance and execution by us in our offices, the original Agreement and chattel paper and shall be admissible for all purposes as the original Agreement. You agree to promptly forward to us the Agreement with your manual signature thereon and upon receipt by us this Agreement with your manual signature thereon shall constitute the chattel paper in lieu of such facsimile transmission.

X_____   _____
Authorized Signer   Authorized Signer

_____   _____
Print Name   Print Name

_____   _____
Title   Date   Title   Date

ATTACH COPY OF CHECK

FOR OFFICE USE ONLY

ACH start date _____ 1, 2002   Lease #:_____

Scenario 3

Lease Agreement – Schedule A

Schedule "A"

Lease #: 32002

This Equipment Schedule "A" is to be attached to and become part of the lease dated _____ .

Quantity	Equipment Description	Serial #
1	1993 Utility Reefer Model 48102	

Supplier Information

SUPER TRUCKS
905 North Lake Way
Yakima   WA 98901

Scenario 3
Lease Agreement – Photo ID

Signer Identification Addendum
(Must Be Completed For All Signers)

Lease #: _32002_

Please include a copy of your valid driver's license including photo and signature.
(front & back may be required in certain states)

ATTACH PHOTO IDENTIFICATION WITH SIGNATURE

Photocopy Clear & Legible Driver's License Here

X_____
Signature of Driver's License Bearer

REVA200

Scenario 3
Insurance Request

Lessor: YOUR COMPANY NAME   Lease #: ___32002___
           YOUR COMPANY ADDRESS

INSURANCE AUTHORIZATION

To: AAAAA INSURANCE
       _____   Please input your insurance
       _____   information on the left.
       _____

Phone: (800) XXX-XXXX
Contact: Erica

We have entered into an equipment lease agreement for the equipment shown on the attached Lease Copy. This equipment is located as stated on the Lease.

This is a net lease and we are responsible for the full equipment cost in the amount of $ 13,953.25

Please see that we immediately have ALL RISK coverage for liability and full replacement cost of the equipment and that (FUNDING SOURCE) is shown as **LOSS PAYEE** and **ADDITIONAL INSURED** on the policy. Please forward a Certificate of Insurance and Loss Payable/Additional Insured Clause to:

                    FUNDING SOURCE (LESSOR)
           _____
           _____

Concurrent Certificates of Insurance, thirty (30) days notice in the event of cancellation or alteration, and general correspondence should be sent to the above addresses as well.

Sincerely,

            Lessee: COMPANY C _____
            X _____
            BY: ___ William Kent, Owner _____
            DATE EXECUTED BY LESSEE _____

Scenario 3
Assignment of Lease

Schedule Assignment of Lease

Date:_____ Lease Agreement Dated:_____Lease#_____32002_____

Lessee:__Company C_____

Leased Equipment

See Schedule "A" of this assigned Lease.

FOR VALUE RECEIVED, _____LUCRATIVE LEASING_____, (Assignor), the receipt and sufficiency of which Assignor acknowledges, does hereby sell, assign and transfer to **PAWNEE LEASING CORPORATION**, (Assignee) its successors and assigns, the annexed equipment lease agreement, any collateral agreement, any additional collateral in the form of stocks, bonds, certificates of deposit, any other agreement related to the above referenced lease agreement, and UCC-1 between Assignor, as lessor, and the lessee identified above, together with all of Assignor's rights, title and interest, and all ancillary rights in and to the equipment described therein, and all of the Assignor's rights and remedies thereunder, including, but not limited to, the right to collect any and all rental payments due and to become due thereon, the right to perfect any additional collateral or collateral agreement, and all monies due or to become due in connection with the exercise by the lessee of any option, if any, to purchase the equipment, and further including the right in Assignee's name to take all proceedings, legal, equitable or other, that Assignor might take, save for this assignment. The equipment in this assigned lease is new unless otherwise disclosed and the consideration paid by Assignee does not include any service or other item of value that has not been disclosed on the lease agreement or the invoice provided to Assignor. To the best of Assignor's knowledge all parties to the lease were competent at the time of execution, there is no undisclosed agreement, concession or litigation of any nature affecting the lease, and there are no valid defenses in law or equity to the lease as it exists in the hands of the Assignee after this assignment. Assignor has full and perfect title to convey the lease and equipment free of any encumbrance, lien, or any other interest of third parties, the equipment which is the subject of this lease has been shipped and installed in accordance with the lease and on the dates specified, no condition exists that would permit the lessee to not pay the lease payments in full and the Assignor is authorized to do business in the state of lessee's location. Assignor has provided Assignee all information about the lessee, the equipment, the credit investigation, and the vendor that is known to Assignor. The terms and conditions of the lease agreement shall survive this Assignment. The terms of this Assignment shall be binding upon the heirs and successors of the parties.

If this document is executed by you and thereafter sent to us by facsimile transmission, then until such time as we have received this document with your manual signature thereon, such facsimile transmission shall constitute, upon acceptance and execution by us in our offices, the original document and chattel paper and shall be admissible for all purposes as the original document. You agree to promptly forward to us the document with your manual signature thereon and upon receipt by us this document with your manual signature thereon shall constitute the chattel paper in lieu of such facsimile transmission.

WITNESS: ASSIGNOR: LUCRATIVE LEASING

_____   _____
                                                              Authorized Signer

                                                       _____
                                                                       Title

                                                       _____
                                                                Company Name

Scenario 3
Broker Fee Invoice

BROKER FEE INVOICE

LESSOR:............................... LUCRATIVE LEASING

LESSEE NAME:........................ COMPANY C

APPROVAL NUMBER:............... 32002

TOTAL LEASE AMOUNT:........... $ 13,953.75

MONTHLY PAYMENT:.............. $ 481.68

RATE FACTORS:...................... Buy: .03002   Sell: .03452

OF ADVANCED PAYMENTS:.... 20% Security Deposit

PURCHASE OPTION:.................. FMV
      Broker Commission........... $ 2,093.06   Points: 15
      + Doc fees collected .... $ 415.00
      - Docs fees required by bank $ 350.00
             Sub-Total $ 2,158.06
Less Advanced Money Received . . . . $ 3,140.75

NET COMMISSION DUE........... $ (982.69) Broker Pays Funding Source

Please Standard Overnight BROKER & VENDOR checks via Federal Express or UPS.

Please send broker check to: LUCRATIVE LEASING

   FedEx #: (Account #)

Scenario 3

Insurance Binder

Scenario 3
Condition Report

LOCAL ████████

TRAILER DESCRIPTION & CONDITION REPORT

STOCK # 1109 YEAR 93 MAKE Utility VIN ████████

WEIGHT 17820
LENGTH 48
OUTSIDE HEIGHT
WIDTH 102
FRAMED
FRAMELESS X
FRAME (STEEL/ALUM) Steel
END DUMP
BELLY DUMP
SPREAD AXLE Yes
FIXED AXLE
FLOOR TYPE Ex Alum
FLOOR CONDITION Excellent
TIRE SIZE 11·24 5
RUBBER % 75%
WHEELS Steel
BRAKES 70%
TYPE FIFTH WHEEL
SUSPENSION TYPE Air Ride
INSIDE LINING Kemlite
METAL CONDITION Excellent
REFRIGERAITON UNIT Thermo King
YEAR 93
MAKE
MODEL SB D
SERIAL #
HOURS Approx 46°° or 4700
PRICE $ 13,500
NOTES: Trailer in Excellent Condition

Scenario 3
Vendor Invoice

Invoice

SUPER TRUCKS
905 North Lake Way
Yakima, WA 98901

(800) XXX-XXXX

DATE	INVOICE #
10/19/2002	3

BILL TO	SHIP TO
Lucrative Leasing	COMPANY C 600 Accord Street. Grandview, WA 98880

P.O. NUMBER	TERMS	REP	SHIP	VIA	F.O.B.	PROJECT
	Lease		10/19/2002			

QUANTITY	ITEM CODE	DESCRIPTION	PRICE EACH	AMOUNT
1		1993 Utility Reefer Model #48102		$13,953.25

| | Total | $13,953.25 |

In Conclusion, it is important to follow through on all of your lease applications. Take them as far as they can go. You will find many times that while one aspect of an applicant is weak; another may be stronger than normal enabling you to offset the weakness.

Many equipment lease brokers who fail at this business fail because they do not have the drive to work hard and/or are shy about requesting tax returns and financials. Do not be fearful about requesting a financial package from your client. You are helping your client acquire equipment which is important to the growth of his/her company. Lastly, in Scenario 3, LL charged 15 percent commission on an already expensive rate. This was because no other leasing company could get this guy a lease. In a situation where you work this hard and dig this deep to approve a lease, you have the opportunity to make some good money if you choose to do so.

SECTION 12

DOCUMENTATION EXAMPLES

In This Section:

- Documentation Examples

Documentation Examples (also available on Cd-Rom)

The following examples have been put on a Cd-Rom which you can purchase on our website www.Theleasingexpert.com. Feel free to utilize all of the following documents for use with your new or existing company. REGARDING THE LEASE CONTRACT DOCUMENTS: The use of the generic lease documentation is unlawful. The lease documents have been created at the expense of funding sources. Funding sources will supply you with lease documents. If you grow to a point where you will require your own lease documentation, it would be best to consult an attorney and have some created which you have proprietary ownership of.

Example A.   Lease Application

> This lease application is perfect to start with and you can put your company information at the top: Company Name, Address and Phones. The lease application asks for all of the pertinent information from your potential customer.

Example B.   Bank Reference Sheet

> As you read in Section 5, "Process the Application", you will be required to get a bank reference on your customers. This blank reference sheet is a good document for you to utilize for obtaining bank references. Fax this form to the reference for a rating on your customer.

Example C.   Trade Reference Sheet

> See Example B. description.

Example D.   Comparable Loan Reference Sheet

> See Example B. description

Example E.   Credit Authorization

> Sometimes, if the applicant does not sign the bottom of the lease application, or you find out that you need additional signatures as requested by a funding source for a particular lease application, this form can be used to obtain those.

Example F.   Vendor Profile

> It is not important to print this one out right away. The vendor profile is requested by a funding source when they are having trouble obtaining historical data on a vendor for one of your deals or when a vendor requires money up front. Vendor profiles are usually very simple forms that the vendor completes which includes information such as: exact name of the business, address, officers of the company, time in business, number of sales people, etc. Each funding source will have their own version of a vendor profile, so don't worry about using this one unless you need it.

Example G.   Turn Down (Decline) Letter

> According to the law, you have to send letters to the customers you turn down. You could use this letter as a starting point. Ask the credit reporting agency that you order your credit bureaus through for more information on this topic.

Example H.   Lease Proposal / Commitment Fee Letter

On lease transactions that look like they are going to take some time to work because of poor credit history, or some other company turmoil, you may want to get a proposal signed along with a commitment fee so that you do not work for nothing if they decide to "walk away" after you put a lot of time into the deal. This is a good example of one. There are many others as well. A commitment fee letter is also good when someone is requesting a very large dollar amount. It keeps them loyal to you while you seek out the hard-to-get funds.

Example I.   Documentation Request Worksheet

You should print one of these out right away. This is the worksheet that you will complete when you are ready to prepare documentation for a deal. This worksheet outlines all of the pertinent information needed for processing the lease documents, including how much your commission is!

Example J.   Generic Lease Documents

There will be no examples of funding source documents. Every funding source has their own version of documents. This entire section focuses on generic documents. Generic documents are standardized forms that are used by most leasing companies in the country. They cover all of the legalities necessary for documenting a lease contract.

J-1   Lease Agreement

J-2   Purchase Agreement

J-3   Equipment Schedule "A"

J-4   Personal Guaranty

J-5   Corporate Guaranty

J-6   Resolution of Board of Directors

J-7   Change LOCATION Addendum

J-8   Change TERM OF LEASE Addendum

J-9   Change LEGAL NAME & ADDRESS OF LESSEE Addendum

J-10   Change EQUIPMENT DESCRIPTION Addendum

J-11   Assignment of Lease

J-12   Assignment of Invoice

J-13   Disclaimer of Ownership

J-14   Landlord Waiver

Example K.   Insurance Request Letter

As mentioned in the "Funding" section of Section 5, the insurance request letter is utilized in the final stages of a lease transaction to obtain the liability insurance information of the lessee in order to get liability insurance coverage for the funding source funding the lease. Feel free to use this one. You will also find that funding sources all have their own version of this form too.

Example L.   Documentation Cover Letter

This letter is optional for you to use when sending documentation out yourself. It is a standard form that requests the usual items. When sending out this letter, I use a highlighter to emphasize photocopying the ID and the amount of money they are supposed to mail in with the signed lease documents. Feel free to use this one or create your own using this one as a reference.

Example M.   Tax Returns – Individual/Personal

Individual tax returns will always be required when your lease applicant falls short of some of the lending criteria of your funding source. For example, strong personal tax returns can offset the applicant's weaknesses of not having a lot of money in the bank at the time they are requesting money, or maybe having too much debt on their credit bureau.

Example N.   Tax Returns – Schedule C

The Schedule C is a form that is only included in individual/personal tax returns when the company is a sole proprietorship. The Schedule C displays income from business activity. If your funding source requests a full financial package on a sole proprietorship, then you will ask for 2 years of the personal tax returns and Schedule C's for both years.

Example O.   Tax Returns – Corporation

If your applicant is incorporated, then they will have an entire 2nd set of tax returns for each year for their corporation's life. A corporation is a separate entity from the individual. If your funding sources ask you for a full financial package on a corporation, then you will ask the applicant for both his/her last 2 years personal tax returns and 2 years corporate returns.

Example P.   Tax Returns – S Corporation

An S-corporation is just another form of corporation, the same rules as described Example O. applies to an S-corporation.

Example Q.   Personal Financial Statement

A Personal Financial Statement always accompanies a full financial package that you send on a lease applicant to your funding source. This will show your applicant's current net worth. It identifies whether a person owns real estate, cars, stocks, cash, bank accounts, etc. It also makes them list debts and liabilities. You can use this form or funding sources will also have a version that you can use.

Example R.   Vendor Invoice Sample

As mentioned in the "Funding" section of Section 5, the vendor invoice is key to funding your lease. This is a general idea of what the invoice should look like when complete.

Example S.   Broker Fee Invoice

Broker fee invoices come in all shapes and sizes. I developed this broker fee invoice for my company and use it all of the time. It defines all the pertinent details of the lease terms and your commission. I will send this along to the funding source with the lessee's completed documents. The funding sources will have their own broker fee invoices for you if you do not choose to use this one.

Example T.   Thank You & Assignment of Lease Letter

This is an example of a letter, thanking your lessee for doing business with you and letting them know that they will be making payments to funding source X, not your company. The funding source will let the customer know where to send payments.

Example U.   Fax Cover Letter

The Fax Cover Letter will be used many times daily. Use this or design your own. Put your company name, address, phone numbers and logo if you have one.

Example V.   Rate Factor Sheet

In Section 6 you learned how to calculate lease payments using rate factors. This is an example of a rate factor sheet that a funding source will provide you once you are approved with them to do business. You will have rate factor sheets for each different funding source. All funding sources have different rate factors. The rate factors for higher risk deals will be much higher than those for strong companies. Organize all your different rate factor sheets in a 3-ring binder for easy access when quoting customers and vendors.

Example W.   Equipment Condition Report

Often when you are trying to approve a lease applicant for used equipment, the funding source will request an equipment condition report. Feel free to use this one. Funding sources will almost always provide one if you do not have one.

Example X.   Lead Qualification Sheet: End User

If you choose to telemarket for lessees directly, this is a good script to use until you develop your own.

Example Y.   Lead Qualification Sheet: Vendor

In Section 5, I discussed the 3-call vendor prospecting cycle. This is the worksheet that you can use as a guide to finding prospective vendors.

Example Z.   Tax Returns - Schedule K-1

Like the Schedule C, the Schedule K is a form included in personal tax returns to show income generated from a partnership.

Example A
Lease Application

Lease Application

VENDOR INFORMATION

Vendor Name

Vendor Address	City	State	Zip

Contact Person	Telephone number ( )

Equipment Cost $ _____

Initial Term _____

Equipment Description _____

LESSEE COMPANY INFORMATION

Company Name

Company Address	City	County	State	Zip

Signer	Titln	Telephone number ( )

Special Requirements _____

Nature of Business	Type of business __ Non-Profit __ Proprietorship __ Partnership __ Corporation	No. of Years In Business

PERSONAL INFORMATION ON OFFICERS, PARTNERS, OR GUARANTORS

Name	Title	Social Security Number		Driver's License Number
Home Address	City	State	Zip	How Long? / Home Phone Number ( )
Previous Address	City	State	Zip	Own / Rent Present Home?
Name	Title	Social Security Number		Driver's License Number
Home Address	City	State	Zip	How Long? / Home Phone Number ( )
Previous Address	City	State	Zip	Own / Rent Present Home?

COMPANY BANK REFERENCES - TWO YEAR HISTORY

Name of Bank/Branch	How Long?	Chkg. Acct. # / Loan Acct. #	Telephone No. ( )	Contact Officer
Name of Bank/Branch	How Long?	Chkg. Acct. # / Loan Acct. #	Telephone No. ( )	Contact Officer
Name of Bank/Branch	How Long?	Chkg. Acct. # / Loan Acct. #	Telephone No. ( )	Contact Officer

TRADE REFERENCES - TWO YEAR HISTORY

Name of Supplier	City/State	Telephone No. ( )	Contact Person
Name of Supplier	City/State	Telephone No. ( )	Contact Person
Name of Supplier	City/State	Telephone No. ( )	Contact Person

I/we hereby authorize you to whom this application is made, or your agents, to investigate my/our credit worthiness and will provide financial statements, tax returns, etc., as you deem necessary. I/we agree that the security deposit is not refundable unless the application is rejected by Lessor. By the execution of the lease agreement, I/we warrant that the information submitted herein is true and correct and hereby authorized references contained herein to release any necessary information. Further, I/we warrant it is understood that Lessor reserves the right to reverse any credit decision if the information contained herein is found to be incorrect, and I/we will indemnify Lessor for any and all costs incurred with this application for credit including any cost incurred in the placement or reservation of the intended leased equipment based on the information contained herein.

Signature X	Date:

Example B
Bank Reference Sheet

BANK RATING REQUEST _____

TO: _____   RE: _____

_____   _____

ATTN: _____   _____

ACCOUNT #: _____

CREDIT MANAGER,

THE ABOVE NAMED PARTY HAS APPLIED FOR CREDIT IN CONNECTION WITH AN EQUIPMENT LEASE/PURCHASE. WE WOULD APPRECIATE RECEIVING THE FOLLOWING INFORMATION AS A CREDIT REFERENCE ON THEIR ACCOUNT. ANY INFORMATION PROVIDED WILL BE HELD IN THE STRICTEST CONFIDENCE.

DATE OPENED: _____   AVERAGE BALANCE: _____

OF NSF'S: _____   # OF OD'S: _____   IF CLOSED, WHEN? _____
(within last 6 months)   (within last 6 months)

RATING AND/OR COMMENTS: _____

NAME EXACTLY AS IT APPEARS ON THE ACCOUNT: _____

_____

ARE THERE ANY LOANS/NOTES/LINES OF CREDIT?   YES   NO
IF YES, PLEASE DETAIL BELOW:
TYPE   OPEN DATE   HIGH CREDIT   BALANCE   (UN) SECURED?   RATING

_____

INFORMATION SUPPLIED BY: _____
TITLE: _____

AS A COURTESY TO OUR MUTUAL CUSTOMER, PLEASE REPLY BY FAX OR PHONE WITHIN FOUR HOURS FROM THE TIME YOU RECEIVE THIS REQUEST.
PLEASE FAX TO: (YOUR FAX #)   **OR   CALL** (YOUR PHONE #)

THANK YOU!

_____   _____   _____
CREDIT MANAGER   **DATE**   **TIME**

Example C
Trade Reference Sheet

TRADE REFERENCE REQUEST

TO: _____   RE: _____

_____   _____

ATTN: _____   _____

ACCOUNT #: _____

CREDIT MANAGER,

THE ABOVE NAMED PARTY HAS APPLIED FOR CREDIT IN CONNECTION WITH AN EQUIPMENT LEASE/PURCHASE. WE WOULD APPRECIATE RECEIVING THE FOLLOWING INFORMATION AS A CREDIT REFERENCE ON THEIR ACCOUNT. ANY INFORMATION PROVIDED WILL BE HELD IN THE STRICTEST CONFIDENCE.

DATE OPENED: _____   HIGH CREDIT: _____

BALANCE? _____ CURRENT? YES NO TERMS: _____

PAYMENT HISTORY: PROMPT SLOW   *If slow, how many days on average:* _____

GOODS / SERVICES YOU SUPPLY TO THEM: _____

COMMENTS:

_____

_____

_____

INFORMATION SUPPLIED BY: _____
                    TITLE: _____

AS A COURTESY TO OUR MUTUAL CUSTOMER, PLEASE REPLY BY FAX OR PHONE WITHIN FOUR HOURS FROM THE TIME YOU RECEIVE THIS REQUEST.

PLEASE FAX TO: (YOUR FAX NUMBER)   OR   CALL (YOUR PHONE NUMBER)

THANK YOU!

_____   _____ _____
CREDIT MANAGER   DATE   TIME

Example D

Comparable Loan Reference Sheet

LOAN REFERENCE REQUEST

TO: _____   RE: _____
_____   _____
_____
ATTN: _____

ACCOUNT #: _____

CREDIT MANAGER,

THE ABOVE NAMED PARTY HAS APPLIED FOR A CREDIT ACCOUNT WITH OUR COMPANY. WE WOULD APPRECIATE RECEIVING THE FOLLOWING INFORMATION AS A CREDIT REFERENCE ON THEIR ACCOUNT. ANY INFORMATION PROVIDED WILL BE HELD IN THE STRICTEST CONFIDENCE.

DATE OPENED: _____   TERM: _____

ORIGINAL BALANCE: _____

CURRENT BALANCE: _____   # LATES: _____ x 30 _____ X 60 _____ x 90

RATING AND/OR COMMENTS: _____

INFORMATION SUPPLIED BY: _____
TITLE: _____

AS A COURTESY TO OUR MUTUAL CUSTOMER, PLEASE REPLY BY FAX OR PHONE WITHIN **FOUR HOURS** FROM THE TIME YOU RECEIVE THIS REQUEST.
PLEASE FAX TO: (YOUR FAX NUMBER HERE)   **OR**   **CALL** (YOUR PHONE NUMBER HERE)

THANK YOU!

_____   _____ _____PST
CREDIT MANAGER   **DATE**   **TIME**

Example E
Credit Authorization

CREDIT AUTHORIZATION

AUTHORIZATION TO RELEASE INFORMATION

I/We authorize (YOUR COMPANY NAME HERE) and its funding sources to make whatever credit inquiries it deems necessary in connection with my credit application. I authorize and instruct any person or consumer-reporting agency to comply and furnish any information it may have or obtain in response to such credit inquiries.

_____   _____
Signature   Date

Example F
Vendor Profile

Vendor Profile

Company Name:_____

Address:_____

City:_____ State:_____ Zip:_____

Phone:_____ Fax:_____ E-mail:_____

President/Owner:_____

Sales Manager:_____

Corporation:_____ Partnership:_____ Proprietorship:_____

Equipment Type(s) Sold:_____

_____

Personal Information of Owner(s)/ Stockholder(s) (Required if Closely-Held)

Name:_____
                                                          Title

Address:_____
              Street   City   State   Zip

Social Security Number:_____ Percentage Owned_____%

Name:_____
                                                          Title

Address:_____
              Street   City   State   Zip

Social Security Number:_____ Percentage Owned_____%

Trades (Manufacturers of Equipment Sold)

Name:_____	Name:_____
Contact:_____	Contact:_____
Account #:_____	Account #:_____
Phone:_____	Phone:_____

Bank

Name:_____	Phone:_____
Contact:_____	Account #:_____

REV4200

Example G
Turn Down (Decline) Letter

DATE

BUSINESS, INC.
123 Main Street
Seattle, WA 98000

Dear Mr. Business,

Thank you for the opportunity to consider your request for credit. We regret that we are unable to approve your application at this time.

In reviewing your application we received information from one of the three major credit reporting agencies. Their only role was to provide us with the credit information about you. Therefore, they will be unable to supply the reason why your request for credit cannot be approved at this time.

The principal factor which contributed to this decision was the following:

_____Inability to establish comparable debt	_____Bankruptcy
_____Minimal Banking Average	_____Type of Collateral
_____Time in Business	_____Derogatory Personal Credit
_____Insufficient income for amount of credit requested	_____Derogatory Business Credit
_____Other_____	
_____Pay history with current funding source	_____ _____

Thank you again for considering First Sierra Financial. If you have any questions about our decision please feel free to contact us at (800) 662-6703.

Sincerely,
(YOUR COMPANY NAME)

(YOUR NAME)
Account Manager

Example H
Lease Proposal / Commitment Fee Letter

Lease Proposal

Date: _____

Lessee: _____

Structure: Lease

Equipment: _____

Equipment Cost: $_____ + APPLICABLE TAXES

Payment: $_____ + APPLICABLE TAXES

Term: _____ Months

End of Lease Purchase Option: _____

Personal Guaranty: _____

Documentation Fee: $_____ (one-time, payable with balance of security deposit)

Payments Collected: By ACH authorization on 5th day of each month during lease term.

PAYMENT/ADVANCE: The payments shall be payable monthly, with the security deposit equal to: _____ due prior to funding.

OPERATING EXPENSES: All operating expenses, including insurance, maintenance and taxes will be the responsibility of the lessee.

GUARANTORS: Personal guarantee of the principals will be required.

PERFORMANCE & EXPENSE DEPOSIT: First monthly payment of $_____ In the event proposed lease transaction is approved and booked, said payment will be applied to the advance rental payment provided for in the lease agreement. If the proposed lease is not approved, said payment will be returned. In the event the said proposed lease is not booked at the election of the proposed lessee for any reason, the above stated deposit will be retained in its entirely by _____ as compensation for expenses incurred in investigating the credit of proposed lessee and as compensation for other costs and expenses including general overhead expenses incurred by _____ in the proposed transaction.

THE PROVISIONS OF THIS LEASE PROPOSAL DO NOT AND SHALL NOT BE INTERPRETED TO CONSTITUTE A COMMITMENT BY_____, TO ACCEPT THIS TRANSACTION.

DATE: _____   _____

                         BY: _____

THE ABOVE TERMS AND CONDITIONS HAVE BEEN READ AND UNDERSTOOD BY PROPOSED LESSEE AND ARE HEREBY AGREED TO.

DATE: _____   BY:_____
                                 Name and Title

Example I
Documentation Request

DOCUMENTATION REQUEST WORKSHEET

SALES REPRESENTATIVE: _____ DATE: _____

LESSEE INFORMATION

COMPLETE LESSEE NAME: _____

BILLING ADDRESS: _____

CITY, STATE, ZIP: _____ PHONE: (____) _____

EQUIPMENT LOCATION: _____

SIGNER: _____ TITLE: _____ PG: YES NO

SIGNER: _____ TITLE: _____ PG: YES NO

VENDOR AND EQUIPMENT INFORMATION

VENDOR NAME: _____
STREET ADDRESS: _____
PHONE: (_____) _____ CONTACT PERSON: _____

EQUIPMENT LEASE TERMS

LEASE AMOUNT: $ _____ SALES TAX INCLUDED: YES   NO

LEASE TERM: _____ MONTHS   BUY-OUT: 10% PUT $1.00 OTHER_____

LEASE PAYMENT: $ _____ MONTHLY TAX (%): $_____

ADVANCED PAYMENTS: 1 ONLY   1+1   10% SEC.   OTHER _____

FACTORS: *Buy Rate:* _____ *Sell Rate:* _____
GROSS COMMISSION   (%): $ _____

DOCUMENTATION SHIPPING INFORMATION

SEND DOCUMENTS TO:

(   ) FED-X TO LESSEE AT LOCATION ABOVE

(   ) FED-X TO LESSEE AT FOLLOWING LOCATION: _____
                                                 _____
                                                 _____

Example J-1
Generic Lease Agreement

LESSOR	LEASE NUMBER

FULL LEGAL NAME AND ADDRESS OF LESSEE	SUPPLIER OF EQUIPMENT (COMPLETE ADDRESS)

JOINTLY AND SEVERALLY RESPONSIBLE

QUANTITY	DESCRIPTION, MODEL #, CATALOG #, SERIAL # OR OTHER IDENTIFICATION

EQUIPMENT LEASED

EQUIPMENT LOCATION IF DIFFERENT

STREET ADDRESS _____

CITY _____ COUNTY _____ STATE _____ ZIP _____

TERMS	AMOUNT OF EACH PAYMENT (PLUS SALES TAX, IF APPLICABLE)	MONTHLY OTHER/SPECIFY	TERM OF LEASE (NO. OF MONTHS)	NO. OF PAYMENTS	SECURITY DEPOSIT

TERMS AND CONDITIONS OF LEASE

1. **LEASE.** Lessee hereby leases from Lessor, and Lessor leases to Lessee, the personal property described above, together with any replacement parts, additions, repairs or accessories now or hereafter incorporated in or affixed to it (hereinafter referred to as the "Equipment").

2. **ACCEPTANCE OF EQUIPMENT.** Lessee agrees to inspect the Equipment and to execute an Acknowledgment and Acceptance of Equipment by Lessee notice, as provided by Lessor, after the Equipment has been delivered and after Lessee is satisfied that the Equipment is satisfactory in every respect. Lessee hereby authorizes Lessor to insert in this Lease serial numbers or other identifying data with respect to the Equipment.

3. **DISCLAIMER OF WARRANTIES AND CLAIMS; LIMITATION OF REMEDIES. THERE ARE NO WARRANTIES BY OR ON BEHALF OF LESSOR.** Lessee acknowledges and agrees by his signature below as follows:

(a) LESSOR MAKES NO WARRANTIES EITHER EXPRESS OR IMPLIED AS TO THE CONDITION OF THE EQUIPMENT, ITS MERCHANTABILITY, ITS FITNESS OR SUITABILITY FOR ANY PARTICULAR PURPOSE, ITS DESIGN, ITS CAPACITY, ITS QUALITY, OR WITH RESPECT TO ANY CHARACTERISTICS OF THE EQUIPMENT;

(b) Lessee has fully inspected the Equipment which it has requested Lessor to acquire and lease to Lessee, and the Equipment is in good condition and to Lessee's complete satisfaction;

(c) Lessee leases the Equipment "as is" and with all faults;

(d) Lessee specifically acknowledges that the Equipment is leased to Lessee solely for commercial or business purposes and not for personal, family, household, or agricultural purposes;

(e) If the Equipment is not properly installed, does not operate as represented or warranted by the supplier or manufacturer, or is unsatisfactory for any reason, regardless of cause or consequence, Lessee's only remedy, if any, shall be against the supplier or manufacturer of the Equipment and not against Lessor;

(f) Provided Lessee is not in default under this Lease, Lessor assigns to Lessee solely for the purpose of making and prosecuting any such claim, all of the rights which Lessor has against the supplier or the manufacturer of the Equipment;

(g) LESSEE SHALL HAVE NO REMEDY FOR CONSEQUENTIAL OR INCIDENTAL DAMAGES AGAINST LESSOR; and

(h) NO DEFECT, DAMAGE, OR UNFITNESS OF THE EQUIPMENT FOR ANY PURPOSE SHALL RELIEVE LESSEE OF THE OBLIGATION TO PAY RENT OR RELIEVE LESSEE OF ANY OTHER OBLIGATION UNDER THIS LEASE.

INITIALS _____

The parties have specifically negotiated and agreed to the foregoing paragraph.

4. **STATUTORY FINANCE LEASE.** Lessee agrees and acknowledges that it is the intent of both parties to this Lease that it qualify as a statutory finance lease under Article 2A of the Uniform Commercial Code. Lessee acknowledges and agrees that Lessee has selected both (1) the Equipment; and (2) the supplier from whom Lessor is to purchase the Equipment. Lessee acknowledges that Lessor has not participated in any way in Lessee's selection of the Equipment or of the supplier, and Lessor has not selected, manufactured, or supplied the Equipment.

LESSEE IS ADVISED THAT IT MAY HAVE RIGHTS UNDER THE CONTRACT EVIDENCING THE LESSOR'S PURCHASE OF THE EQUIPMENT FROM THE SUPPLIER CHOSEN BY LESSEE AND THAT LESSEE SHOULD CONTACT THE SUPPLIER OF THE EQUIPMENT FOR A DESCRIPTION OF ANY SUCH RIGHTS.

5. **ASSIGNMENT BY LESSEE PROHIBITED.** WITHOUT LESSOR'S PRIOR WRITTEN CONSENT, LESSEE SHALL NOT ASSIGN THIS LEASE OR SUBLEASE THE EQUIPMENT OR ANY INTEREST THEREIN, OR PLEDGE OR TRANSFER THIS LEASE, OR OTHERWISE DISPOSE OF THE EQUIPMENT COVERED HEREBY.

6. **COMMENCEMENT; RENTAL PAYMENTS; INTERIM RENTALS.** This Lease shall commence upon the written acceptance hereof by Lessor and shall, upon full performance and observance by Lessee of each and every term, condition and covenant set forth in this Lease, any Schedules hereto and any extensions hereof. Rental payments shall be in the amounts and frequency as set forth on the face of this Lease or any Schedules hereto. In addition to regular rentals, Lessee shall pay to Lessor interim rent for the use of the Equipment prior to the due date of the first payment. Interim rent shall be in an amount equal to 1/30th of the monthly rental, multiplied by the number of days elapsing between the date on which the Equipment is accepted by Lessee and the commencement date of this Lease, together with the number of days elapsing between commencement of the Lease and the due date of the first payment. The payment of interim rent shall be due and payable upon Lessee's receipt of invoice from Lessor. The rental period under the Lease shall terminate following the last day of the terms stated on the face hereof or on any Schedule hereto unless such Lease or Schedule has been extended or otherwise modified. Lessor shall have no obligation to Lessee under this Lease if the Equipment, for whatever reason, is not delivered to Lessee within ninety (90) days after Lessee signs the Lease. Lessor shall have no obligation to Lessee under this Lease if Lessee fails to execute and deliver to Lessor an Acknowledgment and Acceptance of Equipment by Lessee acknowledging its acceptance of the Equipment within thirty (30) days after it is delivered to Lessee, with respect to this Lease or any Schedule hereto.

THIS LEASE IS NOT CANCELABLE OR TERMINABLE BY LESSEE.

SEE REVERSE SIDE FOR ADDITIONAL TERMS AND CONDITIONS WHICH ARE A PART OF THIS LEASE.

LESSEE UNDERSTANDS AND ACKNOWLEDGES THAT NO BROKER OR SUPPLIER, NOR ANY SALESMAN, BROKER, OR AGENT OF ANY BROKER OR SUPPLIER, IS AN AGENT OF LESSOR. NO BROKER OR SUPPLIER, NOR ANY SALESMAN, BROKER, OR AGENT OF ANY BROKER OR SUPPLIER, IS AUTHORIZED TO WAIVE OR ALTER ANY TERM OR CONDITION OF THIS LEASE AND NO REPRESENTATION AS TO THE EQUIPMENT OR ANY OTHER MATTER BY THE BROKER OR SUPPLIER, NOR ANY SALESMAN, BROKER, OR AGENT OF ANY BROKER OR SUPPLIER, SHALL IN ANY WAY AFFECT LESSEE'S DUTY TO PAY THE RENTALS AND TO PERFORM LESSEE'S OBLIGATIONS SET FORTH IN THIS LEASE.

7. **CHOICE OF LAW.** This Lease shall not be effective until signed by Lessor at its principal office listed above. This Lease shall be considered to have been made in the state of Lessor's principal place of business listed above and shall be interpreted in accordance with the laws and regulations of the state of Lessor's principal place of business.

Lessee agrees to jurisdiction in the state of Lessor's principal place of business listed above in any action, suit or proceeding regarding this Lease, and concedes that it, and each of them, transacted business in the state of Lessor's principal place of business listed above by entering into this Lease. In the event of any legal action with regard to this Lease or the equipment covered hereby, Lessee agrees that venue may be had in the County of Lessor's principal place of business.

LESSEE: _____

LESSOR: _____

_____ DATE _____

_____ DATE _____

_____ DATE _____

FORM 104 REV. 2/97

Example J-1 2

Generic Lease Agreement (Page 2)

8. SECURITY DEPOSIT. As security for the prompt and full payment of the amounts due under this Lease, and Lessee's complete performance of all of its obligations under this Lease, and any extension or renewal hereof, Lessee has deposited with Lessor the security amount set forth in the section above as "Security Deposit." In the event any default shall be made in the performance of any of Lessee's obligations under this Lease, Lessor shall have the right, but shall not be obligated, to apply the security deposit to the curing of such default. Within 10 days after Lessor mails notice to Lessee that Lessor has applied any portion of the security deposit to the curing of any default, Lessee shall restore said security deposit to the full amount set forth above. On the expiration or earlier termination or cancellation of this Lease, or any extension or renewal period, provided Lessee has paid all of the rent called for and fully performed all other provisions of this Lease, Lessor will return to the Lessee any then remaining balance of said security deposit, without interest. Said security deposit may be commingled with Lessor's other funds.

9. LIMITED PREARRANGED AMENDMENTS; SPECIFIC POWER OF ATTORNEY. In the event it is necessary to amend the terms of this Lease to reflect a change in one or more of the following conditions:

    (a) Lessor's actual cost of procuring the Equipment, or

    (b) Lessor's actual cost of providing the Equipment to Lessee, or

    (c) A change in rental payments as a result of (1) or (2), above, or

    (d) Description of the Equipment;

Lessee agrees that any such amendment shall be described in a letter from Lessor to Lessee, and unless within 15 days after the date of such letter Lessee objects in writing to Lessor, this Lease shall be deemed amended and such amendments shall be incorporated in this Lease herein as if originally and fully performed for Lessee.

    Lessee grants to Lessor a specific power of attorney for Lessor to use as follows: (1) Lessor may sign and file on Lessee's behalf any document Lessor deems necessary to perfect or protect Lessor's interest in the Equipment or pursuant to the Uniform Commercial Code; and (2) Lessor may sign, endorse or negotiate for Lessee's benefit any instrument representing proceeds from any policy of insurance covering the Equipment.

10. LOCATION. The Equipment shall be kept at the location specified above or, if none is specified, at Lessee's address as set forth above and shall not be removed without Lessor's prior written consent.

11. USE. Lessee shall use the Equipment in a careful manner, make all necessary repairs at Lessee's expense, and comply with all laws relating to its possession, use, or maintenance, and shall not make any alterations, additions, or improvements to the Equipment without Lessor's prior written consent. All additions, repairs or improvements made to the Equipment shall belong to Lessor.

12. OWNERSHIP; PERSONALTY. The Equipment is, and shall remain, the property of Lessor, and Lessee shall have no right, title or interest in the Equipment except as expressly set forth in this Lease. The Equipment shall remain personal property even though installed in or attached to real property.

13. SURRENDER. By this Lease, Lessee acquires no ownership rights in the Equipment, and has no option to purchase same. Upon the expiration, or earlier termination or cancellation of this Lease, or in the event of a default under Paragraph 21, hereof, Lessee, at its expense, shall return the Equipment in good repair, ordinary wear and tear resulting from proper use thereof alone excepted, by delivering it, packed and ready for shipment, to such place or carrier as Lessor may specify.

14. RENEWAL. At the expiration of the Lease, Lessee shall return the Equipment in accordance with Paragraph 13, hereof. At Lessee's option, this Lease may be continued on a month-to-month basis until 30 days after Lessee returns the Equipment to Lessor. In the event the Lease is so continued, Lessee shall pay to Lessor rentals in the same periodic amount indexed under "Amount of Each Payment," above.

15. LOSS AND DAMAGE. Lessee shall at all times after signing this Lease bear the entire risk of loss, theft, damage or destruction of the Equipment from any cause whatsoever, and no loss, theft, damage or destruction of the Equipment shall relieve Lessee of the obligation to pay rent or to comply with any other obligation under this Lease. In the event of damage to any part of the Equipment, Lessee shall immediately place the same in good repair at Lessee's expense. If any part of the Equipment is lost, stolen, destroyed, or damaged beyond repair, Lessee shall, at Lessee's option, do one of the following:

    (a) Replace the same with like equipment in good repair, acceptable to Lessor; or

    (b) Pay Lessor in cash the following: (i) all amounts due by Lessee to Lessor under this Lease as to the date of the loss; (ii) the accelerated balance of the total amounts due for the remaining term of this Lease attributable to said items, discounted to present value at a discount rate of 8% as of the date of loss; and, (iii) the Lessor's estimate as of the time this Lease was entered into of Lessor's residual interest in the Equipment discounted to present value at a discount rate of 8%, as of the date of loss. Upon Lessor's receipt of payment as set forth above, Lessee shall be entitled to title to the Equipment without any warranties. If insurance proceeds are used to fully comply with this subparagraph, the balance of any such proceeds shall go to Lessee to compensate for loss of use of the Equipment for the remaining term of the Lease.

16. INSURANCE; LIENS; TAXES. Lessee shall provide and maintain insurance against loss, theft, damage, or destruction of the Equipment in an amount not less than the full replacement value of the Equipment, with loss payable to Lessor. Lessee also shall provide and maintain comprehensive general all-risk liability insurance insuring but not limited to product liability coverage, insuring Lessor and Lessee, with a severability of interest endorsement, or its equivalent, against any and all loss or liability for all damages, either to persons or property or otherwise, which might result from or happen in connection with the condition, use, or operation of the Equipment, with such limits and with an insurer satisfactory to Lessor. Each policy shall expressly provide that said insurance as to Lessor and its assigns shall not be invalidated by any act, omission, or neglect of Lessee and cannot be cancelled without 30 days' prior written notice to Lessor. As to each policy Lessee shall furnish to Lessor a certificate of insurance from the insurer, which certificate shall evidence the insurance coverage required by this paragraph. Lessor shall have no obligation to ascertain the existence of or provide any insurance coverage for the Equipment or for Lessee's benefit. If Lessee fails to provide such insurance, Lessor will have the right, but no obligation, to have such insurance protecting Lessor placed at Lessee's expense. Such placement will result in no increase in Lessee's periodic payments, said increase being attributable to Lessee's costs of obtaining such insurance and any customary charges or fees of Lessor's or its designee associated with such insurance.

    Lessee shall keep the Equipment free and clear of all levies, liens, and encumbrances. Lessee shall pay all charges and taxes (local, state, and federal) which may now or hereafter be imposed upon the ownership, leasing, rental, sale, purchase, possession, or use of the Equipment excluding, however, all taxes on or measured by Lessor's net income. If Lessee fails to pay said charges or taxes, Lessor shall have the right, but shall not be obligated, to pay such charges or taxes. In that event, Lessor shall notify Lessee of such payment and Lessee shall repay to Lessor the cost thereof within 15 days after such notice is mailed to Lessee.

17. INDEMNITY. Lessee shall indemnify Lessor against any claims, actions, damages, or liabilities, including all attorney fees, arising out of or connected with Equipment, without limitation. Such indemnification shall survive the expiration, cancellation, or termination of this Lease. Lessee waives any immunity Lessee may have under any industrial insurance act, with regard to indemnification of Lessor.

18. ASSIGNMENT BY LESSOR. Any assignee of Lessor shall have all of the rights but none of the obligations of Lessor under this Lease. Lessee shall recognize and hereby consents to any assignment of this Lease by Lessor, and shall not assert against the assignee any defense, counterclaim, or setoff that Lessee may have against Lessor. Subject to the foregoing, this Lease inures to the benefit of and is binding upon the heirs, devisees, personal representatives, survivors, successors in interest, and assigns of the parties hereto.

19. SERVICE CHARGES; INTEREST. If Lessee shall fail to make any payment required by this Lease within 10 days of the due date thereof, Lessee shall pay to Lessor a service charge of 5% of the amount due, provided, however, that not more than one such service charge shall be made on any delinquent payment, regardless of the length of the delinquency. In addition to the foregoing service charge, Lessor shall pay to Lessor a $100 default fee with respect to any payment which becomes thirty (30) days past due. In addition, Lessee shall pay to Lessor any actual additional expenses incurred by Lessor in collection efforts, including but not limited to long-distance telephone charges and travel expenses. Lessee shall pay to Lessor interest on any delinquent payment or amount due under this Lease from the due date thereof until paid, at the lesser of the maximum rate of interest allowed by law or 10% per annum.

20. TIME OF ESSENCE. Time is of the essence of this Lease, and this provision shall not be impliedly waived by the acceptance on occasion of late or deficient performance.

21. DEFAULT. Lessee shall be in default if:

    (a) Lessee shall fail to make any payment due under the terms of this Lease for a period of 10 days from the due date thereof; or

    (b) Lessee shall fail to observe, keep, or perform any provision of this Lease, and such failure shall continue for a period of 10 days; or

    (c) Lessee has made any misleading or false statement in connection with application for or performance of this Lease; or

    (d) The Equipment or any part thereof shall be subject to any lien, levy, seizure, assignment, transfer, bulk transfer, encumbrance, application, attachment, execution, sublease, or sale without prior written consent of Lessor, or if Lessor shall abandon the Equipment or permit any other entity or person to use the Equipment without the prior written consent of Lessor; or

    (e) Lessee dies or ceases to exist, or

    (f) Lessee defaults on any other agreement it has with Lessor, or

    (g) Any guarantor of this Lease defaults on any obligation to Lessor or any of the above listed events of default occur with respect to any guarantor or any such guarantor files or has filed against it a petition under the bankruptcy laws.

22. REMEDIES. If Lessee is in default, Lessor, with or without notice to Lessee, shall have the right to exercise any one or more of the following remedies, concurrently or separately, and without any election of remedies being deemed to have been made:

    (a) Lessor may enter upon Lessee's premises and without any court order or other process of law may repossess and remove the Equipment, or render the Equipment unusable without removal, either with or without notice to Lessee. Lessee hereby waives any trespass or right of action for damages by reason of such entry, removal or disabling. Any such repossession shall not constitute a termination of this Lease unless Lessor so notifies Lessee in writing;

    (b) Lessor may require Lessee, at its expense, to return the Equipment in good repair, ordinary wear and tear resulting from proper use thereof alone excepted, by delivering it, packed and ready for shipment, to such place or carrier as Lessor may specify;

    (c) Lessor may cancel or terminate this Lease and may retain any and all prior payments paid by Lessee;

    (d) Lessor may declare all sums due and to become due under this Lease immediately due and payable, including as to any or all items of Equipment, without notice or demand to Lessee;

    (e) Lessor may re-lease the Equipment, without notice to Lessee, to any third party upon such terms and conditions as Lessor alone shall determine, or may sell the Equipment, without notice to Lessee, at private or public sale, at which sale Lessor may be the purchaser;

    (f) Lessor may sue for and recover from Lessee the sum of all unpaid rents and other payments due under this Lease then accrued, all accelerated future payments due under this Lease, discounted to their present value at a discount rate of 8% as of the date of default, plus Lessor's estimate at the time this Lease was entered into of Lessor's residual interest in the Equipment, reduced to present value at a discount rate of 8% as of the date of default, less the net proceeds of disposition, if any, of the Equipment;

    (g) To pursue any other remedy available at law, by statute or in equity.

No right or remedy herein conferred upon or reserved to Lessor is exclusive of any other right or remedy herein, or by law or by equity provided or permitted, but each shall be cumulative of every other right or remedy given hereunder or now or hereafter existing by law or equity or by statute or otherwise, and may be enforced concurrently therewith or from time to time. No single or partial exercise by Lessor of any right or remedy hereunder shall preclude any other or further exercise of any other right or remedy.

23. MULTIPLE LESSEES. Lessor may, with the consent of any one of the Lessees hereunder, modify, extend, or change any of the terms hereof without consent or knowledge of the others, without in any way releasing, waiving, or impairing any right granted to Lessor against the others. Lessees and each of them are jointly and severally responsible and liable to Lessor under this Lease.

24. EXPENSE OF ENFORCEMENT. In the event of any legal action with respect to this Lease, the prevailing party in any such action shall be entitled to reasonable attorney fees, including attorney fees incurred at the trial level, including action in bankruptcy court, on appeal or review, or incurred without action, suits, or proceedings, together with all costs and expenses incurred in pursuit thereof.

25. ENTIRE AGREEMENT; NO ORAL MODIFICATIONS; NO WAIVER. This instrument constitutes the entire agreement between Lessor and Lessee. No provision of this Lease shall be modified or rescinded unless in writing signed by a representative of Lessor. Waiver by Lessor of any provision hereof in one instance shall not constitute a waiver as to any other instance.

26. SEVERABILITY. This Lease is intended to constitute a valid and enforceable legal instrument, and no provision of this Lease that may be deemed unenforceable shall in any way invalidate any other provision or provisions hereof, all of which shall remain in full force and effect.

Example J-2
Generic Purchase Agreement

PURCHASE AGREEMENT

The Lease Rental Agreement ("Lease") dated _____, _____ between
_____ ("Lessor") and _____
(Lessee), is hereby supplemented and amended to include therein the following:

Lessor agrees to sell and Lessee agrees to purchase, effective as of the expiration of the term of this Lease, all, but not less than all, of the equipment described in the Lease for a purchase price of $_____ (plus applicable sales tax).

The Lessor will execute and deliver to the Lessee a Bill of Sale describing the Equipment purchased pursuant to this Purchase Agreement. The Bill of Sale shall be without recourse to the Lessor. The Equipment is sold "As Is, Where Is, With All Faults." Except as provided in the Lease, Lessor makes no representations or warranties, express or implied, with respect to the Equipment.

Dated: _____

(LESSOR)   (LESSEE)

By:_____   By:_____

Title:_____   Title:_____

Date:_____   Date:_____

Example J-3
Generic Equipment Schedule A

EQUIPMENT SCHEDULE "A"

LEASE #

This Equipment Schedule "A" is to be attached to and become part of that Schedule of Leased Equipment dated _____

_____ , _____ by and between the undersigned and

(Lessor).

QTY	DESCRIPTION	MODEL NO.	SERIAL NO.
Vendor:			

This Equipment Schedule "A" is hereby verified as correct by the undersigned Lessee, who acknowledges receipt of a copy.

Lessee: _____

Signature: X _____

Title: _____

Example J-4
Generic Personal Guaranty

PERSONAL GUARANTY

To induce _____ _____ ("Lessor") to lease equipment to
_____ _____ (the "Lessee") pursuant to Lease No. _____
or pursuant to Master Lease No. _____ and all Supplements thereto (cross out and complete as required) (the "Lease").

1. The undersigned hereby absolutely and unconditionally guarantees to Lessor full and prompt payment and performance when due of each and every obligation of Lessee under the Lease.
2. The undersigned hereby waives (i) notice of the acceptance hereof by Lessor and of the creation and existence of the Lease and (ii) any and all defenses otherwise available to a guarantor or accommodation party.
3. This Guaranty is absolute and unconditional, and the liability of the undersigned hereunder shall not be affected or impaired in any way by any of the following, each of which Lessor may agree to without the consent of the undersigned: (a) any extension or renewal of the Lease whether or not for longer than the original period; (b) any change in the terms of payment or other terms of the Lease or any collateral therefor or any exchanged, release of, or failure to obtain any collateral therefor, (c) any waiver or forbearance granted to Lessee or any other person; and (d) the application or failure to apply in any particular manner any payments or credits on the Lease or any other obligation Lessee may owe to Lessor.
4. Lessor shall not be required before exercising and enforcing its rights under the Guaranty first to resort for payment under the Lease to Lessee or to any other person or to any collateral. The undersigned agrees not to obtain reimbursement or payment from Lessee or any other person obligated with respect to the Lease or from any collateral for the Lease until the obligations under the Lease have been fully satisfied.
5. The undersigned shall be and remain liable for any deficiency following foreclosure of any mortgage or security interest securing the Lease whether or not the liability of Lessee under the Lease is discharged by such foreclosure.
6. The undersigned shall be and remain liable for any deficiency following the initiation of bankruptcy or other insolvency actions affecting the Lease or the Lessee, whether or not the liability of the Lessee is discharged in whole or in part by such action.
7. The undersigned agrees to pay all costs, expenses and attorneys' fees paid or incurred by Lessor in endeavoring to enforce the Lease and this Guaranty.
8. If any payment from the Lessee or anyone else is applied to the Lease and is thereafter set aside, recovered, rescinded, or required to be returned for any reason (including as a preference in the bankruptcy of Lessee), the obligations under the Lease to which such payment was applied shall for purposes of this Guaranty be deemed to have continued in existence notwithstanding such application, and this guaranty shall be enforceable as to such obligations as fully as if such applications had never been made.
9. If more than one person signs this Guaranty, then the liability of the undersigned hereunder shall be joint and several, and this Guaranty shall be enforceable in full against each of the undersigned.
10. This Guaranty shall be binding upon the estate, heirs, successors and assigns of the undersigned, and shall inure to the benefit of the successors and assigns of Lessor.
11. By signing this Personal Guaranty, the undersigned authorizes Lessor to obtain their Credit Bureau Reports for credit and collection purposes.

CONSENT TO LAW, JURISDICTION AND VENUE. The subject Lease shall be deemed fully executed and performed in the state of Lessor's or its Assignee's principal place of business and shall be governed by and construed in accordance with the law thereof. If the Lessor or its Assignee shall bring any judicial proceeding in relation to any matter arising under the Lease Agreement and/or this guaranty, the undersigned hereby irrevocably agrees that any such matter may be adjudged or determined in any court or courts in the state of the Lessor's or its Assignee's principal place of business, or any U.S. federal court sitting in the state of the Lessor's or its Assignee's principal place of business, or in any court or courts in Lessee's state of residence, or in any other court having jurisdiction over the lessee or assets of the Lessee, all at the sole election of the Lessor. The undersigned hereby irrevocably submits generally and unconditionally to the jurisdiction of any such court so elected by Lessor or its Assignee in relation to such matters.

Dated _____ , _____ .

_____
Name of Guarantor

_____
Signature

_____
Home Address

_____
Street

_____
City/State   Zip Code

0341

Example J-5
Generic Corporate Guaranty

CORPORATE GUARANTY

To induce_____ ("Lessor") to lease equipment to
_____(the "Lessee") pursuant to Lease No._____ **871940**
or pursuant to Master Lease No. _____ and all Supplements thereto (cross out and complete as required) (the "Lease").

1. The undersigned hereby absolutely and unconditionallyGuarantees to Lessor full and prompt payment and performance when due of each and every obligation of Lessee under the Lease.
2. The undersigned hereby waives (i) notice of the acceptance hereof by Lessor and of the creation and existence of the Lease and (ii) any and all defenses otherwise available to a guarantor or accommodation party.
3. This Guaranty is absolute and unconditional, and the liability of the undersigned hereunder shall not be affected or impaired in any way by any of the following, each of which Lessor may agree to without the consent of the undersigned: (a) any extension or renewal of the Lease whether or not for longer than the original period; (b) any change in the terms of payment or other terms of the Lease or any collateral therefor or any exchange, release of, or failure to obtain any collateral therefor; (c) any waiver of forbearance granted to Lessee or any other person liable with respect to the Lease or any release of, compromise with, or failure to assert rights against Lessee or any such other person; and (d) the application or failure to apply in any particular manner any payments or credits on the Lease or any other obligation Lessee may owe to Lessor.
4. Lessor shall not be required before exercising and enforcing its rights under the Guaranty first to resort for payment under the Lease to Lessee or to any other person or to any collateral. The undersigned agrees not to obtain reimbursement or payment from Lessee or any other person obligated with respect to the Lease or from any collateral for the Lease until the obligations under the Lease have been fully satisfied.
5. The undersigned shall be and remain liable for any deficiency following foreclosure of any mortgage or security interest securing the Lease whether or not the liability of Lessee under the Lease is discharged by such foreclosure.
6. The undersigned shall be and remain liable for any deficiency following the initiation of bankruptcy or other insolvency actions affecting the Lease or the Lessee, whether or not the liability of the Lessee is discharged in whole or in part by such action.
7. The undersigned agrees to pay all costs, expenses and attorneys' fees paid or incurred by Lessor in endeavoring to enforce the Lease and this Guaranty.
8. If any payment from the Lessee or anyone else is applied to the Lease and is thereafter set aside, recovered, rescinded, or required to be returned for any reason (including as a preference in the bankruptcy of Lessee), the obligations under the Lease to which such payment was applied shall for purposes of this Guaranty be deemed to have continued in existence notwithstanding such application, and thisGuaranty shall be enforceable as to such obligations as fully as if such applications had never been made.
9. If more than one person signs this Guaranty, then the liability of the undersigned hereunder shall be joint and several, and this Guaranty shall be enforceable in full against each of the undersigned.
10. This Guaranty shall be binding upon the estate, heirs, successors and assigns of the undersigned, and shall inure to the benefit of the successors and assigns of Lessor.

CONSENT TO LAW, JURISDICTION AND VENUE. The subject Lease shall be deemed fully executed and performed in the state of Lessor's or its Assignee's principal place of business and shall be governed by and construed in accordance with the law thereof. If the Lessor or its Assignee shall bring any judicial proceeding in relation to any matter arising under the Lease Agreement and/or this guaranty, the undersigned hereby irrevocably agrees that any such matter may be adjudged or determined in any court or courts in the state of the Lessor's or its Assignee's principal place of business, or any U.S. federal court sitting in the state of the Lessor's or its Assignee's principal place of business, or in any court or courts in Lessee's state of residence, or in any other court having jurisdiction over the lessee or assets of the Lessee, all at the sole election of the Lessor. The undersigned hereby irrevocably submits generally and unconditionally to the jurisdiction of any such court so elected by Lessor or its Assignee in relation to such matters.

Dated_____)_____.

_____
Corporation or Partnership

_____
Signature

_____
Title

_____
Address

0324

Example J-6
Generic Resolution of Board of Directors

Resolution of Board of Directors

Lessor:_____

Corporate Name:_____

A corporation organized and existing under the laws of the state of:_____

Resolved, that the proposed contract between this Corporation and the above referenced Lessor was submitted to this meeting, and is hereby accepted, that the President or Vice President are authorized to execute in the name and in behalf of this Corporation, A contract substantially in the form submitted to this meeting.

Resolved, that the Secretary, for the purposes of obtaining credit, is hereby directed to submit to Lessor, or their assigns, a true and correct copy of the list of Shareholders. Such list will name each Shareholder with the number of shares, as listed below, as of the date of this meeting.

I do hereby certify that I am duly elected and qualified Secretary and the keeper of the records and corporate seal of the above named corporation.

_____	_____	_____
Shareholder	Shareholder	Shareholder
_____	_____	_____
Title	Title	Title
_____	_____	_____
% of shares held	% of shares held	% of shares held

(Print officers if not listed above)

President:_____ Vice President:_____

_____
Date   Secretary Signature

(affix seal here)

_____
Print Name

"If additional space is needed, please attach another sheet"

REV4200

Example J-7
Generic Change LOCATION Addendum

LOCATION ADDENDUM TO LEASE AGREEMENT NO. ___ _____

Between _____ , AS LESSOR

AND _____ , AS LESSEE

DATED _____ .

LOCATION: Lessor agrees to amend the Lease Agreement. In regard to the location of the equipment, Lessee must be responsible for maintaining records showing the location of each piece of leased equipment. Lessee will report this location to Lessor upon written request by Lessor. Failure to do so shall constitute a breach of the lease, which default shall be governed by the terms and conditions specified in the Lease Agreement.

Agreed to this _____ _____ day of _____ , _____ .

_____   _____
Lessor   Lessee

_____   _____
Signature   Signature

_____   _____
Title   Title

_____   _____
Date   Date

0321

Example J-8
Generic Change TERM OF LEASE Addendum

ADDENDUM TO LEASE # _____

BETWEEN _____ , AS LESSEE

AND _____ , AS LESSOR

DATED _____

The parties have entered into the above-referenced Lease for the lease of _____ equipment more fully described in said Agreement. In recognition of the inaccuracy of the terms of such Agreement, the parties hereby wish to amend said Lease Agreement as set forth below:

The term of the above referenced lease is (_____) monthly payments of $_____ plus

applicable taxes and a security deposit of $_____.

By signing this Addendum, Lessee acknowledges the above changes to the Lease Agreement and authorizes Lessor to make such changes.

_____   _____
Lessor   Lessee

_____   _____
Signature   Signature

_____   _____
Title   Title

_____   _____
Date   Date

0266

Example J-9
Generic Change LEGAL NAME & ADDRESS OF LESSEE
Addendum

ADDENDUM TO LEASE # _____

BETWEEN _____, AS LESSEE

AND _____,   AS LESSOR.

DATED _____

The parties have entered into the above-referenced Lease for the lease of _____
equipment more fully described in said Agreement. In recognition of the inaccuracy of the legal name of the Lessee,
the parties hereby wish to amend said Lease Agreement as set forth below:

The correct and complete legal name and address of the Lessee's business is:

By signing this Addendum, Lessee acknowledges the above changes to the Lease Agreement and authorizes Lessor
to make such changes,

_____   _____
Lessor   Lessee

_____   _____
Signature   Signature

_____   _____
Title   Title

_____   _____
Date   Date

0269

Example J-10
Generic Change EQUIPMENT DESCRIPTION Addendum

ADDENDUM TO LEASE # _____   _____

BETWEEN _____ _____, AS LESSEE

AND _____,   AS L___

DATED _____, _____

The parties have entered into the above-referenced Lease for the lease of equipment. In recognition of the inaccuracy of the complete description of the equipment, the parties hereby wish to amend said Lease Agreement as set forth below:

The correct and complete description of the equipment for the above mentioned lease is:

By signing this Addendum, Lessee acknowledges the above changes to the Lease Agreement and authorizes Lessor to make such changes.

_____	_____
Lessor	Lessee
_____	_____
Signature	Signature
_____	_____
Title	Title
_____	_____
Date	Date

0268

Example J-11
Generic Assignment of Lease

ASSIGNMENT

RE: Lease No. _____, dated _____, _____

between _____

as Lessee and the undersigned as nominal Lessor (the "Lease").

The undersigned hereby sells, assigns, and transfers to _____ all of the undersigned's right, title, and interest in and to (a) the equipment covered by the Lease and (b) the undersigned's rights as Lessor under the Lease, including the right to receive rent thereunder,

_____
(Name of Lessor)

_____
Signature

_____
Title

_____
Date

0333

Example J-12
Generic Assignment of Invoice

ASSIGNMENT OF INVOICE

ASSIGNOR: ASSIGNEE:

_____   _____
Name   Name

_____   _____
D/B/A   Street

_____   _____
Street   City, State, Zip

_____
City, State, Zip

VENDOR:_____   INVOICE NO.:_____

1. The Assignor hereby assigns to the Assignee all rights to the equipment subject to the terms and conditions of the above referenced invoice, including all revisions thereto, (all the foregoing documents hereinafter referenced as the invoice). Assignee hereby accepts the assignment by Assignor to purchase the equipment in accordance with the terms and conditions of said Invoice and the Assignment.

2. Assignor and Assignee hereby agree that the equipment and other assigned products shall be leased by Assignee or Assignor pursuant to the lease agreement between the parties (the "Lease").

3. Assignor and Assignee agree that title to the equipment shall vest in Assignee on the date this assignment is executed and the invoice price is paid.

4. Assignee and Assignor agree that all rights with respect to warranties, licenses, servicing, training, and other such items shall be for the benefit of Assignor for the term of the lease.

5. Assignor agrees to provide Assignee with a Bill of Sale relating to the assigned equipment, to evidence the passage of title to the equipment and other assigned products to Assignee free and clear of all claims, liens and encumbrances.

6. If the appropriate resale or exemption certificate is not submitted with this document applicable sales tax will be billed to Assignor as part of lease payments.

IN EVIDENCE WHEREOF, THE PARTIES HAVE EXECUTED THIS ASSIGNMENT EFFECTIVE
AS OF THE DATE OF THE SUBJECT INVOICES.

ASSIGNOR: ASSIGNEE:

BY:_____   BY:_____

TITLE:_____   TITLE:_____

DATE:_____   DATE:_____

0954

Example J-13
Generic Disclaimer of Ownership

Disclaimer of Ownership

The undersigned is applying to be the "Lessee" from
"Lessor" in accordance with an Equipment Lease between the two principals, Lease
No.   signed by the Lessee on
"Lease". The asset covered by the Lease is hereinafter referred to ad the "Equipment".

The Equipment will be purchased by Lessor from: ___   _____

_____   _____   _____ __ _____,

Lessee has made a down payment to the Vendor as part of the original purchase order
and its intended that, upon Lessor's receipt of all necessary documentation and
satisfaction of conditions to Lessor entering into the Lease, Lessor shall pay the
Vendor the remaining balance of the purchase price and receive a bill of sale from the
Vendor covering a 100% interest in the Equipment.

The Lessee, being satisfied that its payments under the lease are based only upon
Lessor's payment to the Vendor and not the Lessee's down payment, hereby consents
the vendor transferring the entire ownership in the Equipment to the Lessor, and
effective on the actual transfer of the Equipment to the Lessor disclaims any ownership
interest or rights in the equipment except those the Lessee has by virtue of being the
Lessee under the Lease.

Date: _____

Lessee: _

By: _____

ITS: _____

Example J-14
Generic Landlord Waiver

Landlord Waiver

Lease #:_____

The undersigned is the Holder of an Interest as owner, mortgagee or otherwise ("Holder") in certain real property commonly described as follows (insert address of the property):

_____ .

The Holder has been advised that _____ ("Lessor")
is about to extend credit to (name of "Lessee") _____ to
be secured by a security interest held by Lessor in the following property leased to the lessee: (describe the leased equipment):

_____

_____

The Lessor's extension of credit to the Lessee is conditioned upon the Holder's waiver of any and all claims, interests, or liens he/she/it has or might have with respect to the collateral while it is located on or in the premises, whether or not affixed thereto.

The Holder, intending to be legally bound, does hereby acknowledge that the Lessor is the Holder of a perfected security interest in the leased equipment and hereby waives and disclaims any right, security interest or other lien in or on the leased equipment and expressly acknowledges that, now and forever, the collateral does not constitute a fixture or include fixtures.

The Holder hereby consents that the Lessor may at any time enter the premises and remove the leased equipment without liability for damage to the premises resulting from such removal, and that any costs incurred by the Holder as a result of any such removal shall be the sole responsibility of the Lessee except to the extent that such costs result from the Lessor's gross negligence or willful misconduct.

The Holder will not to seek to levy execution on or foreclose any lien or other security interest in the leased equipment or otherwise apply the value of the leased equipment to satisfy any claim the Holder may have against the Lessor or Lessee, if any. The Holder shall notify any successor in interest it may have with respect to all or any part of the premises of this consent and waiver, which shall be binding upon Holder's personal representatives, successors and assigns.

Property Management Company Name: _____
Authorized Signature: _____
Print Name: _____
Title: _____
Address/ Tele/ Fax: _____
Date: _____

Property Owner Name: _____
Property Owner Address: _____

Property Owner Tele: _____

REV4200

Example K

Insurance Request Letter

Lessor: YOUR COMPANY NAME   Lease #: _____
          YOUR COMPANY ADDRESS

INSURANCE AUTHORIZATION

To: _____   **Please input your insurance**
       _____   **information on the left.**
       _____

Phone: (_____) _____

Contact: _____

We have entered into an equipment lease agreement for the equipment shown on the attached Lease Copy. This equipment is located as stated on the Lease.

This is a net lease and we are responsible for the full equipment cost in the amount of $_____.

Please see that we immediately have ALL RISK coverage for liability and full replacement cost of the equipment and that _____ is shown as **LOSS PAYEE** and **ADDITIONAL INSURED** on the policy. Please forward a Certificate of Insurance and Loss Payable/Additional Insured Clause to:

                    _____
                    _____
                    _____

Concurrent Certificates of Insurance, thirty (30) days notice in the event of cancellation or alteration, and general correspondence should be sent to the above addresses as well.

Sincerely,

                    Lessee: _____
                    X _____
                    BY: _____
                    DATE EXECUTED BY LESSEE _____

Example L
Documentation Cover Letter

PRINT ON TO LETTERHEAD

DATE

ATTN: Joe Business
Business, Inc.
123 Main Street
Seattle, WA 98000

Dear Mr. Business,

Please pay close attention to the following requirements before returning the lease documents.

- Please sign and date each agreement for your equipment lease. **Make sure that all dates are the same throughout all the paperwork.**

- Make a check payable to (Lessor Name) for the total amount of: $X,XXX.XX.

  This amount equals 2 payments of $X (which equals $X + X% tax) plus $X processing fee standard on all transactions.
  * * IMPORTANT: This check must be written from your business account.

- **Please provide your** Federal Tax ID#: _____

- **COPY OF DRIVER'S LICENSE (Joe Business)**

Overnight all original documentation to: **Your Company Name**
                                          Attn: Your Name
                                          Your Address

| FEDERAL EXPRESS |
| ENVELOPE PROVIDED |

Call me with any questions at (Your Phone Number).

Sincerely,

Your Name

Example M

Tax Returns: Individual / Personal

Form **1040** Department of the Treasury — Internal Revenue Service
U.S. Individual Income Tax Return 2001 (99)   IRS Use Only — Do not write or staple in this space.

For the year Jan. 1 - Dec. 31, 2001, or other tax year beginning _____, 2001, ending _____, 20____   OMB No. 1545-0074

Label (See Instructions on page 19.)

L A B E L

H E R E

Your first name and initial | Last name | Your social security number

If a joint return, spouse's first name and initial | Last name | Spouse's social security number

Home address (number and street). If you have a P.O. box, see page 19. | Apt. no.

City, town or post office, state, and ZIP code. If you have a foreign address, see page 19.

Use the IRS label. Otherwise, please print or type.

▲ **Important!** ▲
You must enter your SSN(s) above.

Presidential Election Campaign (See page 19.)

Note. Checking "Yes" will not change your tax or reduce your refund.
Do you, or your spouse if filing a joint return, want $3 to go to this fund? ....▶

	You		Spouse	
	Yes	No	Yes	No

Filing Status

Check only one box.

1 ☐ Single
2 ☐ Married filing joint return (even if only one had income)
3 ☐ Married filing separate return. Enter spouse's social security no. above and full name here. ▶ _____
4 ☐ Head of household (with qualifying person). (See page 19.) If the qualifying person is a child but not your dependent, enter this child's name here. ▶
5 ☐ Qualifying widow(er) with dependent child (year spouse died ▶ _____). (See page 19.)

Exemptions

If more than six dependents, see page 20.

6a ☐ Yourself. If your parent (or someone else) can claim you as a dependent on his or her tax return, **do not check box 6a** ....
b ☐ Spouse ....
c Dependents:

(1) First name Last name	(2) Dependent's social security number	(3) Dependent's relationship to you	(4) ✔ if qualifying child for child tax credit (see page 20)
			☐
			☐
			☐
			☐
			☐

No. of boxes checked on 6a and 6b ____
No. of your children on 6c who:
• lived with you ____
• did not live with you due to divorce or separation (see page 20) ____
Dependents on 6c not entered above ____
Add numbers entered on lines above ▶ ____

d Total number of exemptions claimed ....

Income

Attach Forms W-2 and W-2G here. Also attach Form(s) 1099-R if tax was withheld.

If you did not get a W-2, see page 21.

Enclose, but do not attach, any payment. Also, please use Form 1040-V.

7 Wages, salaries, tips, etc. Attach Form(s) W-2 .... | 7
8a Taxable interest. Attach Schedule B if required .... | 8a
b Tax-exempt interest. Do not include on line 8a .... | 8b |
9 Ordinary dividends. Attach Schedule B if required .... | 9
10 Taxable refunds, credits, or offsets of state and local income taxes (see page 22) .... | 10
11 Alimony received .... | 11
12 Business income or (loss). Attach Schedule C or C-EZ .... | 12
13 Capital gain or (loss). Attach Schedule D if required. If not required, check here ...... ▶ ☐ | 13
14 Other gains or (losses). Attach Form 4797 .... | 14
15a Total IRA distributions ... | 15a | b Taxable amount (see page 23) | 15b
16a Total pensions and annuities ... | 16a | b Taxable amount (see page 23) | 16b
17 Rental real estate, royalties, partnerships, S corporations, trusts, etc. Attach Schedule E ...... | 17
18 Farm income or (loss). Attach Schedule F .... | 18
19 Unemployment compensation .... | 19
20a Social security benefits .. | 20a | b Taxable amount (see page 25) | 20b
21 Other income. List type and amount (see page 27) _____ | 21
22 Add the amounts in the far right column for lines 7 through 21. This is your total income .... ▶ | 22

Adjusted Gross Income

23 IRA deduction (see page 27) .... | 23
24 Student loan interest deduction (see page 28) .... | 24
25 Archer MSA deduction. Attach Form 8853 .... | 25
26 Moving expenses. Attach Form 3903 .... | 26
27 One-half of self-employment tax. Attach Schedule SE .... | 27
28 Self-employed health insurance deduction (see page 30) .... | 28
29 Self-employed SEP, SIMPLE, and qualified plans .... | 29
30 Penalty on early withdrawal of savings .... | 30
31a Alimony paid   b Recipient's SSN ▶ _____ | 31a
32 Add lines 23 through 31a .... | 32
33 Subtract line 32 from line 22. This is your adjusted gross income .... ▶ | 33

For Disclosure, Privacy Act, and Paperwork Reduction Act Notice, see page 72.
ISA
STF FED2611F 1

Form **1040** (2001)

Example N

Tax Returns: Schedule C

SCHEDULE C (Form 1040) Department of the Treasury Internal Revenue Service (99)	Profit or Loss From Business (Sole Proprietorship) ▶ Partnerships, joint ventures, etc., must file Form 1065 or Form 1065-B. ▶ Attach to Form 1040 or Form 1041. ▶ See Instructions for Schedule C (Form 1040).	OMB No. 1545-0074 **2001** Attachment Sequence No. **09**

Name of proprietor		Social security number (SSN)

A	Principal business or profession, including product or service (see page C-1 of the instructions)	B Enter code from pages C-7 & 8 ▶
C	Business name. If no separate business name, leave blank.	D Employer ID number (EIN), if any

E Business address (including suite or room no.) ▶ _____
City, town or post office, state, and ZIP code

F Accounting method: (1) ☐ Cash   (2) ☐ Accrual   (3) ☐ Other (specify) ▶ _____

G Did you "materially participate" in the operation of this business during 2001? If "No," see page C-2 for limit on losses . . . . ☐ Yes ☐ No

H If you started or acquired this business during 2001, check here . . . . ▶ ☐

Part I   Income

1	Gross receipts or sales. Caution. If this income was reported to you on Form W-2 and the "Statutory employee" box on that form was checked, see page C-2 and check here . . . . ▶ ☐	1	
2	Returns and allowances	2	
3	Subtract line 2 from line 1	3	
4	Cost of goods sold (from line 42 on page 2)	4	
5	Gross profit. Subtract line 4 from line 3	5	
6	Other income, including Federal and state gasoline or fuel tax credit or refund (see page C-3)	6	
7	Gross income. Add lines 5 and 6 . . . . ▶	7	

Part II   Expenses. Enter expenses for business use of your home only on line 30.

8	Advertising	8		19	Pension and profit-sharing plans	19	
9	Bad debts from sales or services (see page C-3)	9		20	Rent or lease (see page C-4):		
10	Car and truck expenses (see page C-3)	10		a	Vehicles, machinery, and equipment	20a	
				b	Other business property	20b	
11	Commissions and fees	11		21	Repairs and maintenance . . .	21	
12	Depletion	12		22	Supplies (not included in Part III)	22	
13	Depreciation and section 179 expense deduction (not included in Part III) (see page C-3)	13		23	Taxes and licenses	23	
				24	Travel, meals, and entertainment:		
14	Employee benefit programs (other than on line 19)	14		a	Travel	24a	
15	Insurance (other than health) . . .	15		b	Meals and entertainment .		
16	Interest:			c	Enter nondeductible amount included on line 24b (see page C-5)		
a	Mortgage (paid to banks, etc.) . . .	16a		d	Subtract line 24c from line 24b . .	24d	
b	Other	16b		25	Utilities	25	
17	Legal and professional services .	17		26	Wages (less employment credits)	26	
18	Office expense	18		27	Other expenses (from line 48 on page 2)	27	

28	Total expenses before expenses for business use of home. Add lines 8 through 27 in columns . . . . ▶	28	
29	Tentative profit (loss). Subtract line 28 from line 7	29	
30	Expenses for business use of your home. Attach Form 8829	30	
31	Net profit or (loss). Subtract line 30 from line 29. • If a profit, enter on Form 1040, line 12, and also on Schedule SE, line 2 (statutory employees, see page C-5). Estates and trusts, enter on Form 1041, line 3. • If a loss, you must go on to line 32.	31	
32	If you have a loss, check the box that describes your investment in this activity (see page C-6). • If you checked 32a, enter the loss on Form 1040, line 12, and also on Schedule SE, line 2 (statutory employees, see page C-5). Estates and trusts, enter on Form 1041, line 3. • If you checked 32b, you must attach Form 6198.	32a ☐ All investment is at risk. 32b ☐ Some investment is not at risk.	

For Paperwork Reduction Act Notice, see Form 1040 instructions.
ISA
STF FED2615F.1

Schedule C (Form 1040) 2001

Example O

Tax Returns: Corporation

Form **1120**	U.S. Corporation Income Tax Return	OMB No. 1545-0123
Department of the Treasury Internal Revenue Service	For calendar year 2001 or tax year beginning _____, 2001, ending _____, 20 ___ ▶ Instructions are separate. See page 20 for Paperwork Reduction Act Notice.	**2001**

A Check if a:		Use IRS label. Other-wise, print or type.	Name	B Employer identification number
1 Consolidated return (attach Form 851)	☐			
2 Personal holding co. (attach Sch. PH)	☐		Number, street, and room or suite no. (If a P.O. box, see page 7 of instructions.)	C Date incorporated
3 Personal service corp. (as defined in Temporary Regs. sec. 1.441-4T — see instructions)	☐		City or town, state, and ZIP code	D Total assets (see page 8 of instructions)

E Check applicable boxes (1) ☐ Initial return (2) ☐ Final return (3) ☐ Name change (4) ☐ Address change 5

Income	1a	Gross receipts or sales _____ b Less returns and allowances _____ c Bal ▶	1c	
	2	Cost of goods sold (Schedule A, line 8)	2	
	3	Gross profit. Subtract line 2 from line 1c	3	
	4	Dividends (Schedule C, line 19)	4	
	5	Interest	5	
	6	Gross rents	6	
	7	Gross royalties	7	
	8	Capital gain net income (attach Schedule D (Form 1120))	8	
	9	Net gain or (loss) from Form 4797, Part II, line 18 (attach Form 4797)	9	
	10	Other income (see page 8 of instructions — attach schedule)	10	
	11	**Total income.** Add lines 3 through 10 ▶	11	
Deductions (See instructions for limitations on deductions.)	12	Compensation of officers (Schedule E, line 4)	12	
	13	Salaries and wages (less employment credits)	13	
	14	Repairs and maintenance	14	
	15	Bad debts	15	
	16	Rents	16	
	17	Taxes and licenses	17	
	18	Interest	18	
	19	Charitable contributions (see page 10 of instructions for 10% limitation)	19	
	20	Depreciation (attach Form 4562) 20		
	21	Less depreciation claimed on Schedule A and elsewhere on return 21a	21b	
	22	Depletion	22	
	23	Advertising	23	
	24	Pension, profit-sharing, etc., plans	24	
	25	Employee benefit programs	25	
	26	Other deductions (attach schedule)	26	
	27	**Total deductions.** Add lines 12 through 26 ▶	27	
	28	Taxable income before net operating loss deduction and special deductions. Subtract line 27 from line 11	28	
	29	**Less:** a Net operating loss (NOL) deduction (see page 13 of instructions) 29a		
		b Special deductions (Schedule C, line 20) 29b	29c	
Tax and Payments	30	**Taxable income.** Subtract line 29c from line 28	30	
	31	**Total tax** (Schedule J, line 11)	31	
	32	**Payments:** a 2000 overpayment credited to 2001 32a		
		b 2001 estimated tax payments 32b		
		c Less 2001 refund applied for on Form 4466 ..... 32c ( ) d Bal ▶ 32d		
		e Tax deposited with Form 7004	32e	
		f Credit for tax paid on undistributed capital gains (attach Form 2439) 32f		
		g Credit for Federal tax on fuels (attach Form 4136). See instructions 32g	32h	
	33	Estimated tax penalty (see page 14 of instructions). Check if Form 2220 is attached .... ▶ ☐	33	
	34	Tax due. If line 32h is smaller than the total of lines 31 and 33, enter amount owed	34	
	35	Overpayment. If line 32h is larger than the total of lines 31 and 33, enter amount overpaid	35	
	36	Enter amount of line 35 you want: Credited to 2002 estimated tax ▶ Refunded ▶	36	

Sign Here

Under penalties of perjury, I declare that I have examined this return, including accompanying schedules and statements, and to the best of my knowledge and belief, it is true, correct, and complete. Declaration of preparer (other than taxpayer) is based on all information of which preparer has any knowledge.

		May the IRS discuss this return with the preparer shown below (see instructions)? ☐ Yes ☐ No
▶ Signature of officer	Date	▶ Title

Paid Preparer's Use Only	Preparer's signature ▶		Date		Check if self-employed ☐	Preparer's SSN or PTIN
	Firm's name (or yours if self-employed), address, and ZIP code				EIN	
					Phone no.	

ISA
STF FED3043F.1

Form **1120** (2001)

Example P

Tax Returns: S Corporation

Form **1120S**	**U.S. Income Tax Return for an S Corporation**	OMB No. 1545-0130
Department of the Treasury Internal Revenue Service	▶ Do not file this form unless the corporation has timely filed Form 2553 to elect to be an S corporation. ▶ See separate instructions.	**2001**

For calendar year 2001, or tax year beginning _____, 2001, and ending _____ , 20 ___

A Effective date of election as an S corporation	Use IRS label. Other-wise, print or type.	Name		C Employer identification number
		Number, street, and room or suite no. (If a P.O. box, see page 11 of the instructions.)		D Date Incorporated
B Business code no. (see pages 29 - 31)		City or town, state, and ZIP code		E Total assets (see page 11) $

F Check applicable boxes: (1) ☐ Initial return   (2) ☐ Final return   (3) ☐ Name change   (4) ☐ Address change   (5) ☐ Amended return
G Enter number of shareholders in the corporation at end of the tax year .... ▶

Caution: *Include only trade or business income and expenses on lines 1a through 21. See page 11 of the instructions for more information.*

Income	1a	Gross receipts or sales		**b** Less returns and allowances	**c** Bal ▶	1c
	2	Cost of goods sold (Schedule A, line 8)				2
	3	Gross profit. Subtract line 2 from line 1c				3
	4	Net gain (loss) from Form 4797, Part II, line 18 *(attach Form 4797)* ...				4
	5	Other income (loss) *(attach schedule)*				5
	6	Total income (loss). Combine lines 3 through 5 .... ▶				6
Deductions (see page 12 of the instructions for limitations)	7	Compensation of officers				7
	8	Salaries and wages (less employment credits)				8
	9	Repairs and maintenance				9
	10	Bad debts				10
	11	Rents				11
	12	Taxes and licenses				12
	13	Interest				13
	14a	Depreciation *(if required, attach Form 4562)*	14a			
	b	Depreciation claimed on Schedule A and elsewhere on return	14b			
	c	Subtract line 14b from line 14a				14c
	15	Depletion (Do not deduct oil and gas depletion.)				15
	16	Advertising				16
	17	Pension, profit-sharing, etc., plans				17
	18	Employee benefit programs				18
	19	Other deductions *(attach schedule)*				19
	20	Total deductions. Add the amounts shown in the far right column for lines 7 through 19 .... ▶				20
	21	Ordinary income (loss) from trade or business activities. Subtract line 20 from line 6				21
Tax and Payments	22	Tax: a Excess net passive income tax *(attach schedule)*	22a			
	b	Tax from Schedule D (Form 1120S)	22b			
	c	Add lines 22a and 22b (see page 16 of the instructions for additional taxes)				22c
	23	Payments: a 2001 estimated tax payments and amount applied from 2000 return	23a			
	b	Tax deposited with Form 7004	23b			
	c	Credit for Federal tax paid on fuels *(attach Form 4136)*	23c			
	d	Add lines 23a through 23c				23d
	24	Estimated tax penalty. Check if Form 2220 is attached .... ▶ ☐				24
	25	Tax due. If the total of lines 22c and 24 is larger than line 23d, enter amount owed. See page 4 of the instructions for depository method of payment .... ▶				25
	26	Overpayment. If line 23d is larger than the total of lines 22c and 24, enter amount overpaid ...... ▶				26
	27	Enter amount of line 26 you want: Credited to 2002 estimated tax ▶ _____ Refunded ▶				27

Sign Here	Under penalties of perjury, I declare that I have examined this return, including accompanying schedules and statements, and to the best of my knowledge and belief, it is true, correct, and complete. Declaration of preparer (other than taxpayer) is based on all information of which preparer has any knowledge.	
	▶ _____ Signature of officer _____ Date ▶ _____ Title	May the IRS discuss this return with the preparer shown below (see Instructions)? ☐ Yes ☐ No

Paid Preparer's Use Only	Preparer's signature ▶	Date	Check if self-employed ☐	Preparer's SSN or PTIN
	Firm's name (or yours if self-employed), address, and ZIP code ▶		EIN	
			Phone no.	

For Paperwork Reduction Act Notice, see the separate instructions.
ISA
STF FED4219F.1

Form **1120S** (2001)

Example Q
Personal Financial Statement

PERSONAL FINANCIAL STATEMENT	CONFIDENTIAL

IMPORTANT: DIRECTIONS TO APPLICANT

To: _____

Address: _____

_____

_____

Personal Financial Statement as of _____ (DATE)

APPLICANT'S NAME(S): _____

_____

HOME ADDRESS _____

_____

HOME PHONE _____

Read directions before completing Financial Statement.
Please check appropriate box

☐ Individual credit—If relying on your own income and assets and not the income and assets of a spouse or another person as a basis for extension or repayment or credit, complete the Financial Statement below only as it applies to you, individually. Do not provide any information about a spouse or other person. Sign the Financial Statement.

☐ Joint Credit

☐ Individual relying upon income or assets of spouse or other person.

If applying for joint credit or for individual credit relying on income or assets of a spouse or another person for extension and repayment of credit requested, complete the Financial Statement below. Include information about income, assets and liabilities of the spouse or other person. Both Applicant and Spouse or Co-Applicant sign this statement.

Please do not leave any questions unanswered. Use "no" or "none" where necessary.

Assets	In Even Dollars	Liabilities and Net Worth	In Even Dollars
Cash on hand and in Banks—See Schedule A	$	Notes Payable: This Bank—See Schedule A	$
U.S. Government Securities—See Schedule B		Notes Payable: Other Institutions—See Schedule A	
Listed Securities—See Schedule B			
Unlisted Securities—See Schedule B		Notes Payable—Relatives	
Other Equity Interests—See Schedule B		Notes Payable—Others	
Accounts and Notes Receivable		Accounts and Bills Due	
Real Estate Owned—See Schedule C		Unpaid Taxes	
Mortgages and Land Contracts Receivable—See Schedule D		Real Estate Mortgages Payable—See Schedule C or D	
Cash Value Life Insurance—See Schedule E		Land Contracts Payable—See Schedule C or D	
Other Assets: Itemize		Life Insurance Loans—See Schedule E	
		Other Liabilities: Itemize	
		TOTAL LIABILITIES	$
		NET WORTH	$
TOTAL ASSETS	$	TOTAL LIABILITIES AND NET WORTH	$

Sources of Income	In Even Dollars	General Information	
Salary	$	Employer	
Bonus and Commissions		Position or Profession	No. Years
Dividends		Employer's Address	
Real Estate Income			Phone No.
*Other Income: Itemize		Partner, officer or owner in any other venture? ☐ No ☐ Yes	
		If so, explain:	
TOTAL	$		
*Alimony, child support or separate maintenance payments need not be disclosed unless relied upon as a basis for extension of credit. If disclosed, payments received under ☐ court order ☐ written agreement ☐ oral understanding.		Are any assets pledged? ☐ No ☐ Yes Detail in Schedule A	
		Income taxes settled through (Date)	

Example R
Vendor Invoice Sample

(VENDOR INFORMATION HERE)

Invoice

Date	Invoice #

Bill To	Ship To
(LESSOR INFORMATION HERE)	(LESSEE INFORMATION HERE)

P.O. Number	Terms	Rep	Ship	Via	F.O.B.	Project
	PAYABLE UPON R...	RH	6/3/2002			

Quantity	Item Code	Description	Price Each	Amount
		(EQUIPMENT DESCRIPTION HERE)		

| | | | **Total** | |

Example S
Broker Fee Invoice

BROKER FEE INVOICE

LESSOR:.................................   _____

LESSEE NAME:..........................   _____

APPROVAL NUMBER:..............   _____

TOTAL LEASE AMOUNT:........... $_____

MONTHLY PAYMENT:.............. $_____

RATE FACTORS:.......................   Buy:_____ Sell:_____

OF ADVANCED PAYMENTS:....   _____

PURCHASE OPTION:..................   _____

     Broker Commission............ $_____ Points: _____

     + Doc fees collected .... $_____

     - Docs fees required by bank $_____

     Sub-Total $_____

Less Advanced Money Received . . . . $_____

NET COMMISSION DUE........... $_____

Please Standard Overnight BROKER & VENDOR checks via Federal Express or UPS.

Please send broker check to: Your Company Name
FedEx #: (Account #)   ATTN: Your Name
     Your Address

     CONTACT: (Your Name) at (Your Phone) with any questions.

Example T
Thank You & Assignment of Lease Letter

(PRINT ON TO YOUR LETTERHEAD)

DATE

Business, Inc.
Attention: Joe Business
123 Main Street
Seattle, WA 98000

RE: Lease # 703876

Dear Mr. Business,

Please accept our sincere thanks for giving our company the opportunity to serve you. Our staff will always do everything possible to merit the confidence you've placed in us.

We would like to advise you that (**FUNDING SOURCE**) is handling the lease schedule for your purchase. You will be receiving all billing statements directly from them. However, if you should have any questions or concerns about your lease, please be sure to contact our office at (**YOUR PHONE**).

Please keep in mind that (**YOUR COMPANY NAME**) can provide your business with lease financing for almost every conceivable kind of new, or used equipment acquisition. From computers to heavy machinery, and from a simple $2,000.00 purchase to $500,000.00 dollar transactions, (**YOUR COMPANY NAME**) appreciates your business no matter the size.

Thank you again for allowing our company to be of service to you. Remember that based on your current lease we can pre-approve you at no charge with just a phone call.

Sincerely,
(YOUR COMPANY NAME)

Your Name
Title

Example U
Fax Cover Letter

FACSIMILE TRANSMITTAL

YOUR COMPANY NAME
STREET ADDRESS
CITY, STATE
ZIP CODE

DATE: _____   PAGES: _____
(Including this page)

TO: Company: _____

Attention: _____

Fax Number: _____

Regarding: _____

FROM: _____

```
YOUR LOGO
HERE
```

TOLL FREE PHONE: (YOUR PHONE) * TOLL FREE FAX: (YOUR FAX)

Example V
Rate Factor Sheet

RATE FACTORS WITH 2 ADVANCE AND 10% PURCHASE OPTION			
MONTHS	$5 - 24,999.99	$25 - 39,999.99	$40 - 75,000
24	.04318	.04275	.04254
30	.03585	.03541	.03518
36	.03098	.03053	.03030
42	.02752	.02705	.02682
48	.02494	.02446	.02423
54	.02295	.02246	.02221
60	.02136	.02086	.02062

RATE FACTORS WITH 2 ADVANCE AND $1 BUY OUT			
MONTHS	$5 - 24,999.99	$25 - 39,999.99	$40 - 75,000
24	.04675	.04636	.04617
30	.03861	.03820	.03800
36	.03320	.03278	.03258
42	.02936	.02893	.02871
48	.02649	.02605	.02583
54	.02427	.02382	.02359
60	.02251	.02205	.02182

- Base Rate with no commission calculated.

- Maximum allowable broker commission is 15 points on transaction sizes $5 - 40,000 and 12 points on $40 - 75,000
- Quotes available for transactions exceeding $75,000.
- Advances represent first month's payment and one payment held as security.
- Billing on the first of every month.
- Some types of equipment may require a 10% put verses an option.

Example W
Equipment Condition Report

Equipment Condition Report

Lease #:_____

Supplier of Equipment (Complete Address)   **Lessee Information (Complete Address)**

_____   _____

_____   _____

_____   _____

_____   _____

Phone # _____   Phone # _____

Fax # _____

Equipment Description: (Include Make, Model, Cost Breakdowns and Serial Numbers)

_____

_____

Current dollar Value of Equipment: $_____   Cost new: $ _____

Date Manufactured: _____   Age: _____   Size: _____

Color: _____ Features: _____

List all attachments, accessories, customizing and/or modifications

_____

_____

If reconditioned, explain when and what was done:

_____

Overall Condition/Appearance:

_____

Appraised By:

Company Name: _____

Co. Address/Tele/Fax: _____

Signature of Appraiser: _____

Print Name: _____

Title: _____

Date: _____

REV4208

Example X

Lead Qualification Sheet: End User

<table>
<tr>
<td rowspan="2">

Your Company Name Here
</td>
<td>
Date Contacted: _____
Date Faxed: _____
Date Mailed: _____
Follow-up Date: _____
</td>
</tr>
<tr>
<td>

END-USER
</td>
</tr>
</table>

Lead Qualification Worksheet

Hello Mr/Mrs _____. This is _____ with (Your Company Name). We specialize in equipment financing and I'm calling to see if you have any upcoming equipment financing requirements that we could quote you on . . . .

If yes, follow with these lead qualification questions . . . . . .

What equipment are you planning to acquire? _____

Have you settled on a vendor? If yes, who? _____

What is the approximate price? _____

How soon do you plan on acquiring this new equipment? _____

If you have any questions, you can reach us directly at: (Your Phone # Here)   **Toll Free!**

Contact Name: _____   Title: _____
Company Name: _____   Phone: _____
Address: _____   Fax: _____
City: _____   State: _____   Zip: _____

COMMENTS:

Example Y

Lead Qualification Sheet: Vendor

YOUR COMPANY NAME HERE	Date Contacted:_____ Date Faxed:_____ Date Mailed: _____ Follow-up Date:_____ **VENDOR**

Lead Qualification Worksheet

Contact Name: _____   Title: _____

Company Name: _____   Phone: _____

Address: _____   Fax: _____

City: _____ State: _____ Zip: _____

DO YOU CURRENTLY OFFER LEASING?   (YES / NO)

DOLLAR RANGE OF EQUIPMENT: $ _____

NUMBER OF LEASES PER MONTH: _____

TYPE OF EQUIPMENT SOLD? _____

WHO DO YOU PRIMARILY USE FOR LEASING? _____

HOW DO YOU CHOOSE LEASING COMPANIES? _____
_____

DO YOU HAVE ANYTHING **GOOD** OR **BAD** TO SAY ABOUT THE FOLKS YOU CURRENTLY WORK WITH? _____

DO YOU HAVE ANYTHING RIGHT NOW THAT YOU WOULD LIKE A QUOTE ON?

IF YES, FAX THE APPLICATION TO: (Your Fax # For Reference)

COMMENTS:

Example Z

Tax Returns: Schedule K-1

SCHEDULE K-1 (Form 1120S) Department of the Treasury Internal Revenue Service	Shareholder's Share of Income, Credits, Deductions, etc. ▶ See separate Instructions. For calendar year 2001 or tax year beginning , 2001, and ending , 20	OMB No. 1545-0130 **2001**

Shareholder's identifying number ▶	Corporation's identifying number ▶
Shareholder's name, address, and ZIP code	Corporation's name, address, and ZIP code

A Shareholder's percentage of stock ownership for tax year (see instructions for Schedule K-1) . . . . . ▶ .... %
B Internal Revenue Service Center where corporation filed its return ▶ ....
C Tax shelter registration number (see instructions for Schedule K-1) . . . . ▶ ....
D Check applicable boxes;   (1) ☐ Final K-1   (2) ☐ Amended K-1

	(a) Pro rata share Items		(b) Amount	(c) Form 1040 filers enter the amount in column (b) on:
Income (Loss)	1 Ordinary income (loss) from trade or business activities	1		See page 4 of the Shareholder's Instructions for Schedule K-1 (Form 1120S).
	2 Net income (loss) from rental real estate activities	2		
	3 Net income (loss) from other rental activities	3		
	4 Portfolio income (loss):			
	a Interest	4a		Sch. B, Part I, line 1
	b Ordinary dividends	4b		Sch. B, Part II, line 5
	c Royalties	4c		Sch. E, Part I, line 4
	d Net short-term capital gain (loss)	4d		Sch. D, line 5, col. (f)
	e (1) Net long-term capital gain (loss)	4e(1)		Sch. D, line 12, col. (f)
	(2) 28% rate gain (loss)	4e(2)		Sch. D, line 12, col. (g)
	(3) Qualified 5-year gain	4e(3)		Line 4 of worksheet for Sch. D, line 29
	f Other portfolio income (loss) (attach schedule)	4f		(Enter on applicable line of your return.)
	5 Net section 1231 gain (loss) (other than due to casualty or theft)	5		See Shareholder's Instructions for Schedule K-1 (Form 1120S).
	6 Other income (loss) (attach schedule)	6		(Enter on applicable line of your return.)
Deductions	7 Charitable contributions (attach schedule)	7		Sch. A, line 15 or 16
	8 Section 179 expense deduction	8		See page 6 of the Shareholder's Instructions for Schedule K-1 (Form 1120S).
	9 Deductions related to portfolio income (loss) (attach schedule) .	9		
	10 Other deductions (attach schedule)	10		
Investment Interest	11a Interest expense on investment debts	11a		Form 4952, line 1
	b (1) Investment income included on lines 4a, 4b, 4c, and 4f above	11b(1)		See Shareholder's Instructions for Schedule K-1 (Form 1120S).
	(2) Investment expenses included on line 9 above	11b(2)		
Credits	12a Credit for alcohol used as fuel	12a		Form 6478, line 10
	b Low-income housing credit:			
	(1) From section 42(j)(5) partnerships	12b(1)		Form 8586, line 5
	(2) Other than on line 12b(1)	12b(2)		
	c Qualified rehabilitation expenditures related to rental real estate activities	12c		See pages 6 and 7 of the Shareholder's Instructions for Schedule K-1 (Form 1120S).
	d Credits (other than credits shown on lines 12b and 12c) related to rental real estate activities	12d		
	e Credits related to other rental activities	12e		
	13 Other credits	13		

For Paperwork Reduction Act Notice, see the Instructions for Form 1120S.   Cat. No. 11520D   Schedule K-1 (Form 1120S) 2001

SECTION 13

GLOSSARY OF LEASING TERMS

In This Section:

- Glossary of Leasing Terms

Glossary of Leasing Terms

Listed below is a glossary of leasing some leasing terms that I personally feel will be beneficial for you to know. Understanding the terms in this glossary will better prepare you to communicate comfortably with professionals in the equipment leasing business. Reading through this glossary will also help you understand some of the methods in this manual more clearly.

Broker

A broker is an intermediary between the lessee and lessor. The broker arranges a leasing transaction between an equipment buyer and a funding source for a broker fee.

Broker Fee

This is the fee or commission paid to the broker for his/her services. Typically, this fee is paid to the broker by the funding source once a lease transaction is complete.

Capital Lease

A lease where at the end of the lease term, the lessee owns the property for a predetermined about of money. An example of a capital lease would be a lease with a $1.00 buyout, or a guaranteed 10% buyout (Put) at the end of the lease term.

Capped Fair Market Value

A statement in a lease agreement which states that the lessee can purchase the equipment at the end of their lease term for fair market value, and that the fair market value will not exceed a certain dollar amount or percentage.

Certificate of Acceptance

A certificate of acceptance is a signed verification by the lessee that they have received the equipment to be leased. Once this document is received by the funding source, the funding source will release funds to the vendor and broker.

Corporation

A general corporation, also known as a "C" corporation, is the most common corporate structure. A general corporation may have an unlimited number of stockholders. Consequently, it is usually chosen by those companies planning to have more than thirty stockholders or large public stock offerings. Since a corporation is a separate legal entity, a stockholder's personal liability is usually limited to the amount of investment in the corporation and no more.

Cross-Corporate Guaranty

A guarantee by one corporation to cover the payments of another corporation if that other corporation was to default on its lease or loan. As a lease broker, you may come across a situation where a corporation you are trying to approve is too new or not creditworthy for the dollar amount they are asking for. It is always smart to ask if they have another corporation that could guarantee the loan for the weaker company. They may have an older company of their own, or have a friend's company that is willing to back them up.

Default

A default occurs if a lessee does not comply will all of the terms of a lease agreement (not making payments, etc.). Generally, after a default, the lessor (funding source) can exercise all of its rights under the lease to repossess the property and seek monetary damages.

Dollar Buyout

An "end of lease" option where the lessee purchases the equipment for $1.00.

Economic Life of Leased Property

The estimated amount of time (measured in years) that leased property can be used with maintenance and normal repairs.

Fair Market Value

Fair market value is the value of the equipment at the end of the lease term which is based upon the economic life of the leased property. It is also measured by the average price a person would pay for the equipment at that given time. The fair market value of the equipment on a lease is not known until the lease is over. At that point, the funding source will research blue book values and call dealers to come to a value conclusion.

Fair Market Value Purchase Option

A fair market value purchase option gives the lessee the option to purchase the equipment on the lease for fair market value, or walk away with nothing. This is known as a true lease.

Financial Statements

Financial statements are statements for a business that provide specific information about its financial position. These statements commonly include: balance sheets, income statements, cash flow statements, personal financial statements, etc. Sometimes these statements will be audited, which means a 3rd party developed them, typically a CPA.

Hell or High Water Clause

This clause in the lease states that no matter what happens in the duration of a lease term, the lessee is responsible for all of the lease payments per the lease agreement.

Interim Rent

Interim rent is a fee that funding sources charge lessees to cover the time lapsed between when the funding source pays the vendor of the equipment and when the first payment is due. This is calculated by dividing the monthly lease payment (including tax if necessary) by the number of days in the month. For example, a lessee signs a lease, received equipment and signs the delivery and acceptance to start the lease on the 15th of the month with a funding source. The funding source pays the vendor on the 16th 15 days before the lessee's first payment is due. The lessee's first billing statement will show the first payment, plus 15 days of interim rent to cover the period between the date the funding source paid the vendor and the lessee's first payment due date. Unfortunately, interim rent does not go towards the balance of the lease. Each funding source handles this differently. Some funding sources do not charge interim rents, while others do. Educate yourself on each of your funding sources so that you can prepare your lessees for a possible extra charge on their first billing statement.

Lease

A lease is a contract between a lessor and lessee which gives the lessee the right to use the leased equipment for an agreed period of time (typically 2-5 years, or 24 to 60 months).

Lease Rate Factor

A lease rate factor is a percentage which when multiplied by the equipment cost provides a periodic rental payment.

Lease Term

The lease term is the fixed number of payments on a lease agreement.

Lessee

A lessee is the user and guarantor of leased equipment per a lease agreement.

Lessor

A lessor is the owner of the leased property being used by the lessee.

Limited Liability Company (LLC)

An LLC is not a corporation, but it offers many of the same advantages. Many small business owners and entrepreneurs prefer LLC's because they combine the limited liability protection of a corporation with the "pass through"" taxation of a sole proprietorship or partnership. LLC's allow greater flexibility in management and business organization over corporations.

Master Lease

A master lease is the same as a Lease agreement, which binds a lessor of equipment and lessee together for a fixed term.

Municipal Lease

A municipal lease is one where the lessee is a public, state or governmental entity. The legal documentation is different than a standard lease because of the unique status of public entities. The rates are typically lower than rates for normal businesses.

Operating Lease

An operating lease is a lease where the lessee makes the payments for the fixed term of the lease without any intention of owning the equipment at the end of the lease. This means that the lessor will be stuck with the equipment at the end of the lease. In an operating lease (a true lease), the lessee should be able to legally deduct their payments as a rental expense.

Partnership

A partnership is a business owned by two or more people who share profits and losses. Owners are personally liable for the partnership's debt.

Personal Guarantee

A personal guarantee, also known as P.G., is the guarantee of and individual to be personally responsible for the obligations under the lease. Personal guarantees are required on almost all leases unless special permission is made by the lessor to not have one. For example, special permission may be given to a corporation that has been in business over 10-15 years with solid financials.

Purchase Option

A purchase option is the option of a lessee to purchase the equipment at the end of a lease or walk away from it altogether, once the obligations of the lease have been satisfied. The purchase option is predetermined before the lease agreement is signed by the lessee.

Refundable Security Deposit

A refundable security deposit is an amount of money requested of the lessee by the lessor to strengthen a deal that may be too weak to approve, or outside of the lessor's credit window. A security deposit makes a lease transaction safer for the lessor. If the lessee makes their payments as agreed, then the security deposit is refunded back to the lessee at the end of the lease.

Remarketing

Remarketing is the process in which a lessor markets and sells equipment that comes back to them at the end of a lease where the lessee does not exercise their option to purchase the equipment. There are remarketing companies that assist lessors in selling equipment that comes back to them at the end of leases. Lessors also remarket equipment that comes back to them by order of default as well.

Residual Value

Residual value is the value of leased equipment at the end of the lease term.

Sale-Leaseback

A sale-leaseback is a lease where a business (lessee) borrows money against equipment they already own or just recently purchased from a funding source (lessor). The business sells the equipment to a lessor and buys it back over the term of a lease by making payments. This is common when a company has to move fast on some equipment at an auction or from a private party sale. The company will buy the equipment and then contact a leasing company to lease/finance the equipment they just bought to get their cash back. Funding sources are picky about sale-leasebacks. Some funding sources will not touch them; others will if they make sense.

Sole proprietorship

A sole proprietorship is a business owned by a single individual. A sole proprietor has unlimited liability for business debt and obligations, but does not have to pay corporate income tax.

Step Down Lease

This is a customized payment plan where the lease payments decrease over the term of the lease.

Step Up Lease

This is a customized payment plan where the lease payments increase over the term of the lease.

Subchapter S Corporation

A Subchapter S Corporation is a general corporation that has elected a special tax status with the IRS after the corporation has been formed. Subchapter S corporations are most appropriate for small business owners and entrepreneurs who prefer to be taxed as if they were still sole proprietors or partners. For many small businesses, the S Corporation offers the best of both worlds, combining the tax advantages of a sole proprietorship or partnership with the limited liability and enduring life of a corporate structure.

Term

The term of the lease is the number of payments or years. The most common terms are 2-5 years (24-60 months). Sometimes when people in the business speak about terms, they are also talking about the dollar amount of the payment, interest rate and "end-of-lease" purchase option.

Vendor

A vendor is a company that sells leasible property and equipment.

Vendor Program

A vendor program is a program developed especially for your vendor by you and your funding source to facilitate a long term relationship. If you come across a vendor that does high volume, but will not work with you unless you can promise better rates and approving the some tough credit occasionally, your funding source may help you secure that vendor. Almost every funding source will make special arrangements for great vendors. Talk to your funding sources about how to put together a vendor program that will out do your competitors.

SECTION 14

RESOURCES & SUGGESTED READINGS

In This Section:

- Resources
- Suggested Readings
- Leasing Associations

Resources & Suggested Readings

Recommended Sites:

WWW.Theleasingexpert.com

- Visit our website for additional information and products to help you build your business.

- Cd-Rom with copies of all sample documents and letterhead

- Additional Marketing Material

WWW.MonitorDaily.com – a huge list of funding sources
WWW.ELAonline.com - a source of great information and statistics

Suggested Readings:

Mayer, David G. *Business Leasing For Dummies*. New York: Hungry Minds, Inc., 2001

Contino, Richard M. *Handbook of Equipment Leasing, A Deal Makers Guide*. Second Edition. New York: Amacom, 1996

The United Association of Equipment Leasing. *The Leasing Professionals Handbook*, Second Edition. 1995

Peter K. Nevitt, Frank J. Fabozzi. *Equipment Leasing*, 4th Edition

Molloy Associates. *Monitor Daily*. Wayne, PA, 2001

Leasing Associations:\n \

Name:	Website:
National Association of Equipment Lease Brokers	*NAELB.org*
United Association of Equipment Leasing	*UAEL.org*
The Association for Equipment Leasing & Finance	*ELAonline.com*
Eastern Association of Equipment Lessors	*EAEL.org*
Certified Lease Profession Foundation	*clpfoundation.org*
Leasing News	*leasingnews.org*

THE EQUIPMENT LEASE BROKER

Documentation CD-ROM

There are three folders on the CD-ROM. One folder contains JPEGs of all example documents from Section 12 of the book. The second folder contains some of those example documents that are usable in text format. The third folder contains the same documents as the second folder, but in Microsoft Word Version 9.0 format. The documents are yours to use with your new equipment leasing business.

www.ingramcontent.com/pod-product-compliance
Lightning Source LLC
Chambersburg PA
CBHW080538220326

41599CB00032B/6305